THE SOCIAL WORK AND K-12 SCHOOLS CASEBOOK

This volume offers a collection of nine case studies from clinical social workers in K-12 schools, each from a phenomenological perspective, with the objective of educating Master of Social Work (MSW) students and early career social work clinicians. Each chapter is framed with pre-reading prompts, reading comprehension questions, and writing assignments. This casebook provides a resource for understanding the range of practice in school social work as well as some of the challenges that school social workers face in today's complex world. Using a phenomenological perspective the contributors stay close to the lived experience of students, teachers, parents, and social workers, revealing a deeper and more nuanced understanding of the genesis and treatment of students' problems in school.

Miriam Jaffe, PhD, is the director of the writing program at the Rutgers University Doctorate in Social Work Program. She specializes in issues of autobiography, life-writing, and the case study method.

Jerry Floersch, LCSW, PhD, is an associate professor at the Rutgers University School of Social Work and the author of *Meds, Money, and Manners: The Case Management of Severe Mental Illness* and co-author of *Qualitative Methods for Practice Research*. His clinical practice focuses upon adolescents and adults.

Jeffrey Longhofer, LCSW, PhD, is an associate professor of social work at Rutgers University and the author of *A–Z of Psychodynamic Practice* and co-author of *On Being and Having a Case Manager*. His clinical practice focuses on children, adolescents, and adults.

Wendy Winograd, LCSW, BCD-P, DSW, works in a school and maintains a private practice in Chatham, NJ where she sees adolescents, adults, and couples and provides individual and group supervision. She has published on female development, work with transgender adolescents, school-based psychotherapy with young children, and mother/daughter relationships.

THE SOCIAL WORK AND K-12 SCHOOLS CASEBOOK

Phenomenological Perspectives

Edited by
Miriam Jaffe, PhD, Jerry Floersch, PhD,
Jeffrey Longhofer, PhD, and
Wendy Winograd, DSW

Routledge
Taylor & Francis Group

NEW YORK AND LONDON

First published 2018
by Routledge
711 Third Avenue, New York, NY 10017

and by Routledge
2 Park Square, Milton Park, Abingdon, Oxon, OX14 4RN

Routledge is an imprint of the Taylor & Francis Group, an informa business

© 2018 Taylor & Francis

The right of Miriam Jaffe, Jerry Floersch, Jeffrey Longhofer, and
Wendy Winograd to be identified as the authors of the editorial
material, and of the authors for their individual chapters, has been
asserted in accordance with sections 77 and 78 of the Copyright,
Designs and Patents Act 1988.

Library of Congress Cataloging-in-Publication Data
A catalog record for this book has been requested

ISBN: 978-1-138-29241-3 (hbk)
ISBN: 978-1-138-29242-0 (pbk)
ISBN: 978-1-315-23291-1 (ebk)

Typeset in Bembo
by Keystroke, Neville Lodge, Tettenhall, Wolverhampton

CONTENTS

NOTES ON CONTRIBUTORS

Karen E. Baker, MSW, LMSW, is a clinical social worker-psychoanalyst who earned her Master of Social Work (MSW) from the University of Michigan in 1983. She has been practicing clinical social work for the past thirty-three years. In 2000, she completed her adult psychoanalytic training with the Michigan Psychoanalytic Council, now known as the Michigan Council for Psychoanalysis and Psychotherapy. As a clinical social worker-psychoanalyst, she maintains a full-time private practice in psychoanalysis and psychotherapy in Ann Arbor, Michigan with children, adolescents, and adults. In addition, she is the child development director of a preschool. She is on the faculty of the Institute for Clinical Social Work, teaching in the distance-learning program and serves as a clinical consultant and dissertation committee member. Karen Baker is a consulting editor of *Psychoanalytic Social Work*. She is the past president of the American Association for Psychoanalysis in Clinical Social Work and continues to serve on the national board as the co-chair of the Child and Adolescent Committee. Prior to earning her MSW, she received a BS in education and taught children with learning disabilities. Her clinical practice areas of interest are child and adolescent development, working with parents, applied psychoanalysis in schools, trauma, and transference/countertransference.

Ralph Cuseglio is a clinical social worker who earned his Bachelor's degree in psychology from Oberlin College, and his Master of Social Work (MSW) and Doctor of Social Work (DSW) from Rutgers University. He is currently an assistant professor of social work at Monmouth University (NJ) where he teaches in clinical social work practice. Dr. Cuseglio has maintained a private psychotherapy practice for several years where he combines a psychodynamic treatment approach with mindfulness-based practices. Dr. Cuseglio served as a high school social worker for nine years in an urban school district working primarily with Latino adolescents and families. In this capacity, he provided supportive and therapeutic counseling to over 500 adolescents in individual and group modalities. He also regularly advises school district personnel and advocates for newly immigrated Latino adolescents and their families in response to school district and legislative policies that pose barriers to student learning and emotional well-being. Dr. Cuseglio has taught in the MSW program at Rutgers University School of Social Work and has been a field supervisor for MSW students for the last five years. Given his extensive experience working with youth, Dr. Cuseglio regularly offers mental health training to court-appointed advocates for children in foster care. Dr. Cuseglio's research interests include the integration of mindfulness-based practices into psychodynamic treatment, client re-enactment and rupture in the therapeutic dyad, countertransference as it relates to Carl Jung's wounded healer archetype, and the impact of mental health issues on individuals' creative capacities.

Lynda R. Fabbo, MSW, LCSW, DSW candidate, received her Bachelor's degree in psychology from Seton Hall University in 1989 and her Master of Social Work (MSW) from Rutgers University in 1994. She began her career working as a crisis intervention therapist with children and families involved in family court from 1990 to 1996. She then provided school-based therapy for at-risk children in several elementary schools for Faye G. Hill Community Consultants from 1997 to 2000. Simultaneously, she was the clinical director for Buzz's Bookworm, Inc., a comprehensive tutoring and advocacy program, where she supervised all mental health services provided to students and families and provided individual, family, and group counseling to special needs children and their families, as well as advocacy and education for special education students within their communities. She conducted educational seminars for parents and various professionals about managing learning disabilities and ADHD. She was a member of a special services department from January 2000 to June 2003 in her role on a child study team and provided case management and assessments for special needs students from preschool through fifth grade and counseling for students. She joined a different child study team in 2005, providing case management and assessments for special needs students, grades six through twelve and for students aged 18–21.

Jerry Floersch, MSW, PhD, Associate Professor, Rutgers University School of Social Work, is a 1998 graduate of the University of Chicago School of Social Service Administration. After earning the Master of Social Work (MSW) from the University of Kansas, he worked as a social worker in drug and alcohol, hospital, mental health, and community settings. He administered a mental health crisis service and played a key role in developing and implementing housing policies and programs for the adult severely mentally ill. He is the author of *Meds, Money, and Manners: The Case Management of Severe Mental Illness*, where, utilizing ethnographic and socio-historical methods, he examined the rise of community support services, the rise of the case manager and case management, and the limits of management models in providing services. He is an NIMH K08 recipient (2004–2009) for training in and development of qualitative methods to study youth subjective experience of psychotropic treatment. His work on psychotropic treatment focuses on the meanings adolescents and young adults make of their medication treatment, including social and psychological "side effects." In 2008, he was recipient of a Case Western Reserve University Presidential Research Initiative award where, as the Principal Investigator, he led a two-year investigation of college student use of mental health services, including psychiatric medications. His book, with Jeffrey Longhofer and Paul Kubek, *On Being and Having a Case Manager*, builds on earlier work in this field by exploring a clinical method for case management practice, and he is co-author of *Qualitative Methods for Practice Research*. He is currently conducting a multisite study of college student use of psychiatric medications.

Russell Healy, MSW, LCSW, DSW, is a clinical social worker in private practice in central New Jersey. He earned his Master of Social Work (MSW) in 1987 and his Doctor of Social Work (DSW) in 2016, both from the Rutgers University School of Social Work. He has also earned 18 credits towards a doctorate in medical humanities from Drew University. Healy is a sexuality and gender specialist. He wrote a chapter on transgender healthcare which was published in *Social Work in Health Settings* (4th edn). Healy also teaches courses on the assessment and treatment of transgender youth and private practice ethics for the Rutgers University School of Social Work's Continuing Education Program. He is a full professional member of the World Professional Association for Transgender Health and has given presentations at the Philadelphia Transgender Health Conference and the United States Professional Association for Transgender Health. Dr. Healy presented a seminar on the assessment and treatment of homosexual sex offenders at the Association for the Treatment of Sexual Abusers national conference in 2002. In 1993, the New Jersey Lesbian and Gay Coalition presented him with their yearly Achievement Award for his work on behalf of lesbian and gay youth. His current interests include exploring how social work ethics and biomedical ethics could be integrated to improve mental health practice.

Miriam Jaffe, Director of the writing program at the Rutgers University Doctorate in Social Work Program, holds a PhD in twentieth-century American literature based in cultural theory and ethnic studies, and she has a dual certification in teaching composition. She focuses on issues of life-writing and auto-ethnography in literature. Though she has published many articles on American literature, she was the guest editor for a special issue of *Writing and Pedagogy* on "Teaching with Technology," and she has authored an article in *Clinical Social Work* on teaching case study composition.

Alexis Kaliades, MSW, LCSW, has practiced as a high school social worker within urban public school districts for over five years. As a school social worker, Alexis Kaliades provides individual and group counseling, crisis intervention, mediation, and acts as a conduit between students, teachers, administration, and families. She works to increase protective factors for students who have endured a range of physical and emotional traumas including self-harm, domestic or relational violence, and incidences of harassment, intimidation, and bullying. She also functions as a member of the Child Study Team where she manages a caseload of students receiving special education and related services. Her work with the youth population began during her Master of Social Work (MSW) studies at Hawaii Pacific University. While earning her Master's degree, she worked as a case manager and counselor for at-risk adolescents with the City & County of Honolulu Youth Services Center and as a research assistant for a project entitled, "Promoting Social Competence and Resilience of Native Hawaiian Youth."

Jeffrey Longhofer, MSW, PhD, is Associate Professor of social work at Rutgers University. He is a clinical social worker and applied anthropologist whose research focuses on health and mental health practice, the cross-cultural study of mental illness, mental health case management, and the roles stigma and shame play in the social and psychological dynamics of practitioner/patient interactions. His recent ethnographic research has been in childcare settings and among children with parents suffering from life-threatening illnesses. His research has appeared in journals including *Psychiatric Services, Culture, Medicine and Psychiatry, Transcultural Psychiatry, Journal of Aging Studies, Qualitative Social Work: Research and Practice, Families, Systems and Health, Social Work and Mental Health, Ethnohistory*, and *Theory and Society*. His books include *On Being and Having a Case Manager* and *A–Z of Psychodynamic Practice*. He has served as the associate editor for the Society for Applied Anthropology journal, *Human Organization*, and editor of the American Anthropological Association journal, *Culture and Agriculture*.

Irma W. Sandoval-Arocho is a clinical social worker who earned her Master of Social Work (MSW) and Doctor of Social Work (DSW) from Rutgers University. She has been practicing school social work for the past thirteen years in an urban public school district and specializes in working with Hispanic/Latino children and families, newly arrived immigrant communities, at-risk youth, trauma, domestic violence, and suicide. Her academic work explores the role of schools in working with traumatized children and immigration in the context of the child and their family. Her experience in working with immigrant comm-unities has provided Dr. Sandoval-Arocho the opportunity to collaborate with the Southern Poverty Law Center as a curriculum writer for the Teaching Tolerance project. In this capacity, Dr. Sandoval-Arocho aims to improve justice and equity for immigrants while diversifying the knowledge base for K-5 student populations about immigration. As a school social worker, Dr. Sandoval-Arocho has also led several successful community outreach campaigns with major corporations and institutions of higher education to meet the needs of the children and families she works with. In addition to her role as a school social worker, she serves as an anti-bullying specialist in the public school district. Dr. Sandoval-Arocho is also experienced in the area of administration, policy, and planning and has served in various administrative capacities in the nonprofit sector from program coordinator to deputy director. Dr. Sandoval-Arocho has taught in both the MSW and DSW programs at the School of Social Work at Rutgers University and has been a field instructor for MSW students.

Jessica Verdicchio, MSW, LCSW, DSW, is a high school social worker. For the past twelve years, Dr. Verdicchio has served as a child study team case manager for special education students. She also provides weekly counseling services and is a leadership advisor to the greater student body. Additionally, Dr. Verdicchio is a part-time lecturer at Rutgers University, a clinical supervisor, and maintains a small private practice. Dr. Verdicchio's therapeutic approach incorporates a variety of cognitive-behavioral, solution-focused, and mindfulness-based therapeutic techniques. Her research interests are in the areas of child and adolescent mental health, the identity formation of affluent adolescents, and holistic approaches to health, wellness, and self-care.

Eric K. Williams, PsyA, MSW, LCSW, DSW, began his social work career at an urban community mental health center as the coordinator of Project RAPP (Reaching Adolescents Prevention Program), a psychotherapeutic after-school program for at-risk adolescents (1992–1996). For the past twenty years Dr. Williams has been a school social worker, providing clinical services in a variety of roles and settings. In addition to this work, Dr. Williams has been an adjunct professor at Hudson County Community College and a part-time lecturer at Rutgers University. He is also an instructor at the New Jersey Institute for Training in Psychoanalysis where he is the director of the Adult Psychoanalytic Program as well as a supervising analyst.

Wendy Winograd, LCSW, BCD-P, DSW, earned her BA and MA in English and American Literature at Brown University and University of Pennsylvania, respectively, and her Master of Social Work (MSW) at New York University. A certified psychoanalyst, she maintains a private practice where she provides psychotherapy to adults, adolescents, and couples as well as clinical supervision to social workers and psychoanalytic candidates. She is a faculty member and training analyst at the New Jersey Institute for Training in Psychoanalysis and the Center for Psychotherapy and Psychoanalysis of New Jersey. She has worked for fifteen years as a school counselor with children aged 3–18. She supervises MSW interns and teaches social work practice as a part-time lecturer at the Rutgers

University School of Social Work. Volunteer activities include leading a consultation group for A Home Within, a national organization that matches children and adolescents who have been in foster care with therapists who offer treatment pro bono and serving as recording secretary and co-chair of the Child and Adolescent Committee on the Executive Board of the American Association for Psychoanalysis in Clinical Social Work. Her current research focuses on the psychoanalytic understanding of the relationship between play, identity, and relationship. She has published on female development, psychoanalytic therapy with transgender adolescents, and mother/daughter relationships and has presented her work nationally and internationally.

1

INTRODUCTION

The Value of Case Studies in School Social Work

M. Jaffe, J. Floersch, J. Longhofer, and W. Winograd

In recent years, the number of children and adolescents in school with psychiatric and medical diagnoses has dramatically increased. In addition, with the passage of the Americans with Disabilities Act (1990), schools are required to meet the varying needs of students with disabilities. As administrators, teachers, parents, and students themselves recognize the relationships among mental health, social skills, and academic achievement, schools are employing more and more social workers to intervene with students whose academic progress may be jeopardized by problems in the social environment (Fazel et al., 2014). In school settings, clinical social workers participate on child study teams, provide resources, counseling support, and psychotherapy. Here, we have gathered nine case studies that communicate the complexities and ambiguities of various aspects of this growing field. The case studies in this volume have been written for students and early career practitioners who are interested in the field of school social work. The author of each chapter is a seasoned expert, and thus, other experienced practitioners of school social work will find a familiar and galvanizing community at hand.

What's in this Book?

We begin with Lynda Fabbo's account of school social work on a child study team in "Educating Marta." Her focus is a multiply disabled student whom Fabbo champions from kindergarten through high school—the entire course of Marta's educational career in a public school district. Fabbo demonstrates how an astute early biopsychosocial evaluation can set a student's trajectory toward success against all odds. She presents the nuances of school social work that are so often lost behind the scenes: how to navigate a conversation about special education with fearful parents, how to persuade resistant colleagues in an age of standardized testing, how to facilitate inclusion and accommodations mandated by an Individualized Education Plan, and how to emotionally support a student with special needs. What Fabbo does not include in this chapter are the notes and e-mails that she still receives from Marta, who writes with updates about college life. "Educating Marta" is a best-case scenario, yet throughout Fabbo's narrative, we can feel the tensions underscoring all that might have gone wrong in launching and sustaining Marta's academic success.

Academic performance and student behavior are often commingled priorities for school social workers. Thus, we turn next to Wendy Winograd, one of the volume's editors, in a chapter that explores the school social worker's role in understanding and managing social and emotional struggles. Proceeding from the assumption that behavior is an expression of inner desires, intentions, wishes, and fears, Winograd illustrates in three composite case examples how working from a psychoanalytically informed, attachment-based perspective allows a school social worker to intervene effectively when dysregulated children interfere with the classroom dynamic and with their own learning. Reluctant to label a child's problematic behavior as pathological, she stresses the importance of collaborating and working with teachers and parents in supporting a child's normative developmental strivings. Moreover, Winograd notes the difficulties of conducting mental health services in a "host setting," because the mission of a school does not always align with the goals of a clinical social worker.

This issue carries over into the assumption that in-house services are unnecessary in affluent school districts and private schools because students' families likely have their basic needs met and can cover the costs of mental health services. Jessica Verdicchio, in her work with an adolescent girl, challenges the notion that more money means fewer problems. Verdicchio looks at how the school social worker as counselor navigates an environment rife with scholastic competition, mean girls armed with social media, and preoccupied parents who attempt to remedy their absence via therapeutic getaways to luxurious destinations without really taking time to know their own children. While affluent students must often keep up the facade of perfection everywhere else, the school social worker may often be the only one privy to the dynamics underlying eating disorders, cutting, and drug and alcohol addiction. With this case study Verdicchio takes the reader into the world of teens at risk of heightened levels of depression, anxiety, and suicide. She shows us how school social work is more necessary than ever before in affluent districts.

In "Healing *In Loco Parentis*: The Use of Schools as Therapeutic Communities," Irma Sandoval-Arocho presents the opposite—perhaps more familiar—side of the coin, so to speak. In the urban school district where Sandoval-Arocho practiced, it was not uncommon for families to be torn apart by immigration, poverty, and institutional racism. She homes in on the story of Leo, a 9-year-old Latino immigrant whose broken family system led to his father's suicide, to illustrate how the school in this community acted as a locus of caring. With the school social worker as central player, the school staff mobilizes to recognize Leo's intergenerational trauma as well as the deep shame that overshadowed his grief. Sandoval-Arocho shows how a school functions as a therapeutic community, and how her role in that community required cultural competence, home visitation, and the transformation of *in loco parentis* from a disciplinary concept into a guardianship to keep children like Leo from suffering alone.

Eric Williams's case study on alternative education program design further expands the boundaries of traditional school social work into the realm of administration. Using systems theory as a theoretical frame, Williams documents his innovative approach to transforming an entire school of at-risk adolescent students and the school staff into a unified family. His task required expertise in mental health, an understanding of adolescent development, knowledge of the cultural underpinnings of the community beyond the school, operationalizing a team of colleagues—and the skill to figure out how all of the moving parts could work together to promote academic achievement and social ability. He moved the school away from crisis management to create a wholly new context for student growth, drawing on the person-in-environment perspective to co-create a new culture in which students were empowered. As a result, students who needed special attention in order to thrive—who were set apart because they needed a better way to become integrated—got it not only from the school social worker and the school staff, but also from each other.

Part of what makes social workers successful in facilitating the inclusion of all people is their value to network knowledge. In "School Social Work and the Sexual and Gender Minority Student in the Twenty-First Century," Russell Healy, an authority in LGBTQ issues, shares his experience as a school social work consultant when he is called in to oversee the case of Jay, a transgender high school student. A belief that transgender adolescents presented a "liability" because of a statistically higher suicide rate led Jay's school administrators to urge the school social worker, Carmen, to refer Jay for services in the community. However, in consultation with Healy, who pushed for in-school counseling, Carmen was able to work with Jay in a school setting, thereby avoiding additional stigma by way of Jay's segregation and isolation from the community. Here we see the results of Healy's supervision of Carmen play out in transgender-affirmative case management. As Carmen learns how to help Jay, we learn the history of the LGBT student in schools, the resources to which school social workers can turn for further understanding LGBT students, why a GSA (Gay/Straight Alliance) is not for everyone, and some techniques that improve LGBT student outcomes. However, the most important takeaway from Healy's case study is his assertion that each sexual minority student be treated as an N of 1: an individual within a specific context. And though we have come a long way, in many regions, in our awareness of gender dysphoria, we can do more to check our assumptions about LGBT students through self-reflexivity to recognize that the truest form of client engagement comes from admitting what one does not know.

These principles—self-reflexivity and humility over fragility—take on a similar shape in Alexis Kaliades's chapter, "Rethinking Disciplinary Strategies: Reflections on White Privilege in School Social Work." Kaliades examines how white privilege and a lack of cultural competence lead to a no-tolerance disciplinary system that reinforces oppressive power dynamics. Being a white social worker among students of color gives Kaliades the opportunity to grapple with the racism that affects the ways students respond to pressures in school. Kaliades's structural role in that institution is revealed when her adolescent client, Tara, is repeatedly punished for the defensive behaviors that serve as a coping mechanism in her low-income neighborhood, whose inhabitants suffer from the effects of racial disparities. Tara lands regularly in Kaliades's office, where Kaliades is expected to counsel Tara toward obedience, but through their conversations, Kaliades comes to understand how Tara's race shapes her experience in ways that the staff—herself included—must work harder to recognize in order to implement fairer and more productive policies that actually serve to counteract staff burnout.

Ralph Cuseglio confronts burnout in a different way. When overwhelmed by an impossible caseload of individual student stressors, he turned to mindfulness meditation as a form of self-care. He then realized that the same mindfulness techniques he had been practicing could serve as the foundational coping mechanism for students; furthermore, the group therapy environment cut down on his individual caseload so that he could solve problems more efficiently. Cuseglio's chapter on "Mindfulness Group Work in the School Setting" showcases the way he encouraged connectivity and compassion toward self and other in an age when people are more plugged into screens than to each other. Cuseglio models how to rationalize the purpose of a group, advertise a group, and manage group dynamics.

Finally, Karen Baker offers a look at the role of a school social worker in a preschool/kindergarten setting with a focus on her work with parents. While most non-therapeutic preschools do not offer social work services, Baker's school depends on social workers to provide meaningful parenting education on the fly, in individual meetings, and in a parent group program. Proceeding from the belief that parents and teachers must be partners in a child's development, Baker examines her work as a family coordinator, illustrating through two parent groups how a psychoanalytic perspective based on understanding the whole child in her whole environment is consistent with the basic social work principles of worth of the individual person and the importance of human relationships.

And the Assignment Questions?

While the case studies taken as a group offer an overview of school social work, each case can be read and studied individually. At the end of each chapter, therefore, we offer teaching resources to facilitate an in-depth encounter with the material in that case. The teaching resources fall into three main categories.

The pre-reading questions introduce general social work topics and help students to assess their own theoretical assumptions about those topics. As prompts for class discussion and/or quick writing exercises, the first set of questions is designed to reveal what students want to learn from reading: what they know and what they do not know. The questions ask students to define key terms and to think about how their own experiences will inform their reading before they even start. We encourage students to identify their preconceived notions and to track how their thinking changes through the act of reading a case study.

The close reading questions that appear after each chapter offer a framework to discuss, with attention to specific sets of words, the details in the case that drive the conceptual argument. Initially, the questions in this section ask for some summary as a way to test the students' more basic understanding of the content. But the secondary close reading questions encourage students to explore the author's motivations and scholarly perspectives.

Prompts for writing privilege the students' voices. Students have been well trained to regurgitate the right answers, but this section puts a variety of answers into conversation with each other. These questions often pair case studies with other case studies and research articles so that students can evaluate how one set of ideas sits in relation to another set of ideas. These pairings often call for students to search the author's references. Students are asked to generate their own ideas about what the case and its theoretical frameworks can teach them about important elements of their own practice. Most centrally, we want students to say why the case matters.

Why Narrative Case Studies?

Generalizations can tell us what school social work might look like, but generalizations are inherently reductive: they promote only stereotypes or caricatures. If you have decided to seriously explore the field of school social work, then you must closely engage with the lived experience of school social workers.

The idea that the narrative case study—a story of practice—is a significant form of knowledge production rests upon the following philosophical claim: practice takes place in open systems, and this reality means that the dominant research aim of generalization, or prediction, is often in tension with what happens in actual practice. Thus, all practice is case specific. The power of the case study is in its integrative potential for theory building and causal explanation. However, the case study can only build theory and causal explanation from context-dependent knowledge.

After all, the world of school social work is not actually made up of discrete agents—social workers and clients—who face each other making choices; in this view, reality is an aggregate of separately distinct acts. As many ecologists would argue, our existence is inevitably intertwined with our natural environments, which generalizable data often fails to capture, even with the best measures. Our aim here is for readers to enter an intersubjective world, not a subject/object world. Hence, each author featured in our text frames his/her case study as subject/object paired interactions. When school social workers choose interventions and explain them through writing, we must recognize the role of their interactive experience and interpretation.

Similarly, we must recognize that any individual social worker cannot control all of the variables in the cases that he/she depicts. Therefore, these case studies strive to capture the uncertainty of their circumstances. Andrew Sayer, in *Why Things Matter to People* (2011), writes that

> events are not predetermined . . . yet when looking back at changes and explaining them, it is easy to imagine that what did happen was always the only things that could have happened . . . One of the temptations of social explanation is to suppress acknowledgements of the fact that at any instant, the future is open.
>
> *p. 15*

The case study approach to examining school social work avoids the assumption that there is an end-point or predetermined goal in writing or reading a case study. The real value of the case study is that it does not pretend to control outcomes through these types of assumptions. Instead, the case study is, as Brandell and Varkas (2001) say, an "entree to information that might otherwise be inaccessible," and its value "lies in its experience-near descriptions of clinical processes . . . Case studies provide examples of what already has been encountered and how difficult situations were handled" (pp. 376–377). To offer an example in a way that is "experience-near" requires in-depth self-reflexivity. The authors of this textbook display their self-reflexivity through the creation of narrative.

Why narrative? In *Narrative Knowing and the Human Sciences* (1988), Donald Polkinghorne defines narrative as "the fundamental scheme for linking individual human actions and events into interrelated aspects of an understandable composite" (p. 13). Narrative links events and connects ideas so that we can discover new knowledge as we create narrative and read it. As individuals, we have a great power to decide and explore what narratives mean, and then, by extension, why they matter to us. Our bodies, our identities, our memories, our cultures, our pasts are all filters for how we create and respond to narrative, and we become aware of such filters when we read and write. Even down to the element of plot, we are prone not only to interpretation through our filters, but also to being persuaded in ways that change our filters. A plot—especially if we think of the word in verb form, to plot—is something that an author chooses for a reason. The narrative theorist Ricoeur (1977) would say that the reason is to authenticate data and justify explanation. Narrative case studies do reason, authenticate, and justify by using practice as plot. Thus, narrative case studies, for our purposes, use plot to relay a sense of the school social work world, offering explanations for events that occur in the open system of client and social worker interactions.

Why "Phenomenological Perspectives"?

Phenomenology is the study of experience from a first person perspective. As such, it privileges subjective experience and focuses on the intention of an individual consciousness toward an object in the field outside of the subject. Significantly, though, as Russon (2003) notes, phenomenology stresses the interpersonal, or social, "the way in which we are inherently 'with' others, rather than being fundamentally 'by ourselves'" (p. 2). Key here is the focus on the interplay between self and other and thus the significance of relationship. Moreover, phenomenology is interested in the "meaning things have in our experience, notably, the significance of objects, events, tools, the flow of time, the self, and others, as these things arise and are experienced in our 'life-world'" (Phenomenology, n.d.).

The case studies in this volume aim to give voice to the lived experience of the various subjectivities that inhabit the school environment, from administrators, to teachers, to students, to the social workers themselves, who are writing the case narratives. Because of its interest in our intentions toward the objects and events in our "life-world," phenomenology is a good fit with the case studies presented here, as each one focuses on the social workers' intentions toward the clients they serve and the colleagues with whom they work. Because of its focus on the flow of time, phenomenology is a good fit with the narrative character of the case studies as the stories unfold in time. Schools are environments where the constituents—students—are in a constant state of development and change, thus offering a particularly apt look at the impact of time on human experience. Finally, because of its respect for the significance of relationships in the unfolding and creation of identity and self, phenomenology is a good fit with the philosophy of social work itself, which has always privileged the relationship between social worker and client as a key, if not *the* key in the healing process. Indeed, in each of the case studies, it is the unique relationship between the writer and his/her students that results in empathic understanding, effective intervention, and relief of suffering.

We hope that these narrative case studies as an aggregate will offer a deep understanding of what it means and feels like to inhabit a school. Students of school social work will no doubt be interested in the lived experience of the individual social worker. The self-reflexivity that is demanded by the phenomenological perspective and the narrative case study writing offers such insight into the mind of the writer, thus conveying the importance of understanding and empathizing with all who inhabit the school environment.

References

Brandell, J. R., and Varkas, T. (2001). Narrative case studies. In B. A. Thyer (Ed.), *The handbook of social work research methods* (pp. 376–396). Thousand Oaks, CA: Sage Publications, Inc.

Fazel, M., Hoagwood, K., Stephan, S., and Ford, T. (2014). Mental health interventions in schools in high-income countries. *The Lancet Psychiatry, 1*(5), 377–387.

Phenomenology (n.d.). In *Stanford Encyclopedia online.* Accessed online February 28, 2017 at https://plato.stanford.edu/entries/phenomenology/#1.

Polkinghorne, D. E. (1988). *Narrative knowing and the human sciences.* Albany, NY: State University of New York Press.

Ricoeur, P. (1977). *Narrative truth and historical truth: Meaning and interpretation in psychoanalysis.* New York: Norton.

Russon, J. (2003). *Human experience: Philosophy, neurosis and the elements of everyday life.* Albany, NY: State University of New York Press.

Sayer, A. (2011). *Why things matter to people: Social science, values and ethical life.* New York: Cambridge University Press.

2

EDUCATING MARTA

A School Social Worker's Role on a Child Study Team

Lynda R. Fabbo

Pre-Reading Questions

1. What is a disability? What do you know about the laws that protect individuals with disabilities?
2. What roles does a school social worker play on a child study team? Who are the other members on the team? What is the purpose of the team?
3. What is "mainstreaming" and what are your thoughts about it? Do you have any personal experience with mainstreaming involving yourself or someone you know?

Introduction

The community center was a bright and inviting space with colorful murals of jungle animals painted on the walls. There were bins of toys in every corner and a wooden play kitchen stocked with little pots and pans and plastic food. When Ms. Gutierrez greeted me, I commented on how lovely the center was. She smiled and proudly told me that she and the other parents from the church held fundraisers to acquire the toys and the arts and crafts supplies that the children use during playtime, and she explained how the moms took turns preparing snacks for the children each week. A community center with a playgroup room was something she worked hard with others to create and maintain for the neighborhood. I took a seat on the periphery of the room, and I started my observation of her 4-year-old daughter, Marta.

Marta, Mr. and Ms. Gutierrez's only child, was born with a genetic disorder that is characterized by excessive physical growth during the first few years of life as well as cognitive impairment later in life. Most notable is her craniofacial configuration that includes a prominent forehead, widely spaced eyes with down slanting eyelids, a high narrow palate, and a long narrow face and head that is somewhat larger than her body. She first entered the special services system through an early intervention program that the state provides for children born with developmental disabilities, a step that was initiated by her physician. Marta received physical and occupational therapies at home to address the low muscle tone that her condition caused, as well as speech/language therapy. When Marta turned two and a half, the early intervention program referred her to the public school special education program for evaluation, and they recommended placement into their handicapped preschool program available for children until they enter kindergarten; however, Mr. and Ms. Gutierrez opted not to continue in the program. Ms. Gutierrez continued working with Marta at home, and she eventually enrolled Marta in the local playgroup where I first observed her. When Marta was old enough to enter kindergarten, her mother brought her to the neighborhood school to register her, and based on her health information, the school referred her to the special education department for an evaluation. Ms. Gutierrez met with the team and agreed to have Marta evaluated prior to her entering kindergarten. I was at the community center to conduct my part of the evaluation: a social assessment that involved an observation of Marta and an interview with her parents.

Since she was physically much larger than the other children, I spotted her rather quickly. She had on a pink polka-dotted dress and little white sneakers and an enormous bow in her hair. I wondered if her mother was trying to somehow disguise her larger physical size with the size of the bow. The first thing I noticed about her, other than her size, was her incredibly expressive eyes. She spoke volumes with her furrowing eyebrows and flirtatious blinks. She was not verbal at all, yet she communicated effectively with the other children through her facial expressions and subtle hand gestures. She found her way to a bin of wooden blocks in a corner of the room and emptied it onto a woolen, red area rug. She was stacking the blocks in a tower when a little boy in the group noticed her tower and walked over to her and kicked it over, causing the blocks to scatter. I expected Marta to do what any typical 4-year-old would do: to cry or run to her mother. But Marta did not do that. She looked up at him, gave him a little smile, and stacked the blocks again, and he kicked them down. This was incredibly funny to both of them, and they roared with laughter. The little boy then sat next to Marta and began building a tower himself and then knocking it down. Marta abandoned her block building at this point and decided to just hand the blocks to the little boy who kept smashing his tower over and over again. They had created some sort of game and were enjoying it immensely. I wrote in my notes, "Marta has a sweet endearing way, exuding a gentle kindness to the other children that clearly enjoy her company." I was very impressed with her ability to manage the situation at her age the way she did. She was able to capture the attention of this rather rambunctious boy in a game without saying a word. I watched Marta for about an hour, and she involved several other children in similar ways. She seemed to understand how to read social situations and to engage in cooperative play. She was even-tempered, emotionally regulated, and incredibly aware of all that was going on around her, even of strangers sent there to observe, which I learned when it was snack time. The children eagerly took their places around a little table waiting for the moms to pour juice into cups and pass out the snacks, but Marta did not. Instead, she came over to where I was sitting, looked at me and blinked her long lashes twice, took my hand and gently led me to the table. She had not acknowledged me prior to this moment, but clearly she knew I was there and in her own very hospitable way was offering me (a guest) some of her snack. I accepted her silent invitation and while sitting at the little table sharing in the group's snack time, I realized what a keen perception of the social construct around her she had, and I was impressed by her ability to successfully participate. This was the strength around which a child study team could build an academic program. Marta was incredibly connected to her "typical" peers, and despite her learning difficulties, she was an integral part of her community. This was a valuable resource to her now, and it would prove valuable to her in the future. I concluded, in my mind, that my official recommendation would be for the district to find a way to meet her complicated educational needs within her neighborhood school and not in a self-contained special education classroom across town. I then wondered exactly how I was going to relay this to a team of professionals with a stack of standardized tests that purported otherwise. I sighed, and Marta handed me a pretzel stick.

What is Disabled?

Modern movements for the rights of individuals with disabilities have been diligent in separating disability from illness in an attempt to reframe how disabled people have been seen under the dominant medical model construct. Under this construct, a disabled person is medically assessed, diagnosed, and treated most often in isolation (Laing, 1971). Their disabling condition is seen as an illness in need of curing or healing, when in fact not all disabled people are sick. Most disabled people are relatively physically stable and do not need continual medical intervention, yet they are continued to be "treated" as ill. Under the purview of the medical model, a disability is located solely within the person and needs to be ameliorated or eradicated for the individual to successfully function in society and they are often alienated as a result (Wendell, 2013). Conversely, the social construct approach to disability locates the issues to be that of society's neglect of differing abilities which leads to total exclusion and subsequent oppression. The disabling factor is not a problem located in the person, but an environmental problem. However, this model mostly takes into account those with physical or sensory impairments which can be easier to accommodate through physical adaptation (Shakespeare, 2013). Learning disabilities, and other disabilities such as autism, can pose very different challenges that cannot necessarily be cured or physically adapted to, which is why an approach located somewhere in between these models needs to be considered.

The World Health Organization revised the classification of functioning and disability in recognition of the importance of the full participation of persons with disabilities and in recognition that the terms used in classifying such people can be stigmatizing (WHO, 2007). But what does participation mean and how is this facilitated successfully? In a study by Hammel et al. (2008), this question was posed to a group of diversely disabled people to ascertain what participation meant to them in order to characterize it and to identify the barriers and supports that they required to experience it. The result of the study yielded that there was no gold standard for participation. The participants reported needing to be free to pursue participation on their own terms and in their own way based on their personal experiences and the experiences that they had in their different communities. Participation was viewed as a relational right and a responsibility between disabled people and their environments, and it was based on individual experience.

Children born with disabilities are generally healthy-bodied with varied abilities that need to be recognized and encouraged. How they exist in their environments and how their environments respond to them will determine whether or not they are successfully included. As a school social worker, my goal for every student with whom I work is for her educational experience to prepare her for a lifetime of meaningful, valuable inclusion in her community as independently as possible and to provide her with the ability to access the necessary resources to facilitate and adapt this inclusion as she desires. My goal is to help the child and her family formulate and realize how this goal will manifest within her family, school, and community. To achieve this goal, I continually assess the various strengths and challenges that emerge during a child's development and experience and formulate a working trajectory of success. This trajectory of success is a living plan that includes factors such as a child's personal character-istics and abilities as they emerge and develop, her family's available support and culture, the overarching bureaucracy governing her education, and the community resources available to facilitate her education. Although these trajectories are very different for each student, my ideal goal remains the same—that students with disabilities will find their meaningful place in the community. The following case study composite of Marta illustrates how this is done at various junctures in her educational program from the perspective of a school social worker on a child study team.

Marta's Parents

Family dynamics shift dramatically when a child with disabilities is born into it. The initial shock of the diagnosis is often replaced by negative emotions, and parents will adapt in many different ways. Some will be able to effectively mobilize with acceptance and flexibility, others may freeze in various degrees of rigidity, and some may completely resist or deny their child's disability altogether. The overall stress level of these parents increases, and they often develop anxiety and can be extremely overprotective of their children (Falik, 1995). They can feel intruded upon as the involved professionals ask personal questions repeatedly to gather background developmental information. If parents themselves have had negative experiences in the past because of their own learning or physical issues, the process of evaluating their child could trigger traumatic feelings. Some parents may also blame each other or themselves for having caused their child's disabling condition in some way, and feelings of shame and guilt develop. Family characteristics such as marital status, ethnic background, and income affect how parents interact with their child's school and community, and how they influence their child to adapt and respond to their environment. Parents' perception of their child's abilities, their confidence that they can help provide for their child's special needs, and their belief that they are effective members of the educational team are also important factors to consider when creating a bridge between home and school (Eccles and Harold, 1993). They reinvent themselves, deciding how they want the world to see them and how they will present themselves and their family to their community, and this new identity will often change as the child grows and develops.

A child's primary experience with her parents will determine how she will view and learn from her world. Parents are the meditational entities that establish the framework for how their child will learn and respond to the various stimuli she encounters. It is through them, as conduits, that the child will learn how to interact with her world and how she interprets the way the world interacts with her. The essential support a child needs to function in life comes directly from her family's need and her school's need to facilitate positive interaction, which thus establishes a strong and healthy home-school connection. Providing help is one part of the equation when working with children overcoming academic and social challenges, but ensuring that the offered help is positively received is far more important. A child will look to her parents and family to learn how to receive help from the other significant teachers and adults in her life, which is why it is important to establish a healthy, positive network to support development and learning (Comer and Haynes, 1991). Parental involvement will directly affect a child's successful participation in her education.

When I called Marta's parents to set up a meeting, Mr. Gutierrez answered and presented himself as the spokesperson for the family. I sensed his reluctance to participate when he told me that each day and time I offered to meet with him and his wife was not convenient for them. I told him I would accommodate any day and time that would work for them, and he requested we meet very early in the morning so that he would not miss work, and he informed me he could only stay for a limited amount of time. I realized I would have to tread lightly around Mr. Gutierrez, who was exhibiting a resistance to the process. I wondered if this was why the family pulled Marta out of the early intervention program. I didn't want them to pull her again, especially after I saw how positively she interacted with her peers and her future social potential, so I needed to engage him directly in the process. I wanted to ensure that Marta's parents felt heard and understood and knew I respected their opinions and input. If any plan for Marta to succeed in school was going to be effective, then creating a healthy working relationship with her parents would be crucial, so I agreed to meet with them the morning and day Mr. Gutierrez requested.

Mr. and Ms. Gutierrez came into the office together, and I offered them a seat at our conference room table. There were other offices attached to this conference space, and the workers in these offices shut their doors as is our practice when one of us needs privacy. Mr. Gutierrez looked at the closing doors and then at me for explanation, and I assured him we wouldn't be disturbed and that their privacy would be respected. He nodded and relaxed in his chair, indicating he was willing to continue. My goal for this interview was to explore their resilience and flexibility as parents of a special needs child, as well as to collect a detailed family history as part of my social/emotional assessment of Marta. I also wanted to establish a healthy rapport with her parents, hoping to engage them, especially her father, in the evaluation and planning process. Before I could make recommendations to the school regarding how best to educate Marta from a social and emotional perspective, I needed to understand the current climate of her life. I needed to assess how she functioned in her home and in her community, and I needed to identify the sources of strength and empowerment in her world, as well as to identify problematic areas.

I took out my interview questionnaire and simultaneously handed a copy of it to Mr. Gutierrez. I typically do not do this, but I wanted to put him at ease, and I thought giving him a copy of the questionnaire might help. He nodded his head in thanks and read the document. The items on the questionnaire asked basic demographic information about him and his wife and developmental questions about Marta. I asked him if he wouldn't mind answering the questions and whether there were any questions that he did not want to answer. He took a few moments to read it over, and he agreed to proceed.

I went through the questionnaire, asking them some basic information such as their ages and occupations and where they were from. Mr. and Ms. Gutierrez met and married in Puerto Rico, where they were both born. They came to the States in their early twenties and lived with extended family until they were able to afford their own home. They had Marta, their only child, about ten years later, in their early thirties, when they were more financially stable. Mr. Gutierrez worked in construction as a foreman, and Ms. Gutierrez was a nurse; however, she stopped working when Marta was born so that she could stay home to take care of her. Both Mr. and Ms. Gutierrez were very active in their church and in their community, and they lived on the same block as many of their extended family members.

When most of the questionnaire was filled out, Mr. Gutierrez said he needed to leave for work, and he turned to his wife, assuring her he approved of her remaining there with me alone to finish the interview. I thanked him for his time, and I proceeded to complete my interview with Ms. Gutierrez. I hoped his entrusting his wife to be with me alone was an indication of new willingness to participate in the process. Ms. Gutierrez seemed relieved by her husband's departure, and her demeanor changed dramatically. The demure polite smile she maintained in her husband's presence disappeared as she looked directly into my eyes and asked if she could tell me some things that were not on the questionnaire. She needed to speak "off the record," so I put down my pen and pushed the questionnaire aside signaling my receptiveness. She apologized for her husband's initial resistant behavior and explained that he could be very overprotective of Marta, but she felt that he was easing into the process.

Ms. Gutierrez told me that she and her husband waited a long time to have a child, and that her husband felt this was maybe why Marta was born with the disorder. She said her husband often blamed himself for not making enough money when they were a younger couple, feeling that their older age had something to do with Marta's condition. Mr. and Ms. Gutierrez did not know there was anything wrong with Marta while Ms. Gutierrez was pregnant with her and found out about her condition when she was born. I asked her how they eventually came to terms with Marta's condition and how they handled her needs when she was a baby, and she said that many members of their church were supportive. She shared that her husband did not want anyone to see Marta for a long time. He was afraid people would stare at her because she looked different, and he feared they would not accept her. Ms. Gutierrez fought with her husband about this because she knew it was not possible to keep her hidden, and she wanted her daughter to be part of the world. As Marta got older and her personality blossomed, Ms. Gutierrez insisted that Marta be with other children. Eventually, Mr. Gutierrez agreed to bring Marta to church activities and family events. He became suspicious and defensive when the early intervention team was involved, and he insisted they leave the family alone. He was afraid of the evaluation being conducted and was concerned that Marta would be put in an institution. I now better understood Mr. Gutierrez's resistance. He was afraid for his daughter's future, and he didn't know if people would be as understanding toward her as she would need them to be. I understood this vulnerability and appreciated why he was so overprotective of his Marta. I wondered if it would help to show him how others with similar situations fared. Maybe if he could connect with other parents like him, he would feel better about the evaluation process and be open to learning about how we could help Marta.

Ms. Gutierrez then changed her tone and began to ask me some questions. Will Marta be able to learn what other children learn? Will the kids in the public school make fun of her? Will she find her place in the world? Will she be happy? The future was unknown, and this was terrifying. I tried my best to answer her questions without too many specifics because the nature of Marta's genetic condition offered a very broad range of possibilities. Ms. Gutierrez needed this opportunity to speak candidly, and I wondered if she and her husband were still at odds about the evaluation and the services that may follow. I felt that she needed to ask these questions by herself, and she needed time to process answers. I sensed she was struggling to visualize what Marta's future could look like, and she needed some vision to work toward. Much was unknowable about Marta's future at this point, which was difficult to explain to Marta's parents without being too discouraging or unrealistically hopeful. Raising a special needs child is a lifelong process that needs to unfold in the least damaging way to the family unit. If the family cannot sustain the stress of raising a special needs child, then the child suffers. I asked Ms. Gutierrez what her main goal was for Marta's future, my final question in the interview, and she said she just wanted to make sure Marta was among people who cared about her and that she was not alone.

I had the same goal in mind. I wanted her to be included in her community as independently and as successfully as possible, and I wanted her to be able to access the resources she would need to be able to do so. I felt this was a very good starting point for my working with Marta's parents, not just because we had similar goals in mind, but also because her mother was willing to have the conversation about Marta's future. I have seen what happens to families who are not willing to discuss or acknowledge their child's future. They get stuck in denial for refusing to plan for the future until it is too late to effect any choices, and the child and the family suffer. It is best when the family is open to the conversation because it indicates that they are able to mobilize necessary resources on their child's behalf, and I felt Marta's mother could do this, but first I had to mobilize the team.

The Team

To understand the role of a child study team member in a public school setting, it is necessary to be cognizant of the mandate under which they work that created the Special Education system. Public Law 94–142, called the Education for All Handicapped Children Act, was enacted on November 19, 1975, and was later renamed the Individuals with Disabilities Education Act (IDEA) in 1990. This law ensures that all handicapped children would have a right to an education, and it establishes a process by which state and local educational agencies could be held accountable for providing educational services for all handicapped children. The Special Education Code was created to further ensure all students with disabilities receive "a free, appropriate public (special) education including related services based on the student's unique needs and not on the student's disability in the least restrictive environment" (US Department of Education, 2010). In order to do this, the code specifies that a multi-disciplinary team be assembled who are required to conduct evaluations, create Individualized Educational Plans (IEPs) with measurable goals and objectives, and ensure these IEPs are being accurately followed and appropriately reviewed within very specific timelines. The IEP team must consist of parents, teachers, and other pertinent professionals who are qualified to administer standardized testing in order to establish a child's learning potential and achievement. This team most typically comprised of a school psychologist, a learning disabilities teacher consultant (LDTC), a school social worker, and possibly other professionals, such as a speech/language therapist, behavioral specialist, and occupational and physical therapists, depending on the area of disability identified or suspected in the child.

The IEP is a written plan that is reviewed at least yearly and describes in detail a child's specialized education program. It includes a description of the child's disabling condition and how the condition interferes with her ability to effectively access education. The plan must outline how the team plans to address a child's difficulties and must include measurable goals and short-term objectives or benchmarks and provide data-driven methods and results. This document is also considered a legally binding contract between the parent and the school and is the document that is scrutinized when taken to court. It drives the budget for in-school services, transportation, and out-of-district placements. If it is not written in the IEP, then it does not happen.

What is not outlined here, for the sake of brevity, is the legal paperwork required, the very specific timelines involved in the entire process, the case manager's obligation to have the correct attendees at the correct meetings, and the many courses of mediation and due process available to parents that do not agree. The code is a lengthy, legal document that can be confusing, and it is often misinterpreted, which is why parents seek advocates or procure legal representation and why special education departments have lawyers regularly retained. Child study team members, especially social workers, who hold professional licenses in addition to school certification credentials, take great care to stay within the legal parameters when working with students, because their licenses can be at risk, which can be quite challenging when trying to find creative ways to educate children. The benefit of having a multi-disciplinary team working with a special needs child far outweighs the challenges occasionally presented by differing professional opinions. The range of skills and knowledge made available by the team for special needs children is valuable and very necessary. Having different professionals with different theoretical backgrounds examine a student typically results in a plethora of recommendations and resources. However, the differing theoretical backgrounds can at times clash as a student's multiple needs compete for attention. For instance, a speech language therapist may feel pragmatic language deficiencies are more in need of correction than a reading issue that is identified by a learning consultant. A school psychologist might consider supporting a child's processing issues in a way that pulls him out of a class in which the school social worker feels he thrives socially. The team is challenged with meeting a student's needs by formulating a plan that incorporates all their specialized professional input. Most of the time, the team concurs and the work is complementary, but there are times when differing professional backgrounds and perspectives cause a dissention in the planning process which, in fact, happened when we were formulating a plan for Marta.

Prior to the formal IEP meeting with Marta's parents, the team met to discuss their findings and recommendations. The school psychologist and learning consultant who focused their evaluation on Marta's cognitive ability and achievement determined that although Marta's cognitive ability was at the lower end of the average range, her achievement was considered significantly below her same aged peers. This, coupled with her physical condition and subsequent need for occupational, physical and speech therapies, warranted their recommendation that she be placed in a self-contained classroom in one of the district's schools located several miles from her neighborhood. Here, they argued, she could get all these necessary therapies in one place and receive remedial education as well in a small group. Although I agreed that Marta would benefit from the various therapies we could offer her, I felt that pulling her out of her community school and placing her in this highly specialized setting would be detrimental to her emotional and social needs. I had no doubt that Marta would make new friends in this school, but so many of the students there were from communities that were further away. The children in this particular school traveled some distance for the services and there was no opportunity for relationships to evolve once the school day ended. I was concerned that Marta's and her family's connection to the neighborhood and community could not be maintained if Marta attended a school so far away. The Gutierrez family did not drive, and having Marta in a school across town would mean that Ms. Gutierrez could not be part of the school as she was in the community center where Marta attended preschool and playgroup. I felt that Ms. Gutierrez would continue to need the support of the parents in her community as Marta grew, especially since her husband was ambivalent and somewhat resistant to the process. Marta needed the support and connection to her peers, and so did her mother. Moving Marta to the specialized school would have required a total reorganization of Mr. and Ms. Gutierrez's support system.

We are working in a challenging system that contradicts itself. The child study team and the laws under which it was created and governed are all designed to ensure effective and meaningful education for disabled children in the least restrictive placement possible. These rules and regulations are designed to safeguard students from unnecessary segregation from their peers; however, this whole process was created under a medical model, which by design leads to exclusion and labeling (Areheart, 2008). Removing the barriers to educating

Marta in her community required that we diagnose her and develop a treatment plan to "fix" her. In doing so, her disability presented the team with several significant obstacles that varied in importance depending on the different professionals examining them. Moreover, the school psychologist and LDTC operate directly under a medical model construct as they administer standardized testing to the student designed to compare and categorize children's functioning among their peers. They are required to locate the areas of dysfunction in a child's cognitive ability and academic functioning and to create a "treatment" plan to address these identified areas using data-driven methodology. To some degree, school social workers also operate under the medical model in that we assess a child's social and emotional functioning for psychopathology; however, we also assess their overall environment and their relationships with their family and peers. This person-in-environment perspective examines individual behavior in light of the environmental contexts in which that person lives and acts (Corcoran and Roberts, 2015), rather than the medical model, which ignores the social environment.

Professionals in social public programs, such as schools, are accountable to public preferences and to the larger society, and must simultaneously act in a person's best interest (Lipsky, 2010). We had different ideas of what was in Marta's best interest because we had different professional orientations and subsequent opinions as we often do by design. In my opinion, Marta was able to sustain reciprocating meaningful social interactions. In this respect she was "normal." Her strength was in her ability to relate to her peers, a skill that I knew from experience is not easily taught and very necessary to succeed in life. Being able to access resources now and in the future is very important to people with varying needs and Marta's demonstrated ability to do so was, I felt, the key skill on which we needed to base her educational programming. I was asking the team to abandon their test results and statistical charts—test results that they would be accountable for explaining and documenting in the IEP, a legally binding document to which they were committing their professional recommendations— and consider an alternative that could not be currently quantified. I was asking them to throw out their standardized tests and solely consider my assessment of her future ability to successfully interact with her peers to drive the plan we were mandated to collaboratively write, and the plan to which we would all be held accountable. I was asking them to go against the grain, and herein lay the dilemma.

When a key person involved is not working toward the same goal, or has a competing or hidden agenda, problematic issues can arise that can derail a plan. An important function of the school social worker is to positively influence the people in the child's environment to create, or to continue to provide, an atmosphere conducive to maintaining the child's trajectory for success. Relationships with all the people involved at various levels need to be cultivated and massaged continually to ensure flexibility and understanding. One can mandate the delivery of a service, or an educational modification, but if the person directly involved in providing that service to the child is not personally and relationally invested, it will most likely be ineffective, and can even be damaging. All involved in executing the child's plan, even when we have constraints and demands that pull us in opposing directions, must focus on what is best for the child. When conflict does arise, I approach the situation with this mindset even if I suspect an alternative agenda. I convey, to whomever is in conflict with the plan, a willingness to listen to their perspective and encourage discussion until a resolution can be reached. Marta's educational plan would be complicated, and we would all be held accountable for her success and her failure. Everyone's perspective needed to be considered and shared.

Prior to the team's making a final decision on Marta's placement, the team asked me to consult with Marta's receiving teacher to ascertain her opinion on Marta's placement in her classroom. I approached the teacher and was, surprisingly, met with resistance. Before I could even finish outlining the proposed program for Marta, the teacher articulated a number of reasons why the placement would not be beneficial. I had worked with this teacher in the past, and I sensed that there may be another agenda involved. One of the reasons I even considered this teacher's classroom at all was because of her past flexibility and success with other students, so I took the time to sit with her to explore her concerns. We talked about her current students and their progress and some of our past students who did well in her classroom. This put her at ease and reminded her of our past joint successes and of our positive working relationship. She eventually shared with me that there was a new rating system that was put into place in the school to assess a teacher's effectiveness which directly affected teachers' salaries and tenure. This teacher was concerned about having a student such as Marta with severe learning issues in her classroom for fear that she would not be able to help Marta pass the state-required examination which could reflect poorly on her as an educator. There it was. I understood why she was initially resistant. I knew of this new rating system and that it posed a certain complication for the teachers who worked with the special education students. The rating system was still being honed to account for the differences among various professionals, myself included, and many people feared being wrongly assessed. I assured her that the team and I would work with her and support her regarding the new testing procedures, which relieved the teacher. The root of her resistance was revealed and addressed: we could now move forward with planning for Marta.

With the receiving teacher's support, the team eventually agreed to plan for Marta in her community school. It also helped that the law required us to provide Marta with a free and appropriate education in the least restrictive environment available, and my proposed plan was doing just that. For once, the overarching law was helpful and on my side. The next challenge would be mobilizing the school and the administration.

Working with Faculty and Administration

In my opinion, children have an innate desire to function successfully in the world in a comfortable, healthy, and happy way. When children perceive a lack of resources to meet the demands of their environment, their well-being is disturbed and their ability to function is diminished or damaged. Their emotional state is negatively affected and their ability to learn and thrive is thwarted (Boekaerts, 1993). Children with physical or mental disabilities enter the educational system with significantly altered or diminished personal resources. When a child's environment is not flexible, and does not offer opportunity for adaptation, the child suffers. A child with physical and/or learning challenges needs to be and feel wholly accepted as a learner to thrive.

The successful participation of special needs students in a general education classroom depends on many factors, including appropriate curriculum modification and an observed social validity by the teachers implementing the inclusion and by the students receiving it (Harrower, 1999). It is not enough for a special needs child to be present in the classroom with general education peers. She needs to be able to socially benefit from interacting in the classroom. Teachers also need to see this benefit to be able to best adapt their teaching methods to enable the student to be successful in the classroom. To facilitate this success, Marta's teachers worked closely together to modify the curriculum and make adjustments in the classroom to optimize her participation. Marta's special education teacher would pre-teach concepts to Marta so she had some prior knowledge of the presented lesson, and she was able to successfully participate in the class. This process, called *priming* (Wilde et al., 1992), also helped her socially as the other children saw her as an active member in their classroom and as a potential friend.

Socially, Marta thrived. She had many friends in and out of the classroom, and every time I visited her classroom to see how she was doing, she was smiling and positively engaging with someone. Her academic skills were still behind, but her speech and language skills increased dramatically. The gains Marta made were many, and the team eventually committed to keeping her in her neighborhood school for the remainder of her time in elementary school. However, creating and maintaining a collaborative classroom took a great deal of planning by the inclusion teachers, who often had to find time on their own to help meet my goal because they did not have the ample opportunity to plan together during the day. It also involved being able to share the instructional responsibility equally. Special education teachers bring a unique set of skills to the process, and sometimes the general education teachers felt that they were being overly managed in the relationship. Both teachers needed to feel empowered in the process and share in the responsibilities. The relationship between general education and special education teachers is a relationship that needs cultivating and time to develop. When the team teachers figured out how they best worked together and how this positively impacted their students, the partnership solidified. I continually offered resources, support, and insight to help them educate Marta on a daily basis, and I also made sure to acknowledge the gains Marta made because of their effort.

As Marta progressed though the grade levels in the inclusion model classroom, curricular demands increased and more modification had to be made. The teachers did their best to differentiate their instruction as well as the classroom activities so that all the students could participate to the best of their ability. As they progress through the grades and more is required of students academically, children with special needs tend to lag further behind, and the gap between special education and regular education students tends to widen. The challenge was to maintain the social gains made through inclusion while simultaneously providing Marta with the remediation, differentiated instruction, and therapies she needed to maintain her academic skills. A disabled student's participation in school needs to include experiences through which her unique skills can be discovered and cultivated in addition to her acquisition of common skills and knowledge.

At the end of Marta's fourth grade year, the principal of her school informed me that we would have to adjust Marta's educational plan and consider placing her in the self-contained program in the other school. Creating a master schedule for the school that included the inclusionary periods was becoming more and more difficult, and he did not believe that he would be able to provide a viable schedule that would accommodate her needs. Scheduling presented more significant challenges as Marta aged. Moreover, with the need to incorporate the collaborative teaching pairs in the academic subjects, and with the increasing demands made on the teachers, it was becoming harder to find willing participants to put in the extra time needed. The schedule also needed to accommodate the various therapies that Marta received during the week, and as the district's population grew, the staff did not, and traveling from building to building was cutting down on the session times of the therapists. The stress of coordinating the effort was taking its toll. This was a unique situation, and the school was not accustomed to accommodating a student like Marta. I had suspected the principal was beginning to wonder if it was worth all the extra effort, and I knew how easy it could be for him to justify no longer providing the program for Marta in this setting. I suspected that the principal thought that at this age, Marta's family should not factor into the decision about her placement. But I persevered in getting him to adjust his vision of the successful trajectory for Marta. I needed him to see further down the pathway to understand why it was important to keep her program in the school intact. I didn't want scheduling challenges to subvert the program that had been so beneficial to her. I assured the principal that I understood his dilemma, and I truly did. I told him I would discuss alternatives with the team, but I thought that maybe I could change his mind in the meantime.

It happened to have been lunchtime, when he came to me with this dilemma, and I had just completed an observation in the cafeteria. I liked to see how the students socialize during these times, and I saw something I thought he should also see, so I asked him to join me. As we walked to the cafeteria, I directed his attention to a group of girls in a loose huddle. Like typical elementary school girls, they were giggling and talking to each other, whispering secrets through cupped hands into eager ears. The principal looked around, not seeing anything usual and asked me who it was specifically I wanted him to see. I pointed to the girls again and brought his attention to the girl in the center of all the action. It was Marta. She was running the show. The girls were around her, attentively listening to what she was saying, giggling, and happy. I turned to the principal and said, "See those girls around Marta? They are all friends because they spend time together during their day, and no one in that group cares about who looks or learns differently." I explained that through inclusion they learned to be tolerant, caring people who found positive and loving ways to relate to one another. I pointed out how he gave these children this opportunity through his creative scheduling which accommodated the inclusion process—which included Marta. I told him the girls were talking about the sleepover Marta was hosting on the upcoming weekend for her birthday. Marta's mother told her that she and the girls could plan the events for the evening, and they were making a list of all the things they would be doing together. Marta's house was their favorite place to have sleepovers because Mr. Gutierrez had built the girls a clubhouse in the backyard. Seeing my point, he gave me a half smile and said he'd think about what else could be done. I felt his view shift, and he saw her as I did, an essential member of the student body and community who was an integral part of all our lives and without whom we would suffer a loss. I also wanted him to know that her parents, too, were an important part of the school community even though he could not see this directly.

At the end of the day, when I checked my mailbox before going home, I found the master schedule projection for the next two years put there by the principal. He had found a way to fully incorporate the inclusion program. Marta's program would continue for the remainder of her elementary school years. Her family was supportive, and she thrived. But like all developing children, the pre-teen and teen years can prove challenging. The key element now that required most of my intervention and attention was Marta.

Marta

Switching classes every 44 minutes, using lockers in crowded hallways, and changing clothes every day for gym class were difficult at first for Marta, like most middle school students, but she eventually learned how to navigate the middle school obstacles and functioned very well. She still received specialized instruction in her academic areas and received speech/language therapy, but she no longer needed to have physical and occupational therapy in school. For the most part, there was really nothing "special" about her program at all. Marta followed an eight period schedule like everyone else and went to her leveled academic classes like everyone else. The departmentalization of the academics in the middle school program naturally lent itself to an inclusion model, which was a perfect training ground for Marta, and prepared her well for high school. However, high school was different, and peer dynamics shifted as adolescence and identity formation began to take hold.

She was much taller than most of the students in her grade and the grade above her, and as she entered puberty, she became painfully aware of how different her body was. Boys weren't asking her out on dates like they were the other girls, and she started to become withdrawn. Marta never saw herself as different when she was younger, but as she was grew up, her self-image was changing, and as a result she often became overwhelmed with self-doubt. My role in the past had been to empower the adults around Marta so she could gain access to the necessary resources that would provide her with inclusionary opportunity, but now my role was shifting. I needed to empower Marta more directly.

When Marta's fears and concerns became overwhelming, she would come to my office under the pretense that she wanted to discuss her "failing" grades. She would say that she was flunking all her classes and would want to know if she would be promoted the following year. Marta was never academically failing, but her determination to fit in was so strong she could not bear to face the occasional self-doubt that suggested that despite her best efforts she may not be successful in this endeavor. I would show her the grades and comments from her teachers to reassure her that she was working hard. And then she would cry and tell me about whatever was happening in her life that caused her pain. Marta also struggled with her self-esteem. She was becoming aware of her limitations, and she had difficulty accepting her differences. I asked Marta to keep a journal, and to write at least one good thing about herself that she noticed every day, no matter how small it was. It was hard for her to do at first, so I would do it with her. Slowly, the notebook filled with all the attributes she discovered about herself, and her self-esteem improved. Whenever her self-doubt returned, I'd ask her to take out her journal to remind herself of all the things she could do and did, and this always seemed to raise her spirits and restore her confidence. Most adolescents struggle with self-esteem issues, and Marta's experience in a mainstream setting allowed for this normal social dynamic to unfold. She had the opportunity, like her peers, to navigate these emotionally tumultuous times and to emerge more self-determined. I realized this fact one morning when she was waiting for me at my office door. She towered over me. Tall and thin, she was a young woman who had finally grown into her body. Her eyes were the same though, expressive and telling. "I didn't get it . . . I mean . . . She told me I couldn't get in . . . I mean . . ." So many sentences and emotions were fighting to get out. I just wanted to get my office door open and get her out of the hallway before the other kids saw her crying. A high school hallway is not a good place for a meltdown. I opened the door and reached up to gently put my arm around her shoulders and ushered her into the office. She threw her books onto the table and sat in her usual chair and tried again. "I . . . I . . . didn't make it . . . I . . . She . . . I."

I realized what she was talking about. She didn't make the cheerleading squad. I remembered the tryouts were the day before. The coach told her that if she continued practicing and took some dancing lessons during the summer, she would definitely make the squad as a cheerleader in the fall. I continued to hand her tissues and listened to her, and when she came to the end of her tears, she took a deep breath and sobbed, "So . . . do you think I should try out for Color Guard?"

We worked on so many coping skills over the years, and Marta was coping with her heartbreak over not making the squad. She wanted to be a cheerleader, and although not making the squad broke her heart, it didn't break her. She regrouped, internally assessed herself, and decided that she had viable skill set that could be applied in a different way, like in Color Guard.

This made me smile. I knew she was going to be okay out there in the world. I had no doubt that Marta would be an active and valuable part of her community. She already was. I knew that her trajectory of success would continue throughout her lifetime and that she would achieve whatever she put her mind to.

Conclusion

One challenge for the school social worker is to be able to see needs across lifetimes and through various family dynamics and bureaucratic agendas, empowering the key people to perpetuate a positive pathway to success for students. We need to be aware not only of the child, but simultaneously of the child within her family, school, and community and to understand how all these elements impact her ability to be successful. The dilemma of the child study team is to ensure inclusion and full participation, yet to do so, we need to exclude by design. To normalize or generalize a student we need to specialize them, and sometimes this leads to isolation.

A school social worker has to be aware of all the various points of view and experiences of the key players involved in a child's education. Each child and each situation is completely different. Some cases have similarities, but I have never experienced identical situations. I have learned to catalog the various experiences I have had in all the areas that affect a child's life, and I draw from this database when working with children and families and schools. Many cases do not reach the ideal outcome as Marta did, however. Children's time in school is limited, and it may take longer for them to get close to a goal or ideal, and these goals and ideals will change as these children develop into adults and as their disabilities progress. Families aren't always as resilient as Marta's and may not stay together or reform into new configurations. All of these important factors affect a person's trajectory of success, which is why each person needs continual assessing and reworking. Schools can change administrators who hold different philosophies, and that reality can disrupt programs; community climates and available resources can change as well. Individual students change as they grow. They can develop various mental health issues during their school age years which can alter a plan, or they may disengage from the whole process altogether.

With Marta, my role was to first ensure that she had access and opportunity to education within the most supportive setting possible, her community. I knew she would grow and thrive if given the chance to participate. A real chance. As she became a young woman, my role with her shifted, and I worked with her more directly about how to cope and adjust her world. It was time then to teach her how to demand access and opportunity on her own—to be her own mobilizer and advocate. I saw something valuable in the way she interacted with others and how important her community would be to her and was to her parents. I knew they would need support in the future, and I wanted to help fortify this support while she was young and while they were willing. Her parents could have easily become alienated by their daughter's disability and the special education process. They needed to be empowered and engaged, not only so they could care for her later in her life, but also so that they could help reinforce participation in her school and community. If they felt that they were a part of her school and cared about her school, then she would care about it, too, and not see it as a negative aspect in life. At each pivotal juncture illustrated in the case composite of Marta, I assessed her personal functioning, her family life, and her lived experience in her school and community. I examined each element, ensuring that she remained on her trajectory for success. I would determine who needed support, help, or change, so that Marta could continue to experience success, and then I would provide what I could. I was able to do this because I had cultivated a good professional working relationship with the team and the other professionals involved in Marta's education.

Marta graduated high school on time with her peers and attended community college for four years, earning an Associates Degree in child care. I saw Mr. Gutierrez recently, and he told me Marta would be attending a local university in the fall. She wanted to continue her studies and be a teacher. He was beaming with pride as he told me about his daughter; the little girl he once wanted to hide from the world was now on her way to conquering it.

CLOSE READING QUESTIONS

1. List the various roles that Fabbo plays as a school social worker on a child study team in this case study. What is the range of specialized knowledge required in order for Fabbo to perform these responsibilities effectively? Which social work values does she seem most committed to? Cite examples from the text.

2. Other than Marta, who else benefits from inclusion? How are these beneficiaries positively affected by Marta's inclusion? Give specific examples from the case study.

3. Fabbo says that the medical model creates barriers to inclusion for special education students even though the law mandates that special education students be placed in the least restrictive environments possible. What is your interpretation of this assertion?

Prompts for Writing

1. The Individuals with Disabilities Education Act (IDEA) mandates that a multi-disciplinary team be assembled to help children with disabilities. Give a synopsis of the roles of the other members of a child study team. How might a school social worker interact with the other members of this team? Citing examples from Fabbo's case study and/or examples from your own experience, write about the complicated dynamics of the child study team.

2. Research the disability laws in your state. How would the policies in your state affect the social work practice in Fabbo's case study? Offer a critique of these policies using the social work profession's code of ethics. Bonus: use Michael Lipsky's book *Street-Level Bureaucracy* (2010) to think about the school social worker's role as an agent of social change.

3. Pick another case study from this volume and write from the lens of the author about the case of Marta. For example, if Marta had been in the affluent school district that Jessica Verdicchio describes, or had her parents been counseled from the psychoanalytic perspectives that Karen Baker and/or Wendy Winograd describe, how might the case of Marta be different?

References

Areheart, B. A. (2008). When disability isn't just right: The entrenchment of the medical model of disability and the goldilocks dilemma. *Indiana Law Journal, 83*, 181.

Boekaerts, M. (1993). Being concerned with wellbeing and with learning. *Educational Psychologist, 28*(2), 149–167.

Comer, J. P., and Haynes, N. M. (1991). Parent involvement in schools: An ecological approach. *The Elementary School Journal, 91*(3), 271–277.

Corcoran, K., and Roberts, A. R. (2015). *Social workers' desk reference.* New York: Oxford University Press.

Eccles, J. S., and Harold, R. D. (1993). Parent-school involvement during the early adolescent years. *Teachers College Record, 94*, 568–587.

Falik, L. H. (1995). Family patterns of reaction to a child with a learning disability: A mediational perspective. *Journal of Learning Disabilities, 28*(6), 335–341.

Hammel, J., Magasi, S., Heinemann, A., Whiteneck, G., Bogner, J., and Rodriguez, E. (2008). What does participation mean? An insider perspective from people with disabilities. *Disability and Rehabilitation*, 30(19), 1445–1460.

Harrower, J. K. (1999). Educational inclusion of children with severe disabilities. *Journal of Positive Behavior Interventions*, 1(4), 215–230.

Laing, R. D. (1971). *The politics of the family, and other essays* (vol. 5). New York: Psychology Press.

Lipsky, M. (2010). *Street-level bureaucracy, 30th ann. ed.: Dilemmas of the individual in public service*. New York: Russell Sage Foundation.

Shakespeare, T. (2013). The social model of disability. In L. E. Davis (Ed.), *The disability studies reader* (4th edn, pp. 214–221). New York and London: Routledge.

US Department of Education, Office for Civil Rights (2010). *Free appropriate public education for students with disabilities: Requirements under Section 504 of the Rehabilitation Act of 1973*. Washington, DC.

Wendell, S. (2013). Unhealthy disabled: Treating chronic illnesses as disabilities. In L. E. Davis (Ed.), *The disability studies reader* (4th edn, pp. 161–176). New York and London: Routledge.

Wilde, L. D., Koegel, L. K., and Koegel, R. L. (1992). *Increasing success in school through priming: A training manual*. Santa Barbara, CA: University of California Press.

World Health Organization (2007). *International classification of functioning, disability, and health: Children & youth version: ICF-CY*. Geneva: World Health Organization.

3

RESUMING THE FORWARD EDGE OF DEVELOPMENT

Psychoanalytically Informed School-Based Intervention

Wendy Winograd

Pre-Reading Questions

1. What do you know about psychoanalysis? Do you think it has a place in a school social work, particularly with very young children?
2. How do you make sense of dysregulated emotion and dysregulated behavior in young children?
3. What do you think the role of a counselor in an elementary school would be like? What responsibilities and/or specialized knowledge would be required in the counseling of young children?

Introduction

Mentalization or reflective function is a theory to explain the uniquely human capacity to know another's mind and how that capacity develops beginning in infancy and through early childhood. Psychoanalysts Winnicott (1960), Fonagy and Target (1996), Fonagy et al. (2002), Slade (2008), and Fonagy and Allison (2012) as well as philosopher Baron-Cohen (1995) have contributed to the development of this theory of the human mind and in particular to its intersubjective nature. According to Fonagy et al. (2002), reflective function[1] "is the developmental acquisition that permits children to respond not only to another person's behavior, but to the children's conception of others' beliefs, feelings, attitudes, desires, hopes, knowledge, imagination, pretense, deceit, intentions, plans" (p. 24). The understanding of the human capacity to mentalize derives from a joining of psychoanalytic theory, modern attachment theory, empirical ethological research, and neurobiology.

Development proceeds best when the caregiving adults in a child's life provide attachment experiences that nurture the development of mentalization or reflective function. Such attachment experiences involve the provision of attuned mirroring or the understanding and reflecting back to the child the contents of her mind. According to the theory, attuned parents communicate their understanding of a baby's state of mind through facial expression, tone of voice, and gesture. Over time and repeated incidents of reflection, an infant begins to understand her own mind as well as that of the other. It is believed that initial mirroring experiences involve the basic emotions of happiness, sadness, anger, fear, and disgust; ultimately, such mirroring will also reflect an understanding of the child's intention and desire (Fonagy et al., 2002).

In my role as social worker in a small independent elementary school, I work with teachers and parents to provide children with a safe and nurturing environment, one in which their developmental needs can be met, enabling them to progress academically and socially toward becoming productive and moral members of society. I base my understanding of child development on psychoanalytic ideas and on the assumption that given an adequate environment, most children will progress along developmental lines in an expectable manner. Pushing against what she describes as a classical psychoanalytic focus on pathology, Tolpin (2002) maintains that a psychoanalytic understanding based on the needs of a developing self allows for the nurturing of what she terms "forward edge" (p. 168) transferences. She argues for a "theoretical shift that places our clinical accent on the normal development of the self and its constructive forward moves . . . from the trailing edge of pathology of the past to the forward edge of future developmental potential" (p. 187). Building on Tolpin's work, Smaller (2012) describes such progress of the psychological development of the self as "dynamic and instinctually forward moving" (p. 139). Working from a "'forward' or 'leading edge' model of emotional development" (p. 139) allows the clinician to recognize the healthy developmental strivings present in children's behavior and to mobilize such strivings in the interest of a child's growth. Children veer off the leading edge under extreme stress or in conditions of trauma. My job is to work with their teachers and parents to resolve the stress or trauma so that children can return to a normative forward edge of development.

Often, the first sign that a child has fallen off the leading edge of development is emotional dysregulation. At one time or another, most people have witnessed a child who is falling apart, crying inconsolably, or engaged in a full-blown temper tantrum. The normal stresses of school can set off such an event, but why are some children able to contain difficult affect while others are not? Children who have been effectively mirrored develop secure attachment styles, and research shows that a secure attachment and mentalization are key factors in the development of the capacity to self-regulate (Fonagy et al., 2002). Initially, an emotionally dysregulated infant will become regulated only in the presence of a soothing caregiver. In the language of Wilfred Bion (1963), the mother first contains the difficult or toxic affect that is upsetting to the baby. The mother, who is not, herself, dysregulated but who understands the nature of the infant's distress and represents it symbolically, can reflect that representation back to the infant in a form that is more manageable. Over time, due to the repeated experience of having his dysregulated affect mirrored, the infant will begin to be able to utilize the memory of having his distress contained in order to self-regulate. Reflecting behavior without understanding its intention is not attuned mirroring and will forestall rather than facilitate the development of healthy attachment, mentalization, and affect regulation. Fonagy et al.'s (2002) research finds that with consistent provision of attuned affect mirroring in repeated incidents over time, children will internalize the means to self-regulate. Self-regulation is compromised when parents fail to offer consistently attuned affect mirroring during infancy and early childhood. It may also fail under extreme stress or trauma.

Even children who have been adequately mirrored and have developed the capacity to mentalize will, on occasion and under stress, become dysregulated. School social workers are often called upon to step in when such dysregulation leads to social and behavioral problems in the classroom. Keeping a child's intentions, desires, hopes, and fears in mind when attempting to influence her behavior can significantly improve a social worker's chances of helping to soothe a child and returning her to the forward edge of development. Moreover, interventions that utilize attuned affect mirroring are not only more effective but also contribute to a child's development of reflective function, thereby refining her capacity to mentalize. Although the primary mission of schools is academic learning, children are in a continuous process of development of self. Since they spend considerable time in the school environment, it is critical that their developmental needs be understood and met so that they can attend to the academic demands of school. Social workers play a key role in this process in their direct work with children and in their supportive and educational role with teachers and parents.

Marcus: "Not to bite." Too Many Rules for a 5-Year-Old Boy

Called into the principal's office after a kindergartener bit a classmate, I was wondering what would make this 5-year-old bite. At five, well past Freud's oral stage, children may still hit or push, but they usually have enough verbal capacity to manage difficult feelings without biting. Still, under stress or when dysregulated, a child may regress and lose the ability to talk it out. Though school administrators and teachers know that a 5-year-old bite is not unheard of, it nevertheless strikes alarm, due in part to medical concerns about the consequence of a human bite to the victim as well as worries about the reaction of parents. At this moment, my cause for alarm was Marcus, the boy who bit. A bright, African-American boy, Marcus ruled the roost in his classroom with his verbal acuity. So what happened this day? This bite was not the first incident that brought Marcus to my attention. Indeed, I had been working with him quite regularly, in his classroom and in my office, to address his increasingly aggressive behavior. He had begun to have regular temper tantrums, in which he hit his teacher, pulled her hair, and threatened his classmates, incidents most often set off by transitions from one activity to another, when Marcus was forced to stop an activity in which he was immersed.

In the interest of classroom management and in order to contain a roomful of active young children, teachers often employ behavioral interventions. A typical response to Marcus's acting out might be a series of increasingly serious consequences: timeouts, loss of privileges (such as free playtime), and, ultimately, a parent conference. Keeping Marcus's mind in mind, however, I focused instead on his intention. I thought that Marcus must, himself, have felt terribly frightened by his own impulses and by his helplessness to control them. While the visible behavior became the focus of the school's response, I remained curious about how Marcus was or was not experiencing his inner fantasies, wishes, and fears, as well as his loving and aggressive impulses. Moreover, I wondered what was happening to his capacity to mentalize and empathize with the teacher whom he loved and with his classmates whom he considered friends. Why were his aggressive feelings overwhelming his love? Was it the result of a structural impairment in Marcus's development, by a failure of attuned mirroring? Or was it temporarily derailed due to some immediate distress? I was aware that Marcus's father had recently returned to school to pursue a graduate degree. Moreover, six months prior, they had welcomed a baby girl into the family, and Marcus was spending more time with his nanny. I had mentioned to his parents that perhaps Marcus was wrestling with the birth of his sister and the associated feelings of being dethroned or abandoned. Perhaps a deficit of attention was the explanation for Marcus's increasingly problematic behavior, for his inability to tolerate adjusting his attention. At the same time, I wondered if it were something else.

When I arrived at the principal's office, he left me with Marcus, who was sitting at a table drawing a picture. He was not crying, but he looked grave. Marcus and I had a good relationship, but when he looked at me, he did not smile. I sensed that he was ashamed and did not want me to know of his transgression. We had been working together in my office to understand the anger that sometimes overtook him. We were working this out in play with superheroes and super villains. The play was vigorous and intense, but clearly *pretend*. Fonagy and Target (1996) maintain that small children do not yet "regard their own psychological states as 'intentional' (based on what they believe, think, wish or desire), but rather as part of *objective or physical reality*" (p. 219; italics in original). They call this a state of "psychic equivalence" in which internal and external reality are one. At the same time, these youngsters are fully capable of imagining a pretend world, a fully imaginary world, such as the one that Marcus and I created in our superhero game. Fonagy and Target argue that for very young children, the worlds of psychic equivalence and the pretend mode are kept very separate, but that over time, through play, the child can begin to integrate these separate psychic realms and move into a mode of mentalization, in which he understands the relationship between internal mind states, such as intention and desire, and external reality, where behaviors take place. Playing facilitates such integration: "While playing, even the young child has a mentalizing model of psychic experience and sees his mind as representing ideas, desires, and other feelings" (Fonagy et al., 2002, p. 262).

"What are you drawing?" I asked Marcus as I sat down beside him at the table. He pointed to a crudely drawn face with an X where the mouth would be. "Not to bite," he responded. "Shall I write that down?" I asked. He nodded. Next to the face, I wrote the words, "Not to bite." Marcus began to cite rules and asked me to write them on his paper. After a few minutes, the entire page was covered. I recognized many of them as school rules: Not to hit. Not to kick. Not to push. Not to cut in line. No making fun of people if they don't like it. Don't talk when the teacher is talking. Other rules sounded like those he had learned at home: Don't forget stuff at school. Don't make a mess in cars. Always stay close to your mommy and daddy. Don't go outside with no clothes on. By the time we finished, Marcus had recited at least forty rules. How does he keep them all in mind? What happens to his mind when he does? I understood Marcus's drawing and the words he had dictated as the symbolic representation of very important contents in his mind. His desire was to be a good boy and to follow all the rules—not to bite—that he had dictated. However, such a responsibility was daunting and overwhelming in its rigidity. The biting mouth under the X symbolized the opposite impulse—to bite—representing his aggression and the difficulty he had containing all of those strict rules.

Too many rules for a 5-year-old, I thought. How had rules become so much of a focus for so little a boy? How could I help him to be the good boy he wished to be without overwhelming him with rules? It was true, I thought, that there were many rules to follow at school. Did we have too many? At the same time, I wondered about all the rules from home. What was Marcus's home life really like? Shortly after that day, I met with Marcus's parents to talk about rules. As I showed them his drawing, I mentioned, "These are a lot of rules for a 5-year-old. I wonder if the extreme behavior we are seeing and the bite as well are a reaction to experiencing so many constraints." I wondered, too, what was in the mind of his parents? Clearly, they were ambitious, successful members of the community. They had shared their pride in Marcus and hoped that he would grow up to be a college-educated professional someday. I also wondered about their fears. In the aftermath of Trayvon Martin and Michael Brown, what were their concerns about their African-American son?[2] Keeping the minds of the parents in my mind, I asked. As a white social worker, a representative of the school in the aftermath of a disciplinary event, I was concerned about how they might experience my question. "I am sorry if this sounds presumptuous," I ventured cautiously, "but I am wondering if it might be the case that as parents of a black boy, you worry that if he doesn't follow all the rules all the time, he could end up getting killed." Marcus's mother's face fell. "You are exactly right," she said, sadly. In the following moments, the three of us discussed how to allow Marcus appropriate leeway for breaking the rules—for asserting his will and as an outlet for normal aggression—while at the same time helping him to stay safe by learning how to live with limits. The "talk" that African-American parents feel compelled to have with their black boys could come later. After all, Marcus was only five.

We also discussed Marcus's feelings about superheroes and villains, good and evil, and his desire to be good. At five, his developing conscience would be just consolidating. He would be in the process of internalizing messages about right and wrong, of making them his own. It would be important, therefore, to help him develop a conscience that could guide him in the direction of good without inundating him with harsh messages that he was bad. Could he have felt that if he were a better boy, his parents might spend more time with him? Perhaps he imagined that had he been good enough, they would not have needed another child. Was it possible that such fantasies increased the pressure on Marcus to be good, and, concomitantly, the risk of being bad? Were his parents too harsh or perhaps too lenient in their external messages about good and bad, leading to overly harsh internalizations? I noted the stress he must have been feeling because of decreased time with his parents, and I suggested that they seek ways to remediate this by being more available, if at all possible, and if not, by providing him with an opportunity to verbalize any feelings he may have about his father's new work schedule, his sister and the time with his nanny. Focusing with them on being mindful of Marcus's mind and respectful of his intentions and desires, we developed a plan to alleviate the stress that was most likely responsible for his regressed behavior.

A strictly behavioral intervention with Marcus would most probably have involved behavioral consequences. Perhaps he would have lost some privileges at school or at home. Perhaps the teacher and parents would have developed a behavioral chart to focus on positive reinforcement of good behaviors. Such measures may have been successful in controlling Marcus's behavior, at least in the short term. However, we would have missed the opportunity to understand and respond to his intentions. A mentalizing approach that made his intentions the focus of the intervention and provided an attuned mirroring response contributed to his developing ability to understand the contents of his own mind and, as a result, a growing capacity to self-soothe.

Ravi: "I can't stand that I can't do it." Shame and Pride in a 6-Year-Old Boy

I began working with Ravi at the request of his teacher, who was concerned about the self-denigrating statements Ravi made whenever he made a mistake. She reported that despite her best effort to create an atmosphere in the classroom where mistakes were welcome and characterized as opportunities to learn, Ravi dysregulated quickly in the face of an error. "I'm so stupid. I can never do anything right," he would say, and then he would run into the bathroom crying. On a couple of occasions, he banged his head on his desk. At times, he would lash out at his classmates; as a result, he had few friends. The other students were a bit put off by him and perhaps even frightened. The teacher had encouraged the parents to allow me, the social worker, to intervene, but they had declined, insisting that it was just a phase, that he was learning these behaviors from other bad kids in the class, and that he was a good kid and a smart boy. In fact, they protested, testing showed him to be way above his peers. He didn't need a counselor! The teacher continued to try to help Ravi accept his imperfections, but as the school year progressed, the self-punitive talk and behavior escalated. After she told the parents about one particularly painful episode for Ravi, when he characterized himself as a loser and a failure and ranted that no one liked him, they relented and agreed to meet me.

Working with children requires sensitive work with parents, a reality that is no different in a school setting. Ravi was born in the United States to Indian parents who immigrated here for their education. Both were successful professionals, a doctor and an engineer, and had worked very hard for their achievements. While I was aware that many Asian-American parents had very high academic standards for their children, sometimes nearly impossible to meet, I was also reluctant to rely on easy stereotypes when attempting to understand Ravi's problems. It would be important, therefore, to learn directly from his parents what kinds of expectations they had for Ravi.[3] I understood his parents' hesitance to accept help to be related to their pride, a kind of parental narcissism that made it unbearable for them to face their own imperfections and those of their son. The dialectic of pride and shame seemed central to Ravi's problem, and I knew that I would have to be sensitive to his parents' pride and shame as well. I also knew that Ravi had many strengths and that his parents wanted him to feel good about himself and to succeed in school. A strengths-based focus on achieving those goals would, I thought, give me the best chance of engaging his parents in working with me on his behalf.

I began the meeting as I begin most parent meetings by asking them to tell me a little bit about Ravi and about their hopes and concerns. His father began: "We only want Ravi to grow up to be a good citizen who enjoys life and is generally happy." I replied that I thought those were very reasonable expectations. I was concerned, however, about how hard Ravi seemed to be on himself. It was as if he had already determined that he was failing at reaching these goals, and I imagined that it might be very painful for him to feel that way. They acknowledged this, and expressed appreciation that I was concerned about his inner life. They had expected that I would be focused on and critical of his behavior. I wondered if their expectation could be evidence of their own hidden critical feelings of Ravi. I stressed that I was most concerned about how Ravi was feeling in the classroom, believing that if he were in a good frame of mind, he would thrive. My concern, I shared, was that Ravi seemed to be unable to manage feeling any disappointment at all. Indeed, disappointment moved quickly to shame, and the very second something that he experienced as shameful happened, he flew into a rage, either at himself or at someone else. I understood such rage, a powerful feeling, as a defense against the helplessness he felt whenever he recognized that he was in error. Such rage was alternately externalized onto others—his peers or teachers—or internalized against himself.

Developmentally, children Ravi's age are establishing and firming up their conscience. According to psychoanalytic theory, the conscience is comprised of two related agencies: the ego ideal and the superego. Lampl-de Groot (1962) notes that "the ego ideal is originally and essentially a need-satisfying agency, whereas the superego . . . is originally and essentially a restricting and prohibiting agency" (p. 99). Both agencies involve identification with parents. The ego ideal encourages a child to live up to ideals he has learned from his parents, receiving pleasure and gratification from doing so and becoming like the parents he idealizes. The superego takes on the role of the parents' (and society's) demands, meting out punishment against the self when demands are not met. For Ravi, it seemed that the superego was overly developed while the ego ideal was underdeveloped. His drive for perfection made it impossible for him to feel that his work was ever good enough, and even when he was successful or correct, he could not acknowledge it to himself. I explained to Ravi's parents (and later to Ravi) that it seemed he had an inside voice that was very quick to tell him what he was doing wrong, but not one that ever said, "Good job!"

"Is there something I can read about this so that I can be more effective with Ravi," asked his well-intentioned father. "I mean, what is it that I should do to correct this?" Understanding the strong identification between children this age and their parents, I asked how they managed their own shame. Sheepishly, both admitted to being very hard on themselves. Explaining that children learn how to be in the world by identifying with, observing, and learning from their parents, I encouraged Mr. and Mrs. B to pay attention to their own feelings of pride and shame just as we were paying attention to Ravi's. In addition, I offered to work one on one with Ravi to process some of the anger he had at himself for not living up to his own ideals and perhaps to work some of that out in the play with me. I encouraged his parents to do the same.

Ravi's overly harsh and punitive superego created a flood of shameful affect whenever it was engaged. Indeed, the smallest error triggered unmanageable shame that Ravi, alone, could not yet regulate. Part of the solution would be in helping him to soften the punitive voice and develop a supportive counterpart, the ego ideal. However, Ravi also needed attuned mirroring to develop his capacity to mentalize—to know his own mind—and to manage his own emotional states. Paradoxically, as Fonagy et al. (2002) and Bion (1963) discovered, reflecting back the difficult or painful affect without actually feeling it has a soothing effect.

Behavioral interventions that might have punished Ravi for his acting out behavior would have had the effect of re-engaging his superego and amplifying his shame, risking a vicious cycle of a worsening dysregulated affect storm. Verbalizing his distress and speaking with him directly about the shame he was feeling could have the reverse effect; it could actually reduce his feeling of shame.

My work with Ravi, therefore, would focus on representing his shame in play and words. Directed by Ravi himself, through games with puppets and in scenes in the sand tray, in pretend play, Ravi and I created stories that re-enacted his shameful moments, giving him the power to change the outcome as well as work through the feelings. At the same time, the superheroes provided models for pride with whom he could also identify. In Fonagy et al.'s (2002) words, "This type of self-controlled modified reenactment within the safe 'pretend mode' of a fictional representational world provided, therefore, an effective way of helping to cope with the painful memory of the traumatic event" (p. 297), which was, for Ravi, the experience of disappointment and shame. Moreover, the relationship we forged over time allowed me to know Ravi well enough to provide attuned mirroring, and thereby assist in his developing capacity for mentalization, affect regulation, and self-soothing. We had worked out an agreement that in moments when he got very angry, he could ask a teacher for me. I would come as soon as I could and we could talk out his anger. In this way, I became, in Chethik's (2001) terms, "a new object relationship through which developmental experiences . . . may lead to the forging of more enduring and successful adaptations" (p. 9). Over time, his need for me decreased as he became more able to regulate himself. He learned how to talk himself down.

After a year of meeting weekly with Ravi, talking regularly with his parents, and coordinating with his teachers, Ravi's relationships with his peers had improved, he had become more patient with himself, and he had completely stopped running out of the room when faced with a difficult or even impossible task. Still, he continued to struggle with a tendency to blame himself and with the expectation that others would as well. Indeed, once when his entire class had misbehaved and had been issued a joint class punishment, Ravi thought it was his fault. In a regressed moment, he lapsed into a mode of psychic equivalence, in which his inner psychic experience became external reality. He went into a corner to hide, his head in his arms. His classmates lovingly tried to talk him out of it. "Ravi, we were all talking out of turn, it's not your fault," they said. His distress deepened. They could not talk him out of it with reason. I sat with him quietly for a few moments. "You are so upset because you feel that your classmates are mad at you. You wish that you had behaved differently, that it hadn't been your fault." Ravi lifted his head. Only an empathic response that resonated with his feeling, one of attuned mirroring that represented his feeling of responsibility and shame pulled him back. "They are telling you," I continued "that it is not all you. Can you see that now?" Ravi nodded. Knowing that his feelings were not only understandable but understood, he was able to recognize that his feelings of responsibility and guilt were in his own mind and not in those of his peers. The inability to recognize that the contents of his own mind were not identical to that of others had left him temporarily dysregulated. With an affect mirroring, attuned intervention, his ability to regulate quickly returned.

Emily: "What if you don't come back?" Separation Anxiety in a 10-Year-Old Girl

Emily's teacher was at her wits' end. "Emily asks to go to the nurse at least six times a day," she complained, "and there is nothing wrong with her. She's a smart girl, but she is not getting her work done. If it's not the nurse, it's the bathroom. I don't know what I'm going to do with her!" According to Erikson's (1963) model of development, a latency age child is in the phase of industry vs. inferiority. At this point, a child is "set for the 'entrance into life,' except that life must first be school life" and she "now learns to win recognition by producing things" (pp. 258–259). If a child does not manage to become industrious, to master the demands of the school curriculum, she risks developing an identity as inferior.

Ms. C. was a caring teacher who approached Emily with compassion and kindness. However, a cultural bias in favor of individualism and autonomy along with an impatience for dependency and need seemed to underlie Ms. C.'s assumption that Emily was a bit spoiled and just craved attention. Consequently, she devised an intervention to try to eliminate the need rather than to understand or meet it. She tried to reason with Emily, explaining the importance of her doing her schoolwork so she would be ready for sixth grade. Together, she and Emily devised a system by which Emily could go to the bathroom or nurse without asking, but she would only be allowed three trips in a day; the trips would be marked with a check in a chart that Ms. C., who knew Emily liked art, directed her to make. This behavioral intervention provided some relief. Emily did, in fact, cut down on her requests to leave the classroom. Her anxious demeanor, however, intensified with the new limits she faced. Ms. C.'s intervention did not understand or account for Emily's true intention in seeking trips to the nurse. Because it failed to address Emily's dysregulated affect—her intense anxiety—this behavioral intervention could be only partially effective. Now Emily was spending more time in the classroom, as her trips to the nurse were, indeed, limited, but her anxiety in the classroom was increasingly problematic, for her and for her peers. With growing concerns about Emily's academic work, Ms. C. asked her parents if she could spend some time with me.

An initial meeting with Emily's parents led to revelations that explained Emily's apparently irrational health concerns. In the past year, a family friend the same age as Emily's father had died suddenly of a heart attack. He left a wife and twins who were Emily's age. Moreover, Emily's mother had been hospitalized briefly for an appendectomy. The surgery was completely successful and without complication, but Emily was still preoccupied by this hospitalization. Emily was constantly complaining of back pain and because she was always needing to go to the bathroom, they had taken her to the doctor and even to the emergency room on several occasions to rule out an infection. Nothing was wrong with her, her parents explained. But they, like Emily's teacher, could not understand her worries. I offered that perhaps the death of this family friend had made a greater impact on Emily than they had believed and that she hadn't quite accepted that her mother's appendectomy was really okay. We agreed that I would meet weekly with Emily with the ultimate goal of understanding and alleviating her anxiety.

In our first session together, as we walked over to my office, she noted, "I'm coming to see you because I panic. That's why I have to go to the nurse so often. I get this funny feeling, and I'm so scared." "What do you suppose makes you so scared?" I asked in response. "I don't know. I just don't know. I'm afraid my mommy won't pick me up after school." "Has she ever not picked you up when she said she would?" I asked. "No." She paused and then said, "I know she wouldn't forget about me, but still I am so scared that she won't be there, or that Ms. C. won't come to school. I just can't stand it when we have a sub. It has to be Ms. C." Emily herself connected her worries to the death of their family friend. She told me about his surviving children who were her friends. She said that they seemed fine but she knew they were not feeling fine on the inside. Emily also spoke about her great grandmother, who had died when she was in third grade. She was ninety-three. Her parents, she said, told her that ninety-three was very old and that she had died of old age, but Emily missed her and wished she hadn't died.

I was aware that at her age Emily was consolidating an understanding that death is both universal and permanent. These people were not coming back, and one day, Emily, too, would die. She was beginning to know this existential reality. I understood her worries about her own body, including the panicky feelings she had, the backaches, and the worries about an infection, as somatic expressions of her anxiety about her own mortality. The separation anxiety that she revealed in much of her talk seemed to reflect her need for the presence of a soothing other to manage this overwhelming anxiety. At ten, Emily was unusually psychologically minded and quite aware of her own mind. Her ability to mentalize—to understand the contents of her own mind, her intentions and desires as well as that of others—was well established. Fonagy et al. (2002) argue that the capacity for mentalization goes hand in hand with the capacity to self-soothe or self-regulate, due to the fact that they develop along similar lines when an infant's affective states are mirrored by an attuned and attentive caregiver. In Emily's case, however, while her capacity for reflective function was clear, her ability to self-regulate had been compromised. It had, it seemed, been derailed by the circumstances of a traumatic death of a friend, her mother's surgery, and her own transition from a world of childhood fantasy, in which a death might be reversed by a wish, to a world of adult reality, where wishes and fantasies are just wishes and fantasies and death is forever.

The fact that Emily seemed to have some understanding of these matters did not immediately translate into the easing of her anxiety. Work with Emily continued throughout the school year, and in our weekly sessions, she talked about her worries about her health and the health of those she cared about. She also talked about her relationships with peers and conflicts therein. Most weeks, as she talked, she chose to draw. Often she made cards for friends or family, which I understood as transitional objects that soothed during the person's absence.[4] The cards were of hearts, happy people in beautiful clothing, with bright and pastel coloring—the opposite of death. She decorated my office with pictures, leaving a piece of herself with me. Clearly Emily was working out feelings about not being forgotten and not forgetting, part of the dynamics of her separation anxiety. In the meantime, I was able to offer affectively attuned mirroring to her anxious states. Rather than trying to talk her out of them as "not real," or refusing to acknowledge them at all, I provided marked, attuned mirroring. According to Fonagy et al. (2002), mirroring by the caregiver must be *marked* so that the infant (or, in this case, child) is sure that the caregiver's internal feeling is *not* the same as the child's. In other words, it would not have been helpful for Emily had her anxiety elicited anxiety in me. Rather, I needed to reflect her anxiety to her, demonstrate my understanding that hers was real and understandable, given her circumstances, but clearly *mark* that it was not mine. In this way, her capacity to mentalize, to recognize the validity of her own emotion, know that I understood it (which helped her to recognize it), while also knowing that she could not produce that anxiety in me would be strengthened. At the same time, my marked mirroring had a soothing effect. As she began to associate the mentalizing function with self-soothing, she further consolidated her ability to self-regulate.

Discussion

The familiar structure of the classroom, with one or maybe two teachers and a group of students that could range from eight or nine to twenty-five or more, requires teachers to control and contain student behavior such that students are safe and free to learn. When individual students become dysregulated, their behavior threatens not only their own learning but that of their peers as well. Teachers can be called upon to justify their interventions with children to parents and administrators, and they often therefore feel pressured to intervene quickly and firmly. Behavior modification has long been the standard method that schools use to control student behavior. Positive reinforcement of good behavior and the use of consequences to respond to poor behavior are believed to be the most effective interventions.

After biting another child, Marcus was required to go home. Such a decision is made on the basis of a belief that a negative consequence, such as missing school, will teach a child to behave better in the future, ostensibly to avoid such a consequence. It also provides justification to all parents that dangerous behavior, such as biting, is taken seriously. Indeed, suspension from school in elementary grades is increasingly common.[5] Sending Marcus home, however, without meeting his parents to discuss the possible meaning of the bite, without the opportunity to learn from Marcus himself how much he wanted to be a good boy and how difficult that had become for him, would only have served to placate the other parents and would have failed to address the underlying cause of the bite. Although Ravi's teacher was intent on helping him to manage his shame over mistakes, she would no doubt have ultimately punished his aggression toward other students, perhaps with a timeout or by withholding a privilege such as recess or free time. Separation from the group is a common punishment; indeed, throughout human history, shunning or banishment have been used to control behavior. However, in Ravi's case, such a punishment would have no doubt intensified the very shame that was the basis for his behavior in the first place. Emily's teacher was growing frustrated with her needs and did, in fact, create a behavioral intervention, which had the mixed result of limiting the number of trips to the nurse but also increasing Emily's anxiety.

In all three cases, shifting the focus of the intervention away from controlling behavior to containing affect and understanding intent allowed for deeper understanding of the contents of a child's mind and a greater possibility for a healing result. A psychoanalytically informed intervention, one based on an understanding of the role that mentalization and reflective function have in affect regulation, has the potential to move a child who has temporarily wavered back onto the forward edge of development. Attuned mirroring to the child and to her parents allows the school social worker to delve more deeply into the complicated dynamics that influence a child's behavior. Work with parents and teachers is essential when utilizing this model, as a child will need to have her intentions, wishes, desires, and motives thought about, understood, and reflected back by *all* the important caregivers in her life if such forward edge development is to proceed.

Basing one's work on the assumption that children instinctually move along a path of development unless they are derailed by stress or trauma and on the assumption that self-regulation develops in the context of appropriate affect mirroring and with the child's development of the capacity to mentalize requires that the school social worker not only be cognizant of these models of development but also be able to effectively communicate these ideas to teachers and parents. A social worker who stays attuned to the minds of the teachers and parents will be more effective in sharing her perspective on development. In other words, just as with the children we serve, we must attend to the relationships we have with teachers and parents, being mindful of their emotional states and attuned to their struggles. We must balance our goal of bringing a child back to the forward edge of development with the teacher's goals of maintaining an orderly classroom and successfully covering the academic curriculum and the parents' goals of raising successful and happy human beings.

Conclusion

Working from a psychoanalytically informed perspective in a school presents a double challenge for the school social worker, but one, if met, can lead to significant positive results with individual children as well as improved classroom culture in the school. The double challenge is this: first, schools are primarily institutions of learning and not mental health clinics. As social workers in schools, we are working in host settings, and the lens with which we view child development and behavior may be quite different from that of the teachers and administrators. Second, discipline in school is typically organized around behavior modification. It is possible, though, to meet this double challenge. To do so, one needs to be an educator of child development for the other adults in the community. While keeping the minds of teachers in mind and working to understand the lens through which they view the children in their charge, we must respectfully share our understanding of child development and of the individual children we see. But that is not enough. It is also necessary to become an expert in the mind of each individual child. It is only in this way that we can gently challenge the hegemony of the behavioral approach to children and classroom management. Keeping each child's intentions, desires, wishes, fantasies, and fears in mind, seeking an understanding of unconsciousness process that may be revealed in their play, artwork, and verbalizations, and then doing the same for their parents is a tall order indeed but one that if met will result in deep and meaningful relationships with children, parents, and teachers alike.

At times, working in a host setting, particularly in a psychoanalytic mode during a time in history when cognitive behavioral approaches are more familiar in the mainstream, can be lonely. However, in my work with Marcus, Ravi, and Emily, I have learned that truly knowing a child's mind is not only healing for the child but also results in a deep and abiding love, a very effective antidote to loneliness. So many children, even those who do not reveal the difficult contents of their minds in troublesome behavior, are starved for someone to take an interest in their inner lives. The theory of mentalization is an intersubjective one. An infant comes to know her own mind in a relationship with an affectively attuned mother. Likewise, the relationships that school social workers and young children can have when one works from the perspective of mentalization are rich and rewarding for children and social workers alike. Being interested and taking the time to know another's mind is perhaps one definition of love. Indeed, Freud (1906/2006) once said that the psychoanalytic "cure is effected by love" (p. 12). Perhaps, then, it is true that working empathically with children and utilizing the perspective of mentalization is, indeed, a cure through love.

CLOSE READING QUESTIONS

1. How do you define the key terms—mentalization and reflective function, mirroring, transitional objects—in Winograd's case study in your own words? Connect your answers to examples from the text.
2. Winograd writes, "Separation from the group is a common punishment; indeed, throughout human history, shunning or banishment have been used to control behavior." How is this separation from the group related to shame, particularly in the first two vignettes, where the children are non-white? What does Winograd's treatment of the children and their families in these first two vignettes say about her cultural competence?
3. How does Winograd's position as a school social worker uniquely position her to approach student problems in ways that parents and other staff cannot? What have your learned about her psychoanalytic lens? Do you think you would employ any of Winograd's strategies in your own work? If so, which strategies? If not, why?

Prompts for Writing

1. Choose one of the vignettes. Describe how Winograd worked with the child, focusing on advantages and disadvantages of her approach. Then discuss how you imagine a behaviorist would approach the child.
2. Read Kaliades's case study, "The White Privilege of a School Social Worker." Write about the relationship between these two cases and how Winograd's approach to Marcus might apply to Tara.
3. Read the Smaller article referenced in Winograd's case study. How might you utilize the idea of the "forward edge" in work with a child or adolescent client, whether in a school setting or now? What theories of human development that you have learned fit well with this idea of the forward edge?

Notes

1. Reflective function is known as "theory of mind" in developmental psychology.
2. A *Guardian* study found that "young black men were nine times more likely than other Americans to be killed by police officers in 2015 ... [and] recorded a final tally of 1,134 deaths at the hands of law enforcement this year" (Swaine et al., 2015).
3. Amy Chua, author of *Battle Hymn of the Tiger Mother* (2011), is perhaps the most famous example of a justification for the pressure that many immigrant parents impose on their

children. Her book set off considerable controversy in the mental health field over child-rearing practices and how they are culturally situated.

4. Winnicott (1953) defined a transitional object as that which is used by the infant as a bridge from internal to external reality, a bridge to the mother in her absence. We know these objects as the first blanket or teddy bear. An infant will grow out of the need for this object in time, and it loses its intense meaning. "The transitional objects and transitional phenomena belong to the realm of illusion which is at the basis of initiation of experience" (p. 97). I am using the term here to refer to an object that helps to soothe an older child suffering from separation anxiety. I believe that we all make use of such objects throughout life, when, under stress, we struggle with being separated from those we love who help us to contain dysregulated affect.

5. A Stanford University study reported in *The Huffington Post* (Klein, 2016) showed that rates of school suspensions go down when teachers use more empathy. Empathy requires keeping the child's mind in mind.

References

Baron-Cohen, S. (1995). *Mindblindness*. Cambridge, MA: MIT Press.

Bion, W. R. (1963). *Elements of psycho-analysis*. London: Heinemann.

Chethik, M. (2001). The play relationship and the therapeutic alliance. *Psychoanalytic Social Work*, 8, 9–20.

Chua, A. (2011). *Battle hymn of the tiger mother*. London: Bloomsbury Publishing.

Erikson, E. (1963). *Childhood and society*. New York: W. W. Norton & Company.

Fonagy, P., and Allison, E. (2012). What is mentalization? The concept and its foundations in developmental research. In N. Midgley and I. Vrouva (Eds.), *Minding the child: Mentalization-based interventions with children, young people and their families* (pp. 11–34). New York: Routledge.

Fonagy, P., Gergely, G., Jurist, E., and Target, M. (2002) *Affect regulation, mentalization, and the development of the self*. New York: Other Press.

Fonagy, P., and Target, M. (1996). Playing with reality: I. Theory of mind and the normal development of psychic reality. *International Journal of Psycho-Analysis*, 77, 217–233.

Freud, S. (1906/2006). Letter from Sigmund Freud to C. G. Jung, December 6, 1906. *The Freud/Jung letters: The correspondence between Sigmund Freud and C. G. Jung*, Ed. W. McGuire, Trans. R. F. C. Hull and R. Manheim (pp. 11–13). Princeton, NJ: Princeton University Press.

Klein, R. (2016, May 12). The key to reducing school suspensions? Treat kids with empathy, says study. *The Huffington Post*. Accessed online August 16, 2016 at www.huffingtonpost.com/entry/school-suspensions-empathy_us_5733a7f1e4b08f96c1821e9e.

Lampl-de Groot, J. (1962). Ego ideal and superego. *The Psychoanalytic Study of the Child*, 17, 94–106.

Slade, A. (2008). The move from categories to process: Attachment phenomena and clinical evaluation. *Attachment: New Directions in Psychotherapy and Relational Psychoanalysis Journal*, 2, 81–105.

Smaller, M. D. (2012). Psychoanalysis and the forward edge hit the streets: The analytic service to adolescents program (ASAP). *Psychoanalytic Inquiry*, 32, 136–146.

Swaine, J., Laughland, O., Lartey, J., and McCarthy, C. (2015, Dec. 31). Young black men killed by US police at highest rate in year of 1,134 deaths. *Guardian*. Accessed online August 16, 2016 at www.theguardian.com/us-news/2015/dec/31/the-counted-police-killings-2015-young-black-men.

Tolpin, M. (2002). Chapter 11 doing psychoanalysis of normal development: Forward edge transferences. *Progress in Self Psychology*, 18, 167–190.

Winnicott, D. W. (1953). Transitional objects and transitional phenomena: A study of the first not-me possession. *International Journal of Psycho-Analysis*, 34, 89–97.

Winnicott, D. W. (1960). The theory of the parent-infant relationship. *International Journal of Psycho-Analysis*, 41, 585–595.

4

FINDING YOUR "SELFIE"

The New Crisis of the Affluent
Adolescent in School

Jessica Verdicchio

Pre-Reading Questions

1. What are your assumptions about the role of social work with affluent populations? How does such work impinge on or comply with the professional mission of advocating for social justice?
2. Think about the pressures that adolescents face in today's world. How are they different depending upon an adolescent's socioeconomic background? What kinds of biopsychosocial pressures do most adolescents face, regardless of socioeconomic background?
3. What special skills and knowledge is required of a high school social worker?

"Look around. Is there really a need for a social worker in an affluent high school?" one parent inquired of me after a PTA meeting. "Sorry, I mean, the families in our community don't need social services or charity ourselves; we just donate to them." Although somewhat stunned, I simply smiled.

As I walked back to my office, I thought "Was she right?" I began to take note of the decor: bright, cheery walls filled with award-winning student artwork, trophy cases filled to capacity with league, state, and athlete of the week recognitions, and sizeable banners hanging with inspiring quotes from the likes of Einstein and Shakespeare. As I continued through the expansive hallway to the cafeteria, I dodged the long line of students and faculty getting their daily coffee fix and noticed the other food kiosks selling sushi rolls and freshly squeezed organic juices. Most high school cafeterias conjure up the image of mac-n-cheese and boiled hot dogs. This cafeteria was a Whole Foods–Starbucks for teenagers. Several students smiled and waved, and I thought, from the outside, this school appeared to be almost perfect.

From the PTA mother's perspective, I could certainly see why parents and the community at large might think that social work services are unnecessary. With all these well-presented young people who come from affluent homes and who attend a high school that exudes scholastic excellence, how could the students ever need the services of a social worker? Maybe her referent, I reasoned, was one of the urban high schools often profiled in the news: a high school situated in a destitute community with dangerous streets paroled by drug dealers and full of broken families. Perhaps she opined that those are the people who really *need* social work services and, of course, charity. While her comment was jarring, her question was a fair one: do affluent schools need social work services? As a school social worker in an affluent district for over a decade, and having been raised in an area similar to my school community, I understand and recognize the pressures that adolescents face in high performing schools. But for an outsider looking in, looks can be deceiving. The facade of an affluent school is often not enough to make an accurate judgment about the social and emotional well-being of its students.

Many (not all) young people of high school age appear to be making a choice to travel down a dangerous path that places them at risk for a host of social and emotional deficits. One cursory glance at the profiles of school shooters, suicides covered by the media, and the demographics of heroin use document that reality. As this chapter unfolds, I will lay the foundation for understanding the culture of affluence and highlight the role that technology plays in adolescent identity formation. Then I will use Caroline's story, which is a composite case study, to illustrate the pressures and the struggles of affluent teenagers in the school setting. Subsequently, I argue why it is now, perhaps more than ever, that school social workers, with their unique set of clinical expertise and passion for positive change, are integral to raising awareness of, and responding to, the critical issues that impact the mental health of students in affluent schools.

A New At-Risk Population

Adolescence is a transitional phase in our development, spanning from the biological, psychological, and social domains of childhood to those of adulthood. During this time, there is a growing need for adolescents to begin to develop an identity, coupled with an emerging sense of autonomy. In this quest to define and redefine an identity, adolescents explore many facets of themselves and take a series of risks before committing to a specific role or set of values (Marcia, 1980). For some, these risks may be a change in attire or hairstyle, and for others, this self-exploration may manifest itself through experimentation in sexual relation-ships, drug and alcohol use, or pushing the limits with tattoos and piercings.

Identity formation is the key struggle of adolescents, and for many, this pursuit continues throughout the late teens and early twenties as they have experiences separate from those that their parents create for them. It is only after some autonomous experiences that young adults begin to solidify their identity in love, relationships, and at work, all while developing a unique view of the world (Arnett, 2000).

As with many of life's transitions, experiencing identity changes, coupled with new emergent roles and responsibilities, can be quite stressful and challenging under normal circumstances. The journey through adolescence is not a new phenomenon, but there is something about the way teenagers navigate this phase today that is disconcerting. Instead of viewing adolescence as a time for exploration, some are feeling debilitated by high expectations, pressure, and a fear of failure, which has led to a nationwide rise in teenagers reporting symptoms of anxiety and depression. The National Institute of Mental Health (NIMH) estimates that more than 11 percent of 13–18 year olds have been affected by a depressive disorder in their lifetime (Merikangas et al., 2010). Additionally, a 2011 survey by the Center for Disease Control and Prevention (CDCP) reports that nearly one in six high school students has seriously considered suicide and one in twelve has attempted it; suicide remains the third leading cause of death of 10–24 year olds (Center for Disease Control and Prevention, 2014). America's youth is anxious, unhappy, and heading toward a mental health crisis.

In the past several decades, the term "at risk" has been used to refer to the financial, social, and emotional experiences of children and families living in poverty. However, beginning in the late 1990s, researchers uncovered "a new 'at risk' population, a previously unrecognized and unstudied group, that of the affluent teenager" (Levine, 2006, p. 17). According to researchers Luthar and Sexton (2005), "In spite of their economic advantage, they experience among the highest rates of depression, substance abuse, anxiety disorders, somatic complaints, and unhappiness of any group of children in this country" (as cited in Levine, 2006, p. 18).

Luthar and Latandresse's (2005) research suggests: "Growing up in the culture of affluence can connote various psychosocial risks . . . and two sets of factors seem to be implicated, that is, excessive pressures to achieve and isolation from parents (both literal and emotional)" (p. 49). For some, this assertion may be quite surprising; however, to the clinicians who work with this population, such as Dr. Madeline Levine, clinician and author, this is old news. Levine (2006) writes, "There is a disconnect between how affluent adolescents appear on the outside and how they are navigating adolescence internally" (p. 7). Affluent teenagers are children of parents who have deep and often far-reaching political, social, and economic resources, from which they greatly benefit. Economic resources allow teenagers to receive countless hours of individual tutoring, private college counseling, athletic trainers and coaches; even admittance to a university, solely for being a donor's daughter or legacy. With good intentions, these extra supports are designed to give the best possible advantage for success. However, it appears that "Modest setbacks frequently send them into a 'tailspin' as their parents, with good intentions, have attempted to provide only opportunities for success" (p. 7). Moreover, when faced with these challenges, symptoms of depression and anxiety often emerge as adolescents are faced with a new set of emotions that they are unequipped to handle.

Affluent teenagers are a part of the "culture of affluence," a culture that values drive, competition, and material objects, at times over familial ties, kindness, and honesty. This culture places esteem on the exterior and the public persona, while the needs of the inner self can be neglected. This inner emptiness, or an "empty self," creates many voids in a young person's being. Cushman (1990), a well-known clinician and professor in the field of self-psychology and sociocultural contexts, asserts:

> Inner emptiness may be expressed in many ways, such as low self-esteem (the absence of a sense of personal worth), values confusion (the absence of a sense of personal convictions), eating disorders (the compulsion to fill the emptiness with food, or to embody the emptiness by refusing food), drug abuse (the compulsion to fill the emptiness with chemically induced emotional experiences), and chronic consumerism . . . It may also take the form of an absence of personal meaning.
>
> *p. 604*

Adolescents use many of these extrinsic expressions to attempt to fill up their internal emptiness because they are taught or groomed by their culture and media to always desire and to be in need of something. Popular cultural themes, often echoed by various media forms, construct an imposing or artificial self that does not correspond to the adolescent's actual lived reality. Essentially, these media forms are idealized versions of constructed selves. But if affluent adolescents are taught to always "want" or strive for more, the insinuation that who they are is not good enough.

The Origins of Insecurity and the Rise of Social Media

In the past several decades, one could infer that an imaginary bubble protected America's affluent youth from the political, economic, and social struggles of the rest of US society. However, the 1999 Columbine school shooting, the September 11, 2001 terrorist attacks, and the Great Recession economic crisis rapidly brought issues of safety and security to the forefront and garnered intense media attention, spreading a culture of fear. Generally speaking, most enclaves of affluence were and are insulated from street and school violence, job and income loss, and catastrophic events at home. That may have changed in the previous two decades. While most affluent people have not experienced any disruptions directly, the news media amplified a sense of crisis that resonated with the affluent population. As many parents felt a sense of panic and vulnerability, these feelings trickled down to their children.

The massacre at Columbine demonstrated that even America's affluent schools are not immune to mass shootings, a crime that most people erroneously associate with poverty-stricken and crime-infested inner-city schools. After Columbine, schools across the country responded to the increased anxiety of parents, children, and school personnel to prepare for such unpredictable and terrifying events by increasing the number of practice drills. However, simulations such as active shooter, bomb threats, code red and other emergency drills, which are often unannounced, increased the levels of anxiety and insecurity that learners and educators feel within the school setting.

A couple of years later, the 9/11 terror attacks, particularly in the New York metropolitan area, illustrated that in a matter of hours our nation's sense of security could place the young and old alike in a defenseless position. For many families, this feeling of vulnerability changed the way they viewed traveling on airplanes; some families were even too anxious to leave the home. The economic crisis of 2008 further illustrated how exposed affluent families could be when corporate buyouts caused many in the financial industry to lose their jobs, coupled with a significant decline in the housing market due to unstable mortgage providers. This series of events, and perhaps many smaller ripples along the way, led affluent families to feel an increasing need to protect their children and give them every possible opportunity in an unstable, ever-changing world. Essentially, children now entering school come from a world and generation characterized by widespread and pervasive anxiety.

Another key contributor to the development of affluent youth is the role of technology, most notably, social media. There is a general agreement amongst scholars that identity formation is structured by the sociocultural context (Gardiner and Kosmitzki, 2008). The media—print, movies, TV, internet, and the use of cellphones—in the United States has created a culture in which, "images, sounds, and spectacles help produce the fabric of everyday life . . . and provide the materials out of which people forge their very identities" (Kellner, 1995, p. 12). For many young people, the internet subculture is a window to exploring new vistas, some frightening, from their bedrooms.

This present cohort of teens and young adults is unique in that social media has had a significant impact on their development. From the very moment they were born, a digital footprint was created. For this reason, some refer to them as the igeneration—or, as Dr. Jean M. Twenge asserts, "GenMe"—because of the confidence, entitlement, and narcissism that has surfaced through the use of technology (Twenge, 2006). As if on cue, the Oxford Dictionary named "selfie" its 2013 word of the year, which officially means "a photograph that one has taken of oneself, typically one taken with a smartphone or webcam and uploaded to a social media website" (Oxford Dictionary, 2013). In our ever-changing electronic world, "the selfie" attempts to give insight into where you are, what you are doing, and how you are feeling, something that an ordinary text message can't always accomplish. However, selfies are not an accurate portrayal of one's true self. Selfies are about showing the outside world what we want them to see about us, our ideal self; not the darker, inner emotions. As adults, we can see through this persona and realize that a selfie is just a snapshot in someone's day. However, teens view selfies and online personas as a true representation of self and they often compare how they are feeling internally to how others showcase themselves externally, which is a dangerous mistake.

In an era in which social media is prominent, applications such as Facebook, Instagram, Twitter, and Snapchat seemingly define the identity and reputations of adolescents. These applications allow teens to showcase their best selves by controlling what their "friends" or other users see, including insightful quotes, funny tweets, or perfectly edited photographs. However, the concern goes much deeper than the editing of our online personas. Our society is at a crossroads with our ability to connect with others because we do not allow ourselves to be vulnerable. Dr. Sherry Turkle, researcher and author of *Alone Together: Why We Expect More from Technology and Less from Each Other* (2011), fears that we use technology to give us the illusion of connection, but without the emotional risks of friendship. In a 2012 TED Talk, Turkle stated,

> Solitude is where you find yourself so that you can reach out to other people and form real attachments. When we don't have the capacity for solitude, we turn to other people in order to feel less anxious or in order to feel alive. When this happens, we're not able to appreciate who they are . . . if we don't teach our children to be alone, they're only going to know how to be lonely.
>
> *para. 19*

Although the original goal of these applications was to create immediate, positive connections, those same applications can certainly exacerbate the level of anxiety and insecurity that many teenagers experience. If teenagers feel lonely when they are connected, what will happen when they are truly alone?

Excellence Begins Here: The Role of the School

A prominent developmental theorist, Urie Bronfenbrenner, postulates through his ecological model that an individual's upbringing is shaped through a series of interconnected spheres from family, neighborhoods, and schools, to the larger context of values, attitudes, and ideologies held by a culture or subculture (Bronfenbrenner, 1994). This model can be used to visualize the individual adolescent at the core of this discussion and the interdependent relationships and multiple spheres or systems that influence development.

There is a two-way relationship between the school and the community at large in which each influences the development and education of youth. Students and parents bring their cultural practices and the school teaches, echoes, and transmits the values of the past and the larger community. But just as one would like to view schools as a place of positive growth, they are not immune to the pressures associated with the larger culture. Schools, in particular, are the places where the community drama unfolds, and teenagers are not immune to this. There may have been a time, prior to cell phones and modern media, when high school students might have been sheltered from the news and events of the day until after school hours, but with technology, every person is a citizen journalist and every story is only a click away. An unstable global and national economy trickles down to education legislation from our state government forcing more standardized tests, the suicide of a popular alumni athlete, the relentless explosion of social media updates from the latest school shooting, and the argument before school this morning. All the aforementioned factors impact the adolescent, and for many high school students, it is overwhelming and chilling. Most can cope, but many cannot.

In order to compensate for our unstable society, many affluent youth try to gain control by being perfectionists and following a "recipe for success," which usually includes taking honors and AP classes, achieving a 2100 or better on the SAT/ACTs, and holding leadership positions in several clubs and teams. Those credentials will help to gain entry to a highly competitive college, which will lead to a notable graduate school admission or career, home, spouse, car, and vacation home. Unfortunately, in the school setting, educational professionals reinforce this mentality by giving public accolades and awards for every accomplishment. Although schools, with the best of intentions, use this as a way to honor their students, it reinforces the very exterior or facade that the adolescent wants us to see. Now every accomplishment seems to be rewarded, again sending an inaccurate message to students that their efforts will always be publicly applauded.

Affluent teens are trying to live up to both their parents' and society's expectations, all while trying to navigate the turbulent adolescent years. It is nearly impossible to form a stable identity while trying to please everyone and simultaneously portray a perfect image to college admission counselors. Even earning a B to this crowd is greatly distressing, while a C is failure. This strict perception of the meaning of grades is tied so closely to one's sense of worth, it is easy to see how "I failed that test" becomes "I am a failure" in her mind.

Affluent teens are craving someone to listen, judgment free, and a safe place to explore who they are without the fear of others finding out that they may not be perfect after all. School is a natural place for this self-discovery to occur as the learning is already a cornerstone of this social setting. The school social worker's office is its unique little hideaway. It has its own set of rules. Instead of teachers being the experts, adolescents take on that role by learning about themselves and strategies for coping with life situations by processing problems as they occur. As adolescents move forward on their life paths, self-understanding and perseverance are perhaps the greatest skills that teenagers can take with them.

Caroline

"You think you know me? No, seriously. You think you know me because you've been my counselor for three years? You have no idea. I don't even know me. So how can you?" That's how I was greeted after a long Columbus Day weekend during Caroline's senior year. The sassy, yet likable, adolescent I had worked with for the past three years had morphed into a teenager full of angst seemingly overnight, and apparently I was the first person in her path of self-destruction. Her preppy, conservative clothes were replaced by a short, ivory, boho-style dress and six-inch, wedge sandals. She masked her beautiful blue eyes with deep purple contact lenses, long eyelash extensions, and dramatic eye make-up as if attempting to create a barrier between the world and her soul. "I said, 'Do you think you know me? Are you going to answer me or should I just leave?'" I tried to cover up and hide my surprise and concern, but she saw right through me in a matter of seconds. I was in complete awe of the person that stood before me. I had no idea my opening statement, "Caroline, wow, you've transformed into a whole new person," would have evoked such an intense reaction. I was shocked. What just happened?

★ ★ ★

I met Caroline and her parents a few months into her freshman year in high school at a meeting regarding Caroline's apparent academic weaknesses. Normally, I don't attend routine meetings such as this, but at Caroline's school counselor's insistence, I acquiesced. When I arrived at the conference, Caroline was sitting between her parents annotating a book for English class. Caroline's father, dressed in a sharp, black Armani suit, was engrossed in his cell phone, and her mother, a striking blonde, stared at her freshly manicured nails. No one was speaking. I broke the palpable tension by introducing myself and began discussing my role at the high school. "All students are assigned a school counselor to assist with academics and the college process," I began,

> but in addition, there are counseling services available for students and families who may need extra support. I have several positions and roles here, including working with students with learning disabilities, advising our peer leadership program, and counseling students and families experiencing a variety of concerns such as loss, divorce, relationship questions, and stress management.

Both parents simultaneously nodded their heads in tacit agreement and with apparent understanding. Once the group was assembled, Caroline's father began,

Thank you all for attending. We requested this meeting to hear from you the available accommodations or amenities that are available for Caroline. Caroline will be attending an elite university in the future, and it is essential that she has an extra edge or boost because of the competitive nature of this school. Caroline has told us that she hasn't been able to finish her Math Analysis tests by the end of the class period, resulting in a grade of a 89 on the last test. Frankly this is just unacceptable, especially when she is working so hard. Shouldn't her grade reflect not only her knowledge, but her strong work ethic and desire to do well? We've done our research and our team of tutors and college advisors feels that she needs and would greatly benefit from extended time on all assessments. We'd like to sign off on a plan to put this into place today.

I looked around the table and made eye contact with Caroline's school counselor. Now I understood why it was so essential to attend this meeting. Caroline's father is a "snowplow" parent, one who quite literally removes any obstacles (real or perceived) in his daughter's way to ensure success. In my experience with well-meaning parents like these, the teenagers often benefit from a sounding board at school because the stakes seem insurmountable. He continued, "We've already consulted with our attorney and are prepared to take further action, should the school not agree." By the end of the meeting, a plan was in place that gave Caroline her extended time, and Caroline's parents seemed to be pleased with the resolution. As we were adjourning, I said to Caroline, "your counselor thought it would be a good idea if you had an additional person to talk to here at school. I really hope we can work together." I waited a moment for her response. She looked up and said, "Thank you, but I'm not sure I will need to talk to you. Everything is fine." I smiled and said, "I'm here if you change your mind."

A few weeks later, I received a phone call from a teacher asking if I could come up to her classroom and speak to a young girl who seemed to be very distressed. When I got to the classroom, the teacher told me that the student was in the bathroom across the hall and that she was too upset to come out. I walked into the bathroom to find Caroline sitting on the floor with her head in her hands. I asked the other students who were waiting with her to give us a little bit of privacy and gently sat down across from her.

"Hi, Caroline," I began. "It's just you and me in here. Can you tell me a little bit about what happened?"

Um. I'm really not sure. I was taking my math test, and then I started to feel really hot and all of the numbers started getting jumbled on the page. I didn't want to leave the class to go to the bathroom because this test is really important. It's the last one of the trimester. So I don't know . . . I just peed in my seat. I don't think too many people noticed; if they did, maybe they thought it was sweat? But anyway, I finished the test, I think I did well and then came directly in here.

She paused and picked her head up to look at me: "are you going to tell my parents?" I thought for a few moments, and said, "I'm so sorry that happened. It seems like you felt a lot of pressure to do well on this test; is this the first time this happened?" Caroline picked up her head and nodded yes. "Please don't tell my parents," she pleaded. "They will be so embarrassed." "Right now is about you and getting you out of this bathroom and perhaps into some more comfortable clothes. We can talk about your parents another day."

The very next day, Caroline took me up on the offer, and we began our weekly counseling sessions. My meetings with Caroline covered a range of topics including school, home life, and friendships. Although I had already met Caroline's parents, I learned more about the dynamics within her family. Daniel and Ann, Caroline's parents, met in college and married soon after graduation. After briefly living in NYC, they settled into the suburbs where Caroline and her younger brother Colten were born three years apart. Ann's primary role was a wife and mother, while Daniel worked tirelessly to become the CFO of a major pharmaceutical company. Daniel's high-stress job often kept him away from home for weeks at a time, and when he returned, his temper was easily flared.

Caroline shared that Daniel is often on edge because of work-related stress. When he was not talking about work and the latest business acquisition, the focus would be on her. She reported that most of their dinner table discussions involved her grades not being high enough, her work ethic with swimming, or her weight.

It honestly doesn't matter what I do, I am always getting yelled at. I could be up in my room doing homework or chatting online, and he is screaming at me from downstairs. "You only got a 90 on your Math Analysis test? You ordered takeout? You are never going to fit into your skinny jeans eating like that! I thought our goal was to swim at UM. It's not going to happen if you don't give it your all at every practice and meet. Your future depends on it." I mean who needs to hear that all the time? I get it. He thinks I'm not working up to my potential. He doesn't need to keep pressuring and reminding me. I live this life every day. I wish he would just talk to me and ask me what I want.

When Daniel went on one of his hurtful rants, Caroline stayed silent. She would not talk back, argue, or meltdown as other teenagers might; she just took it, leaving all the remarks to fester beneath the surface. To add to this dynamic, Ann would not immediately intervene in these one-sided discussions, leaving Caroline feeling even more unsupported and alone. Instead, Ann would take Caroline on a generous shopping spree for some "retail therapy," treat her to a day at the spa, or jet away for a quick, 10-day trip to the Maldives.

A bright student by nature, academic work and school had always come easily to Caroline. Caroline's parents pushed her to take advanced honors and AP classes so that she could gain entry into an elite college. Prior to the beginning of high school, Caroline's parents outlined her academic schedule for the next four years, which included every AP and honors class she was eligible to take. Academic success, coupled with leadership experience and volunteer work, would get her close to her dream school, but outstanding SAT scores would certainly boost her appeal to colleges. The icing on the cake would be if she were scouted to play college athletics, something her parents had always believed was the definition of true achievement. Essentially, Caroline's parents believed that these elements equated the formula for future success and happiness.

However, Caroline was not sure if she agreed. Caroline knew she wanted to further her education and was well aware of the standards to gain admission into a prestigious institution; after all, they were ingrained in her since she was a young girl. And, even though the relationship with her parents was often in conflict, she always believed that they wanted the best for her and would do just about anything to help her achieve her goals. She recognized that her parents felt that her success in gaining admission into college was a direct reflection of their own parenting, and if she failed to get into an elite school, it would not only be a failure on her part, but also on her parents' parts. She spent a considerable amount of time ruminating about these points but what always seemed to surface was, "would gaining admission to an elite college really make me happy?" She was not sure.

At school, teachers view Caroline as a model student. She is prepared, participates, and is articulate. She often seeks extra help to increase her understanding of the material and to build rapport with her teachers. She is polite, helpful, and a natural leader. After school, she is a captain of the varsity swimming team and truly excels on the debate team, winning multiple awards for her persuasive and passionate speeches. Socially, Caroline maintains a close group of friends, who are among the popular crowd, and she is always invited to lavish sweet 16 parties and other gatherings. She dislikes conflict and "girl drama," but always seems to be in the middle of it because she plays both sides. To compensate, Caroline will often drive her friends around in her new Tesla, take them to sold-out concerts, and do just about anything to secure their continued friendship.

However, this is all part of the facade that Caroline has created to mask her insecurities. For Caroline, school is incredibly stressful, in part because of the self-doubt she carries with her from home. "It's so hard to concentrate," she begins.

> All the things that people say about me get jumbled in my head, and I can't stop thinking about them. It's like I miss entire class periods because I space out thinking about what my dad said during our fight last night, the mean comments on my Insta that I read before school this morning, the text that my friend sent me last period calling me a liar. It's like I'm being fired at

from all sides, and I can't make any of it stop. I feel like I have to spend so much energy on just holding myself together until I get home.

When Caroline arrives home after school, her parents have arranged for multiple private tutors, a bi-weekly organizational coach, and a college counselor for monthly check-ins. After her academic tutoring, she has a few hours of swim practice for her club or school team and sessions with her personal trainer and nutritionist. However, even with the support and positive encouragement from tutors and trainers, Caroline lacks confidence in her ability to achieve. She says, "Sometimes I wonder if the only reason I do well is because I have a full-time staff making sure that I do. If I didn't, my parents would kill me and fire them! I mean do they really not believe that I can do anything myself?"

Caroline was able to progress well through her first three years of high school. She maintained a 4.0 GPA, sustained her membership on the varsity swimming team, and had a verbal offer to swim at UM, the elite school she was being groomed for. Her parents were thrilled; Caroline was apprehensive. She used our weekly counseling sessions to process problems, receive positive encouragement, and, most of all, vent. These sessions allowed her to form a trusting relationship with an adult, a kind of relationship that she had self-admittedly never experienced before. Caroline was used to adult figures of authority who reaffirmed her exterior identity, and it was rare for her to find an adult who encouraged her to explore her fears and doubts without consequence. We had formed a true alliance, which is one of the key factors in working with an adolescent.

I was in shock. Several seconds of sustained eye contact later, I blinked and broke the silence. I asked Caroline to come into my office so we could talk this through. I apologized if my comment had made it seem as if I was unsupportive and unaccepting of her new appearance. My reaction was merely a response indicative of my surprise. She reluctantly sat down and stared at the ceiling. She took a deep breath, closed her eyes and began, "I feel empty. I disgust myself. Don't even look at me right now." She opened her eyes, turned toward me, and repeated in a stronger voice, "Do you ever listen? I said, 'don't look at me.'" I silently obliged and turned my chair toward the window, so that I could only hear her voice. She began to tell her story.

This weekend was awful. I went to UM for my first official visit as a recruit for the swim team. It started off really fun. All the recruits and team members were just hanging out and playing drinking games. I guess I thought I could keep up, but, to be honest, parts of the night are a little blurry. I woke up in the hospital with an IV in my arm. I was so freaked out—you know I hate needles. My parents met me at the hospital, and they were so pissed. My new teammates saw that I was a total lightweight and a complete disaster. So embarrassing. But that's not it. I hooked up with Jake, a guy I barely know. Pictures appeared on my teammates' snapstories from that night and showed us kissing. Jake tweeted at me "HMU" and asked if I was DTF. I obviously wasn't because I puked all over the place about a minute later. Everyone was commenting and saying really gross things and now I'm freaking out because those pics are out there forever. What will the UM coach think of me? I think I've ruined my entire future. I feel sick talking about this. Clearly my parents are upset with me, but it doesn't even come close to how mad I am at myself. I figured I should update my outfit to live up to my insta-reputation. Pretty sure my life is over.

I had so many questions, but I could tell she wasn't in the place where I could press her for more details. This event was still too raw for both of us. So I just sat there waiting and listening, until I heard her exhale and let out a sob. I turned my chair around and watched the tears slowly stream down her face along with her black mascara. "I feel so alone. All I could hear was dad's voice telling me I was nothing." A long silence followed.

"I think he might be right."

I started to say, "Oh Caroline, I'm . . ." but she shook her head and said, "I can't talk about this anymore today. Maybe tomorrow. Will you be around?"

After this disclosure, the once weekly sessions with Caroline became more frequent. I would often arrive at school and find Caroline waiting for me. She always had a new story about her father, a dream to interpret, or a social media post to share. We spent the first few weeks trying to process the events of that night. Sometimes she wanted to talk about it but mostly she just wanted to forget. With the mounting stress of the official college admission decision, six AP classes, a high-pressure swimming season, and the events of that weekend still attacking her on social media, Caroline's moods began to vacillate between anger and listlessness. She began to dodge tests at school, complain of headaches, and avoid going home until she absolutely had to. Up until this point, Caroline compartmentalized her school and home selves. She was able to appear outwardly perfect, all the while struggling with insecurities, anxiety, and looming pressure. However, after the incident over Columbus Day weekend, the barrier between her worlds began to break. It was becoming too difficult for Caroline to keep her emotions inside. This was her breaking point.

With Caroline's permission, I reached out to her parents and spoke to them about my observations during the past few weeks, as well as some of my concerns about her decompensated mental state. I shared that with Caroline's demanding school schedule, it was becoming more challenging to see her for longer than an hour each week and I felt that Caroline needed more support than what could be given during the confines of the school day. I further explained that often school-based counseling is a bridge or supplement to private therapy and suggested it might be helpful to meet with a family therapist who was skilled in working with parents and adolescents, and to assist with the transition to college. Initially, Caroline's parents resisted, telling me, "She knows better than to jeopardize her admission into college. Plus, she looks happy on Instagram." But with further prodding, they agreed to follow through if I thought it was best. Caroline, on the other hand, refused to see a private therapist. "Why should I do that? I have you!" she said. I explained that this therapist would be in addition to me, and could help her and her parents understand what she is experiencing and assist during the transition to college. She hesitantly agreed to give it a try. However, despite the gentlemen's agreement to attend private therapy, Caroline and her parents only attended two sessions with the family therapist, and when it did not "work," they made an appointment with a psychiatrist to medicate away her problems. This just reaffirmed Caroline's belief that she was a burden to them and that they did not want to know what she was really feeling.

"You are going to be so mad at me," Caroline announced as she walked through my office door. Caroline took her usual seat next to my desk and pulled another chair closer, so she could put her feet up. I smiled and turned toward her. The conversation continues below:

CAROLINE: Do you know what today is? It's National Signing Day—the day that college athletes sign a letter of intent to play sports in college. I had been purposely dodging the UM coach's calls, but yesterday on my way home from school I checked my voicemail and there was a message from Tom Connor, my new coach. Coach Connor called me to say that I was officially admitted to UM with a full scholarship to attend. Even better, he was coming to OUR school today for a photo op with the local media.

ME: Okay . . . is this good news?

CAROLINE: Nope, not at all. In fact, this is the worst possible scenario. I don't want to swim in college anymore. I'm not sure I ever did. Do you have any idea how much time goes into collegiate swimming? Hours and hours, plus land workouts and strict diet/nutrition programs. Did I mention the pressure to get a good time on each event? I'm not even sure I want to go to college anymore. I don't know what I want to study, where I want to go, and everyone keeps asking me about it and assumes that I am excited about college. Best years of my life, they keep saying. Ugh, enough. I can't do this anymore.

ME: You can't do what anymore?

CAROLINE: This! Live up to everyone else's expectations. I haven't even told my parents about the Coach Connor call or else they will make me go there. They have no idea about what I want or even care to ask me.

ME: What do they care about then?

CAROLINE: Seriously? You've met them! They only care about what their friends and the other swimming parents think—that they are good parents because I swim at UM.

ME: Is this really about them, though?

CAROLINE: Ummm. Yeah, sort of. Swimming doesn't make me happy anymore. I just happen to be good at it. But frankly, all of the fun has gotten sucked out of it. I feel like I don't have any choices and that my parents are going to be in control of my life forever.

ME: Forever?

CAROLINE: Ugh, no. I don't know. I'm freaking out!

ME: Hmmm, okay, let's take a deep breath and process this a bit. Although you said several things that were concerning to me: feeling like you were not in control of your future, stating that you were giving up and I could go on . . . I'm interested to hear from you where you would like to start. What part of this is the most pressing?

CAROLINE: All of it! Ha-ha. I mean, seriously, all of it. Umm, how do I tell them that I'm unhappy and stressed and that I don't want to swim competitively in college without them being disappointed in me? When they are disappointed, that is hands-down worse than them being angry.

ME: I think that's a good place to start . . . How might you broach this topic with your parents? Do you have any ideas?

CAROLINE: Well yeah, I've been thinking about it and I keep playing out all of the scenarios in my head. I thought about telling them that they really don't know me because they never even asked me what I wanted to do after high school or what my real interests are . . . umm, I thought about telling them that they put too much pressure on me, and that I can't be a perfect daughter. Last night, I thought about telling them that I've been unhappy and lonely for as long as I can remember. But seriously! I'm truly scared for their reaction. So much so that I really don't think I can tell them.

ME: I completely understand being hesitant to discuss these topics with your parents. These are difficult things to discuss no matter how old you are. And even when our relationships with our parents are strained, we still want to make them proud and prevent disappointment. But what would happen if you continued to follow their path for you and not your own?

CAROLINE: I don't even want to think about that! I would probably just hate my whole life. Maybe even more than I do now. I'm not sure I can continue to do this without having a total breakdown. It's going to be really ugly when that happens, and it WILL happen.

ME: Sometimes I think breakdowns are important because they cause you to pause and self-reflect on what is important in life to YOU. Think about it . . . Who do you want to be? Are you proud of the person that you are today? If not, what can you change about yourself starting today to have a better tomorrow?

CAROLINE: I'm not sure I have an answer at the moment . . . can we continue this conversation?

ME: Sure can! I don't expect you to have an immediate answer to those questions because self-reflection takes time, but you should give yourself the time and space to do it. I'm here to listen whenever you are ready.

Unpacking the Narrative

Caroline's narrative illustrates and dramatizes a small fraction of the struggles of an affluent adolescent today. High parental expectations to succeed, pressures and stress associated with social media, an internal emptiness masked by a well-presented facade, and substance use as acceptable means of coping are just some of the issues that surfaced. Many affluent adolescents confront the challenges of growing up and learn to cope, although with varying degrees of stress and strain on themselves and their families. They begin to navigate these complex adventures by leaning on a supportive group of friends and/or team members, speaking to their parents or trusted older siblings, or by using social media to connect with others who share similar experiences. But for some adolescents where the foundation or schema for relationships is flawed, reaching out and trusting others is a difficult task. Caroline's relationship with her parents, and her role within the family, was already strained prior to her entrance into high school. She knew that in her family, "feelings" were not important; the flawless and staged exterior presentation was. Despite her rocky family relationships, Caroline had the upbringing and fortitude that many would envy. Caroline, like many affluent adolescents, felt that by acknowledging her unhappiness when she had the "perfect" college résumé, social capital, and financial means, she appeared ungrateful, or that her unhappiness was unfounded. So, instead of acknowledging and expressing these feelings, she internalized them. She stifled these feelings until she imploded.

Coping mechanisms are the skills that youth learn through experiencing the natural ebbs and flows of life. These proficiencies are rarely formally taught, as we draw on prior experiences to teach us how to respond in similar situations. It is through these meaningful encounters that we learn we can persevere and rebound from setbacks, a much-needed life skill. Some affluent parents attempt to prevent these types of learning events, thinking that setbacks or failure will harm their child's fragile sense of self. However, this is simply not the case. By providing resources that ensure success such as tutors, private coaches, and a road map to college, Caroline's parents sheltered her from experiencing disappointments, setbacks, and failures, which are all crucial to developing a solid sense of self. Also, when the situation was leading to a less than favorable outcome, such as Caroline's Math Analysis grade, her parents rescued her and put a plan in place to give her extended time. However, because of Caroline's many talents, most of the time her experiences were favorable. As a result of this and her parents enabling, Caroline never learned how to persevere. Thus when a major setback surfaced, an upsetting event that included alcohol poisoning and exploitation on social media, she did not have the requisite skills nor the experience to cope. In the absence of coping mechanisms, Caroline gravitated toward what was available and accessible (alcohol and external image changing) and immersed herself in a toxic teen culture rather than addressing, or even considering, the more positive alternatives. When the family culture is to persevere at all costs, often the development of the self is not being explored and fostered at home. However, many students naturally make connections with trusted teachers and use this relationship to explore the "who am I" question. But for others, an inherent power differential exists, as the teacher "grades" the adolescent on her work. As a result of this, at times a fear exists that by exposing the self the teacher might mishandle or misinterpret the perceived magnitude of the problem or worse, use the sensitive personal information against the student in various ways.

Forming a relationship with the school social worker can be a critical step for adolescents who are struggling with the pressures associated with affluence as well as navigating adolescence. The school social worker is frequently familiar with the school context, cliques, pressures, and the complicated web of the school, which for some adolescents is a natural bridge toward seeking mental health services. Furthermore, because of the confidential nature of the relationship, no topic is off limits, which allows for exploration and validation of feelings often in the moment, or within the day, because of the flexibility and accessibility of the social worker. In the world of instant feedback and validation through social media and text messages, teens also expect that therapy, or "feeling better" will also happen immediately. This is often not the case, as relationship building and therapy is a process that takes some time. Unfortunately, this need for an instant resolution is a hazard of society, GenMe, as well as adolescence, such that one is unable to see that those setbacks are temporary or that a future exists beyond high school. In addition, when "feeling better" does not happen immediately, a sense of hopelessness sets in that she will feel this way forever.

In a society where media is ever present, adolescents often send and receive hundreds of messages per day. But sending and receiving these messages through personal devices does not allow for adults to help process the messages, and this isolates parents from partaking in the conversation about life experiences. We are allowing adolescents to take on a greater independent role than they are equipped to handle and thereby reinforcing their emotional distance from one another. In essence, connections through social media are not a substitution for face-to-face conversations and relationships. These in-person interactions cause us to pause, consider another person's perspective, and feel, not just react in an attempt to provide an instantaneous response. However, there is often an inherent fear of exposing our flaws. This vulnerability or apprehension of exposure has direct links to the fear of failure in the culture of affluence. However, if adolescence isn't the time to "fail" or make mistakes, then when is? Isn't making mistakes essential to personal growth?

As adults, we know that taking the time for self-reflection is a key component to our continued development. It allows us to process, understand, and grow from experience. But the essential foundation and purpose of communication has been abandoned and replaced with emoticons and selfies that prevent authentic connections. Additionally, teenagers don't always take the time to feel vulnerable or self-reflect because they are never truly "alone." Always having a phone or device to occupy them and keep them from their innermost thoughts and doubts prevents this type of self-reflection from occurring naturally. Consequently, these are often the thoughts we need to listen to—these uncomfortable introspections force us to learn the most about ourselves.

The Endless Race: New Directions

Bronfenbrenner proposes through his ecological model that development is shaped through a series of interconnected spheres or contexts: relationships between parents and children, extended family, schools, neighborhoods, communities, politics, media, and economic climate valued by a culture or subculture (Bronfenbrenner, 1994). As we come back to the core of this discussion, it will be helpful to keep in mind the interdependent relationships and multiple spheres or systems that influence the individual adolescent. As school social workers, we sometimes have the unique role of causing a ripple effect: using the power of the relationship with a student to trigger change in the other spheres or layers of an adolescent's young life.

While the student is usually the primary "client" in school settings, the school social worker is often required to work with other members of students' context or system, namely parents, teachers/administrators, and other support personnel (private therapists, coaches, agencies, etc.). Although the setting of a high school community is often intimate and connected, it frequently comes with a political overtone, which mirrors that of the larger community. If the community values high academic achievement, then the school social worker must have an understanding of this cultural ideal before embarking on a journey to assist students and families. The school social worker's role is as much about meeting the day-to-day emotional needs of adolescents and families as it is about having an understanding of the larger context of the community.

Community

The culture of affluence places much esteem on educational advancement, the impeccable résumé, materialism, and financial gains, all in an effort to create the "perfect" life. However, in an effort to accomplish this lofty goal, our society neglects the fundamental part of the self, one's identity. By overlooking the internal self and moral compass of affluent adolescents, we are contributing to the creation of a generation of unhappy teens with inner emptiness, lack of passion and an inability to cope. How can we, as a society, continue to grow when so many of our teens are giving up?

In order to create change at a community level, several things might transpire. First, stakeholders in the future of affluent youth—parents, teachers, administrators, community members including private therapists, clergy, and police forces—could hold a town hall meeting to meaningfully listen to and discuss the issues of affluent youth today. From there, they could form smaller committees to take on the multiple issues that were raised including: a political action group to write to senators/assemblymen at a macro level to influence policies, another group to provide workshops or educational services to parents about key topics (social media, parenting, teen suicide, current drug trends), a support network of community mental health providers, and a group to work directly with the schools to help inform and influence school policy on issues such as homework and grading. School social workers should have a seat on each of these committees as they have expertise and necessary skills to facilitate an open dialogue among stakeholders. This process will take time, persistence, and a real buy-in from the larger public.

Parents

Parents play an integral role in the social, emotional, and moral development of their child. As children enter the teenage years, parenting becomes paramount because just as adolescents are craving autonomy, they still need trusted adults to help them navigate new experiences.

Many parents are very aware of the emotional and social struggles of their teenagers and seek support from other parents, school personnel, and outside professionals to gain a deeper understanding of their children. However, there can be resistance from some parents to engage with the school on such topics, as discussing the emotional needs of adolescents is often a sensitive subject. Some deny or dismiss the extent of the teenager's struggles because of her exterior presentation or stellar report card. But it is essential for parents to be aware that high grades alone are not always a positive indicator, especially if the school is observing other things, such as a change in friend group, constant worry, excessive crying, or a need for perfection in the classroom. Additionally, parents should be encouraged to understand and address their own anxieties about their child's future including what it means to be "successful." An awareness of this can pave the way to accepting their child for who she is and fostering a path to their adolescent's sense of identity. The social worker has the expertise to initiate this type of discussion and begin to educate parents on how to open a dialogue with their child to understand what emotions may be lying beneath the surface. It is vital that parents view school personnel as being partners in the journey of raising an emotionally healthy adolescent, just as school social workers need to continually reach out and engage parents in discussions about the mental well-being of their child. Once parents are engaged in an open dialogue, it is vital that they begin to understand that setbacks and failures are an important part of adolescent development and that there are lessons to be learned from them.

Teachers and Schools

In high performing high schools where the academic expectations are elevated, teachers often develop and align their perceived expectations with what they believe the community, parents, and administrators want. For Caroline, the school culture reproduced a case of "student success without failure." Regrettably, the message that Caroline received was that being herself (or her best) wasn't good enough. She had to be "perfect" in school to maintain her reputation, but at home and internally she was struggling.

Teachers have a difficult role in that they have many responsibilities in addition to academic instruction. However, an inherent part of a teacher's role is building relationships with students. Caroline and her teachers built their relationships through extra help sessions, engaging her in classroom discussions and providing feedback on her writing. These are natural entry points into an adolescent's world and could have easily blossomed into a conversation about her interests, the swim team, or her future, thus revealing an area of concern or a strengthening of their relationship. Teachers who take the time to build these relationships with students are often the best allies of school social workers, as they often bring a new perspective or information to add to a picture of an adolescent. Just as it takes a village to raise a child, in many cases it takes a group of caring educators to nurture the adolescent.

In addition to building relationships with students, teachers in affluent settings can help by decreasing the pressure associated with grades, testing, and overall "output." They can take the time to discuss the learning process and emphasize that it is not the end result, the grade, but the process of getting to that grade—effort, determination, completion, and the little steps in between—that is important. Also, they can find the teachable moments in class, ask students to self-reflect on their effort, and have students share their failures and setbacks when reaching a goal. Most of all, teachers should share their stories of successes, setbacks, and failures. It's important for adolescents to see that even teachers can make mistakes growing up and get to a place of success. By sharing and modeling a sense of vulnerability, teenagers can gain an even greater understanding and perhaps appreciation for a life's journey.

Social Workers

In summary, though affluent students are often an under researched population, many serious psychological and social issues are masked by the facade of affluence. It is clear that the affluent have resources most do not have, but that does not minimize the pain that some experience.

In this quest for identity and self-understanding, affluent teens are given the best possible education and upbringing in order to be successful. Thus, when they are disappointed or face a setback, as teenagers inevitably do, they feel as if their whole world just fell apart. Many teenagers are emotionally lost when they get to college because their safety blanket of teachers, counselors, parents, and coaches are not with them to cope with the daily challenges that come with being an adult. Furthermore, many graduate from college, land the perfect job, and then realize that they are unhappy and perhaps have been for some time. For the first time, many don't have a clear plan set out for them by a parent or the larger society. They are forced to think for themselves, solve problems independently, and know that their decisions are finally their own. For many, this is the scariest moment they have yet to face. However, getting to this complex life juncture is not entirely their fault. These teens are conditioned by the culture of affluence to believe that education and wealth buys happiness, and to be happy you need to work hard every moment of the day, and be the best at everything that you do. To some extent, I agree with this mentality, but by instilling this endless external drive into our youth we are completely neglecting the internal drive, understanding of the self, and purpose in life.

The past decade as a social worker in an affluent school community has taught me great lessons about the educational experiences of affluent youth, and the challenges they experience along the way. What has surprised me the most is the number of youth who just want to talk, be heard, connect, and attach. They seek to understand themselves and genuinely want to know what to do in situations that are uncomfortable and unfamiliar. They want to know how to talk to their parents about their feelings. They want to know if it is okay to be selfish and make their own life path instead of following the directions of others. I often find myself asking them, "why do you want to join this club, take this class, go this route? Is it for others? Or yourself?" At some point, it isn't about doing what parents, coaches, and teachers want or expect adolescents to do: it's about the path that the adolescent chooses to take. I believe this ideology; however, it is not the message that adolescents are receiving from our society or their parents. Perhaps this cohort of affluent youth will be the ones to change society's "recipe for success" and to question why we keep perpetuating values that are having a devastating impact on the mental health of youth.

Ultimately, I fear that we are launching our youth prepared academically, but not with the life experiences or coping mechanisms necessary for the real world. We are telling our kids there is only one way to get where they want to go in life: we know it's our personal journey, unique set of beliefs, and maybe a little luck that gets us there. We need to teach our kids that it is the journey, not the destination, that is important and that all of the little unexpected, unanticipated successes and challenges that we have along the way make life what it is: an adventure.

How can we, as social workers, help with this process? We can encourage students to take a social media break or disconnect for one hour every day. We can teach coping skills by building on natural strengths. We can motivate and challenge students to go against the grain, choose happiness and life balance over emptiness and over-commitment. We can educate, process, and laugh with them.

We can help adolescents to see the humor in experiences, and that many uncomfortable life experiences are temporary. We can advise them on the endless options or alternatives in life, even though they may be difficult to talk about or discuss. We can inspire teenagers to fight for their lives and discover their unique purpose in life. Essentially, the role of the school social worker is instrumental in every context of raising an adolescent in the culture of affluence.

CLOSE READING QUESTIONS

1. Verdicchio writes: "There is a two-way relationship between the school and the community at large in which each influences the development and education of youth. Students and parents bring their cultural practices and the school teaches, echoes, and transmits the values of the past and the larger community." What does this statement mean to you? How does Bronfenbrenner's ecological model relate to the social work concept of person-in-environment? Use an example from Verdicchio's case study in your answer.
2. What assertions does Verdicchio make about adolescent development? Are these assertions different from those made by Cuseglio, whose case study emerges from a low-income community?
3. Why do you think Verdicchio cites terrorism as a trigger for anxiety among affluent students?

Prompts for Writing

1. Verdicchio writes that "Affluent teens are craving someone to listen, judgment free, and a safe place to explore who they are without the fear of others finding out that they may not be perfect after all." How does social media impact this need for a listener, and is the school social worker's role potentially altered in the age of social media?
2. Verdicchio recommends that school social workers get involved with the broader community in which the school is located. Write about how you might get involved in the broader community and how it might impact the students and families with whom you practice. Be sure to explore what makes the particular community unique.
3. Verdicchio contends that substance abuse is often considered an acceptable coping mechanism in affluent communities, yet affluent communities are some of the hardest hit by the opioid epidemic and other substance-related crises. Think about the following claim: productive

rather than punitive measures to protect against the consequences of substance abuse emerge only when affluent populations are disproportionately affected. Use the rationale behind this claim as a lens through which to respond to any of the prompts below:

- Why does Caroline's father have the power to "snowplow" the school administration, while Tara's mother in Kaliades's case study cries behind the school social worker's door in response to being steamrolled by the school administration?
- How does Verdicchio's healing *in loco parentis* differ from Sandoval-Arocho's healing *in loco parentis* as demonstrated in "Healing *In Loco Parentis*: The Use of Schools as Therapeutic Communities"? What is the variation in resources that might be available to Caroline and Leo outside the school?
- Outline Caroline's educational agenda and juxtapose it with Marta's (see Fabbo's case study, "Educating Marta"). What is at stake in each one?

References

Arnett, J. J. (2000). Emerging adulthood: A theory of development from the late teens through the twenties. *American Psychologist, 55*(5), 469–480.

Bronfenbrenner, U. (1994). Ecological models of human development. In *International Encyclopedia of Education* (vol. 3, 2nd edn, pp. 1643–1647). Oxford, UK: Elsevier Sciences Ltd.

Center for Disease Control and Prevention (2014). Violence prevention. Accessed online March 10, 2015 at www.cdc.gov/ViolencePrevention/suicide/youth_suicide.html.

Cushman, P. (1990). Why the self is empty: Toward a historically situated psychology. *American Psychologist, 55*(10), 599–611.

Gardiner, H., and Kosmitzki, C. (2008). *Lives across cultures: Cross cultural human development* (4th edn). Boston: Pearson.

Kellner, D. (1995). *Cultural studies, identity and politics between the modern and the postmodern media culture.* [Taylor & Francis Elibrary: 2003].

Levine, M. (2006). *The price of privilege: How parental pressure and material advantage are creating a generation of disconnected and unhappy kids.* New York: Harper Collins Publishers.

Luthar, S. S., and Latandresse, S. J. (2005). Children of the affluent: Challenges to well-being. *Current Directions in Psychological Science, 14*, 49–53.

Luthar, S. S., and Sexton, C. (2005). The high price of affluence. In R. Kail (Ed.), *Advances in child development* (pp. 125–162). San Diego, CA: Academic Press.

Marcia, J. E. (1980). Identity in adolescence. In J. Adelson (Ed.), *Handbook of adolescent psychology* (pp. 159–187). New York: Wiley.

Merikangas, K. R., He, J., Burstein, M., Swanson, S. A., Avenevoli, S., Cui, L., Benjet, C., Georgiades, K., and Swendsen, J. (2010). Lifetime prevalence of mental disorders in US adolescents: Results from the National Comorbidity Study-Adolescent

Supplement (NCS-A). *Journal of the American Academy of Child & Adolescent Psychiatry*, *80*(10), 980–989. DOI: 10.1016/j.jaac.2010.05.017.

Oxford Dictionary (2013). *Oxford Dictionary 2013 Word of the Year*. Accessed online December 5, 2013 at http://blog.oxforddictionaries.com/press-releases/oxford-dictionaries-word-of-the-year-2013/.

Turkle, S. (2011). *Alone together: Why we expect more from technology and less from each other.* New York: Basic Books.

Turkle, S. (2012). Sherry Turkle: Connected but alone? [Video file]. Accessed online April 15, 2013 at www.ted.com/talks/sherry_turkle_alone_together.

Twenge, J. M. (2006). *Generation me: Why today's young Americans are more confident, assertive, entitled and more miserable than ever before.* New York: Simon & Schuster, Inc.

5

HEALING *IN LOCO PARENTIS*

The Use of Schools as Therapeutic Communities

Irma W. Sandoval-Arocho

Pre-Reading Questions

1. Sandoval-Arocho says that the "reality of school social work" is that in large urban districts, many kids go unnoticed. What other realities of school social work do you imagine are present in large urban districts?
2. What are your thoughts about school social workers making home visits?
3. Can you imagine any dangers or harmful outcomes that could emerge from a school that also serves as a therapeutic community?

"¡Levantate! . . . get up!" Leo shouted to his younger brother. Because they slept in the same bed, he also gave his brother a quick strike with his foot, just in case the shouting didn't wake him. Leo offered me a naughty smile as he recalled this interaction and continued talking, "I woke up and I didn't see my father. So, I started getting ready for school." Leo's gaze shifted toward the floor and his happier demeanor disappeared. I wasn't sure what he would reveal, but I sensed by the awkward time lag between words and his sudden change of expression that he needed time for his dialogue to come together. I waited. Inhaling deeply, he continued. "I thought papí went to get something at the bodega . . . he did that sometimes. But when I opened the bathroom door, he was on the floor. There were bottles near him . . . the kind you clean with." Closing his eyes shut, he shook his head from side to side, and after a long pause, he continued. "No se despertaba . . . he wouldn't wake up and I couldn't wake him up." Leo held the sides of his head and stared blankly at the floor. In what seemed to be his last breath, he said, "I called . . . I called for help."

Silence was all that remained as his awareness became dormant. It was the unintentional sound of my squeaky chair that brought him back to the here and now. Startled, he quickly pulled his oversized black hoodie over his head, conveniently covering his eyes. It seemed he was eager to disappear as he sunk down into the chair. I waited for his tears while I blinked mine away. But his tears—they never came.

Death by suicide is a difficult topic to speak of and listen to. When 9-year-old Leo recounted the sight of finding his father after a completed suicide, I listened and grieved alongside him. What could I say to relieve his suffering? Not enough. To resurrect his father? Nothing. The most I could offer Leo was my presence and a solemn, "I'm sorry." I was sorry for the loss of his father, for the loss of his innocence, and for the lack of help. As I absorbed the impact of his words, my own recovered memory of Leo surfaced, and numerous images of him emerged from the previous year. The images that stuck were of Leo in the hallways and in the cafeteria. He played with Pokémon cards like the other boys in his class, and even fooled around in line like they did. But during unscripted moments, when he wasn't being one of the boys, there it was: the empty look that faded his awareness away to a dissociated state.

I have ruminated over these images again and again, thinking that I did not take the necessary action, and that I did not have the right amount of curiosity to get to know Leo.

My attempts at finding forgiveness for myself have led me to think about how easily Leo blended in by following the school rules, and by steering clear of earning a frequent-flyer card to the principal's office. How was it possible not to notice? From an outsider's perspective, it may be difficult to conceive how this was possible, but in an urban school, or any school with more than 1,000 students, identifying those in need becomes an issue of prioritizing. Students whose behaviors cannot be seen outright often go unnoticed. This is by no means an excuse, but it is a reality of school social work. Overcoming that sense of having failed Leo was difficult because, in some way, I felt like an accessory to Leo's hidden pain, like a partner in collateral trauma. It was precisely this internal struggle, and my work with Leo, that prompted an understanding of how difficult it can be to identify some traumatized children, and ultimately reformed my practice as a school social worker.

I realize now that some children, like Leo, must learn to navigate intergenerational trauma. Typically, adult caregivers stand alongside a child, helping to cue and guide him toward healing. But when adult caregivers are overpowered by trauma, their ability to attend to the child's trauma is compromised. What is more, the trauma is not reduced or diminished for the child, and he must still cope with it. He does this by accommodating and adapting in seemingly magical ways, being able to hide fears and pain through laughter and play. Such complex post-traumatic responses between a child and his family construct barriers to seeking help. When we consider that navigating the mental health service delivery system is complicated itself, how do therapeutic interventions become accessible to a child's unseen trauma? I believe school systems, under the premise of *in loco parentis*, can form part of the solution that links children with psychotherapy or counseling when a caregiver avoids seeking help. Extending a school's role can contribute to restoring a child's sense of safety, the cornerstone of trauma treatment. Bridging the premise of *in loco parentis* with a therapeutic community can initiate the groundwork for healing. In fact, the therapeutic community modality is the underlying foundation to trauma-informed approaches to healing, such as Sandra Bloom's Sanctuary Model and David Will and Marjorie Franklin's Planned Environment Therapy (PET). Its emphasis on attachment has contributed to the predominant use of therapeutic communities in residential facilities, but schools, too, have shared components with residential facilities that can benefit and transform children.

In order for schools to be transformed into systems prepared to respond to suffering, the idea of *in loco parentis* must be redefined within a therapeutic community framework. Anyone invested in the well-being of children should validate the call to action for public schools to maximize their potential for developing and nurturing therapeutic community environments, as they can and should be replicated. Schools are a child's secondary system of care and so, justifiably, they can be alternative and well-accepted places for healing. They remain time-honored establishments brimming with teachers and staff who have purposefully chosen to serve children. The therapeutic support I provided Leo as a social worker occurred not in a renowned trauma center or private practice, but rather in one of the oldest known institutions for children: his school.

Standing in the Place of a Parent

The already implicit pact between parents and schools, known as *in loco parentis*, routinely designates teachers as being able to act "in place of the parent." This notion was first coined by Sir William Blackstone in 1765, and evolved from English law in which the role of teachers with students in the absence of a parent was regarded as being imposed by God's divine authority (Blackstone, 1765–1769). Francis Wayland's seminal work, *Elements of Moral Science* (1860), offers the historical context for understanding this concept. It states:

> The authority of instructors is a delegated authority, derived immediately from the parent. He, for the time being, stands to the pupil in loco parentis. Hence, the relation between him and the pupil is analogous to that between parent and child; that is, it is the relation of superiority and inferiority.
>
> *Book 2, Part 2, Division 1, Class 2, Chapter 3*

This historical understanding of the *in loco parentis* doctrine evokes a sense of power through domination and manages to transcend centuries, generations, and even cultures. Consider, for example, that the use of discipline in schools is an accepted part of education and across cultures. Smrekar and Cohen-Vogel's (2001) work on the interaction patterns of schools with minority and low-income parents illustrates this cultural link. Here, a Mexican mother corroborates this norm as she expresses her views on the school's parenting. She states:

> The teacher is like the second parent. School is where their behavior is formed, apart from the home. The school is perhaps more important because I cannot be at home very much; I must work. So the school plays an important role in doing what I cannot.

p. 90

This interview draws attention to the way in which parents rely on schools as a partner in the discipline of children. While school personnel must take advantage of their capacity to act as parent figures, they also must take great care to avoid a power differential of roles in which the school is right and the parent is wrong (Smrekar and Cohen-Vogel, 2001). This role conflict would further cement the premise as it is understood today by affirming that "the right of the instructor is to command; the obligation of the pupil is to obey" (Wayland, 1860, Book 2, Part 2, Division 1, Class 2, Chapter 3). It is easy to conceive, therefore, how the practice of *in loco parentis* in schools has become widely used to manage the behavior of students and to guide the use of disciplinary measures such as corporal punishment.

Although the use of corporal punishment in schools is banned in most states today, nineteen states still allow it (Rollins, 2012). Such punishment typically comes in the form of paddling, with or without parental consent, and is always justified by the historical understanding of *in loco parentis*. Many public school systems, including those that have sanctioned corporal punishment as illegal, still marginalize children, in particular those with trauma, by labeling them under the auspices of special education. They are commonly seen as disruptive, inattentive, and emotionally disturbed. Due to the complex emotional needs some children with special education services may exhibit, they often end up in out-of-district placements or private schools. Tuition for these placements, however, costs districts a lot of money. As costs continue to soar, students once placed in private schools are being brought back to public schools. Federal legislation, such as the Individuals with Disabilities Act (IDEA), supports this response from public schools, as it aligns with its major principles in which students with special needs must be placed in the least restrictive environment as close to their non-disabled peers as possible.

Though some of these children are already identified with chronic and complex trauma, when school systems are ill prepared to address the complex needs of children, they often resort to disciplinary tactics because preventive and educational supports are absent for them. In order to renegotiate the notion of *in loco parentis*, it is important to understand the undeveloped potential of what it means to stand in the place of a parent. The sensible interpretation, for instance, connotes that a pseudo-parent figure would also have nurturing qualities like that of a parent. Yet, the "guardianship qualities" that are characteristic of parents, such as "being supportive [and] protective" (Stuart, 2010, p. 2), have not followed suit, where historical understandings of *in loco parentis* prevail. The prevailing function of *in loco parentis* can be considered oppressive and counter-therapeutic to children.

When students misbehave, schools typically respond using a one-dimensional approach of issuing detentions and suspensions and revoking privileges. These practices are rooted in the historical understanding of *in loco parentis* and, accordingly, are widely accepted as being within the school's purview. However, when we listen to the narratives of parents, we gain another dimension from which to view a school's use of *in loco parentis*. This added dimension accentuates the doctrine's oppressive aspects. Bernhard et al. (2004) acquaint us with a mother's view of discipline of Alfredo, her child. The parent states:

Alfredo was suspended from school. We [with ex-husband] went to talk to the vice-principal and told him that he [the child] recognizes he acted badly, but not to suspend him because he was going to lose the school year. We asked if the child could do some volunteer work as a penalty. The vice principal was totally against it and said that in this school there is no volunteer work . . . So we could not do anything. They don't care about the student as a person, they are only following rules . . . How can they be so rigid?

pp. 56–57

The practice of zero-tolerance, under the guise of *in loco parentis*, follows this rigid pattern of across-the-board rule sanctions that leaves out any consideration of the child as a person. So how has such an insensitive and inconsiderate approach survived for so long? The answer is contained in the historical framework of *in loco parentis*.

School systems are microcosms of society, and must therefore respond accordingly to society. Returning children from out-of-district placements is one such response. Ready or not, schools must be prepared to mainstream them. But what of the many children, like Leo, whose traumatic experiences remain unclassified, unidentified, or unknown? Public schools must be prepared for them, too. It has been found that at least one-quarter of children reach their sixteenth birthday having been exposed to some sort of traumatic event (Costello et al., 2002), and so schools must be considered potential catalysts for healing.

Would that undermine the role of families and overextend the role of school personnel? My experience tells me the answer is "no." Here's why: traumatic events are impacting today's public school children, and urban public school corridors may be full of traumatized children, like Leo. John Fairbank, co-director of the National Center for Child Traumatic Stress, writes, "Through epidemiological research, we now know that a plurality of children and youth experience exposure to one or more traumatic events in their lifetimes" (Fairbank, 2008, p. 3). Events can be considered traumatic to a child, whether the child is a victim, witness, or bystander to an experience that overpowers them (Gerrity and Folcarelli, 2008). In urban areas and with ethnically diverse youth exposure to trauma is more pronounced and prevalent (Mathews et al., 2009; Overstreet and Mathews, 2011). Not surprisingly, "there is [also] a clear gap between mental health needs and the availability and use of service" (Overstreet and Mathews, 2011, p. 743), further complicating within underserved populations the chronic nature of trauma, its aftermath, and the healing involved. Already traumatized children need support. Merging the need for accessible mental health services with the need to support traumatized children just makes good sense. Reinterpreting the use of *in loco parentis* within a therapeutic context has great potential for creating therapeutic communities in schools.

I propose that by reframing the function of *in loco parentis* from "restraint and correction" as asserted by Sir William Blackstone in his well-known commentary to that of "responsibility of care" (Bowden, 2007, p. 485), schools can distance themselves from the punitive connotation that this doctrine currently implies. Undertaking a "responsibility of care" approach allows schools to be not only institutions for learning, but also therapeutic communities. Indeed, the teacher's natural inclination to undertake a responsibility of care practice is not new. Henceforth, in this case study, the term teacher will be broadened to include not just those individuals who prepare students in the classroom, but also school-wide personnel, such as security officers and custodians, who can teach less-measurable subjects such as caring, warmth, and safety. While this dynamic may serve an ad hoc purpose for the teacher, such as achieving a sense of personal reward, bolstering professional reward, or both (Hargreaves, 1998), it can be utilized to intensify the therapeutic potential of school systems. Going forward with the assumption of teacher caring enables one to see just how far a responsibility of care approach can extend. The heroic actions of school teachers and staff in the Newtown, Connecticut, massacre at Sandy Hook Elementary School offers a horrific, yet remarkable, reminder of how schools care for students. Here, the role of teachers as heroes (Rodden, 2000) was rekindled for many, including myself.

Through the responsibility of care lens, the conditions of trust, safety, and protection can be created, enhanced, and/or improved upon. In disenfranchised neighborhoods, more so than in affluent areas, schools tend to embrace a one-stop coordinated service approach to education in order to meet the comprehensive needs of students and their families. For immigrant families especially, these comprehensive school systems bridge the gap that exists between two cultures and, as such, they trust and rely upon schools for care. The findings of the Edward Zigler Center in Child Development and Social Policy at Yale University, from its study entitled *Portrait of Four Schools: Meeting the Needs of Immigrant Students and their Families* (2003), authenticate the significance of comprehensive schools for immigrants. In an interview, an immigrant parent of Mexican descent expresses her sentiment in one such school:

> What I feel for Roundy, for Roundy School, I don't know how to say it! Sincerely I am very grateful to them. I would never know how to repay them. Because the people there—everybody—from the principal, the secretaries, all the workers, all the teachers, everybody looks at you and . . . hi, and how are you, and everybody says hello to you very nicely. They make you feel as though you were part of their own family. So I wouldn't even have the words to thank them, and how to repay them.
>
> *p. 27*

This narrative demonstrates how a responsibility of care approach can be experienced, and we begin to see what it may look like. For me, helping Leo underscored an unforgettable and eye-opening view of the therapeutic potential that a "responsibility of care" (Bowden, 2007, p. 485) approach can be transformed into.

Knowing Leo

Leo was the older of two children born to parents who emigrated from the Dominican Republic. He had been too young to understand the arguments, affairs, and alcohol abuse that stood between his mother and father, and ultimately instigated their estrangement. When his parents separated, Leo separated from his mother by choosing to live with his father. After his father's suicide, Leo no longer had a choice, and returned to live with his mother. His father, who had been his choice, had chosen death.

A part of Leo died with his father. His mother moved Leo and his brother to a neighboring city away from Leo's established friendships, which left him isolated. About one year after Leo entered his new school, he disclosed the secret of his father's suicide to a teacher in the school, who brought Leo to my attention. Some days Leo was rambunctious and alert, and he could be seen rushing the recess line for a chance to play fútbol. Soccer, as it is called in America, was one of Leo's favorite sports. On other days, Leo was observed to have an unrelenting fatigue that could be recognized instantly by paying attention to him. His slow stride, dark circles underneath his almond-shaped brown eyes, and disheveled appearance were the usual telltale signs. His teacher would assign Leo to be the messenger of the day, requiring him to take special messages to the main office, or any other office in the school, in hopes that movement would energize him. Sometimes this worked.

Then, there were days when Leo's stiff face gave off a keep-your-mouth-shut look, and his gruff appearance overwhelmed him. If I had scrutinized him more closely, the vein on his neck was likely throbbing. These were the days when the other kids seemed to instinctively stay away. On one such day, Leo was at the water fountain, and without warning, he turned around and shoved the boy behind him, leaving the boy dumbfounded and on the ground. "¡No me toques! . . . Don't touch me!" he yelled. But this warning came too late: the boy got up from the floor and head-butted Leo to the ground. When the fight was broken up, and Leo seemed less fierce, he explained, "All I remember is that I felt him poke me on the back. I couldn't help it, I just lost it." Though I had been aware of his father's suicide, when Leo eventually narrated his story to me, with his sorrow, I realized I never really knew.

Children like Leo, who are left behind after a suicide, experience an all-too-familiar contradiction elicited by the suicide of a parent, the response of the surviving parent, and parenting dilemma. The dilemma is interwoven in the "telling" (Cain, 2002) of the suicide event, and for Dolores, Leo's mother, his so-called knowing "bought [her] time" (Cain, 2002, p. 124). With this in mind, his mother may have presumed that Leo did not need to be told. After all, he found the body, he called for help, and so, by default, he knew, right? This assumption is wrong for the simple reason that when Leo discovered his father's body he was seven, and his concept of death and its finality was underdeveloped (Willis, 2002). The rationale his mother may have used can best be understood through available research, which has found that there is often a postponement in talking with children after a suicide, and this "delay" (Cain, 2002, p. 127) is closely related to the parents' readiness and ability to cope with the suicide. Leo followed Dolores's silent lead and, in doing so, unwittingly assumed the burden of keeping the secret and of keeping quiet for one year following his father's suicide. As I got to know Leo, I came to realize my empathetic listening might have been the only validation he received about the loss. This acknowledgment enabled Leo to reveal his hidden plea to have never woken up the day he found his father's dead body because then he wouldn't feel so angry. He wouldn't feel so sad and—just maybe—he wouldn't feel.

The avoidance of feeling that was maintained by "living inside a secret" (Imber-Black, 2009, p. 7) seemed for Leo to be an unbeknownst process for regulating normalcy. How else could Leo have kept this kind of trauma hidden for so long? Though no one ever took ownership of how the secret evolved, or even if anyone in the family had explicitly forbade talking about the suicide, I understood that the surviving adults by Leo's side must have cued this response because it was a function of the double bind. Looking back, I can see Leo walking the corridors of the school, with his body seemingly heavy and atrophied by the emotional burden placed on him. It seems to me that Leo had fallen victim to something like what Leonard Shengold terms "soul murder" (Shengold, 1989, p. 2). Shengold examines the term soul murder, and reserves use of this term in the context of cruelty to children. This kind of cruelty involves the over-stimulation and deprivation of feelings, is paired with brainwashing from the abuser, and generates an overall ambiguity in the child about that which is good and that which is bad (Shengold, 1989). To start with, the image of his father's dead body was capable of producing a lasting influence on Leo because "that [kind of] trauma never goes away completely" (Epstein, 2013). The overstimulation of intense feelings this image caused, coupled with the family's stigmatized response (the deprivation of feelings), shaped the gradual destruction of Leo's spirit. The most convincing evidence of soul murder, however, originated with the telling and knowing of the suicide (Cain, 2002). I think back to Leo's narrative of finding his dead father. He was not alone: his younger brother had been home, too. By virtue of finding the body, Leo had to "struggle with the same dilemma that earlier occupied the [his] surviving parent, to tell or not" (Cain, 2002, p. 128).

★ ★ ★

ME: How is your brother doing after your father's suicide?
LEO: We don't talk about him. [Reaches over to grab a toy.] My brother used to think that he was in the hospital.
ME: This must have been hard for you.
LEO: Nah. [Shrugs both shoulders.] Not anymore.
ME: Why?
LEO: [Drops the toy incessantly and avoids eye contact.] He just doesn't ask anymore.
ME: Do you want your brother to know?
LEO: [Pretends not to hear.] Huh?
ME: Do you want your brother to know?
LEO: He's too little. [Stands up to look at the broken clock behind him.] Can I go to lunch now?

In what appears to be emotional parentification, Leo safeguarded his brother from knowing by upholding, or rather withholding, the telling of the suicide. This was like soul murder, and Leo was a living casualty of his father's suicide.

Leo's invisible grief as a "secret bearing child" (Cain, 2002, p. 128) was often enacted at school. The capability of schools to observe children interacting and reacting *in vivo* permits school personnel to be in optimal positions to bear witness to the traumatic responses of children like Leo. This is so because, in school, children practice and learn academic skills; they also practice and learn social and emotional competencies. In the year following the disclosure of his father's suicide, Leo began picking fights with other students in the bathroom and on the playground. In the classroom, his moods became unpredictable, and fluctuated between agitation and lethargy.

A refusal to complete work one day escalated into an explosive moment. "I'm not gonna do this damn work!" Leo shouted irritably, overturning his desk. His pencils and books scattered on the floor. Leo's rage took over the classroom, and Leo's teacher stiffened with apprehension. "Let's go outside, NOW!" she commanded. Leo exited the classroom with heavy footsteps, cursing under his breath, and kicking the garbage can on his way out. He rolled his eyes and turned away from the teacher as she began to talk. She followed his movements and made eye contact. Taking a few deep breaths, she reassured him, "You are not in trouble, Leo. I want to help you. I'm going to get help." Leo's head hung low with remorse as she called for support.

The teacher's unflustered response indicated that she recognized her actions needed to de-escalate the situation, validate her concern for him, and suggest safety. Though not formally trained in trauma treatment, her response was trauma-informed. At that moment, it was the most valuable lesson this teacher could model for Leo. Classroom situations like this demonstrate that school systems are in a unique position to offer children "living and learning" (Kennard, 2004, p. 295) environments through the modality known as a therapeutic community. By definition, therapeutic communities are "structured, psychologically informed environments where the social relationships, structure of the day, and different activities together are all deliberately designed to help people's health and well-being" (The Consortium for Therapeutic Communities, 2013). In psychologically informed school environments, all moments and interactions have the potential to become teachable moments. Teachable moments are unplanned, and children offer just the right amount of spontaneity to initiate them. If you pay close attention to actions, and listen closely to conversations in school hallways, the cafeteria, and on the playground, for example, you will find such moments.

The Teachable Moment

Teachable moments take place when children experience crises. Crisis for Leo became apparent one morning during the school's breakfast program. Leo sat at a corner table in the school cafeteria, and gazed aimlessly at the wall. He appeared withdrawn and lethargic. Submerged in his sweatshirt, he covered his head and laid it down on the table. It were as if he was expecting to be swallowed whole by the cafeteria table. And maybe he would have, had it not been for the hourly cafeteria worker that day. She sat beside him and began a conversation: "You're not gonna eat your muffin? They only give these muffins out once a month." Leo did not respond. "The bell is gonna ring soon," she continued. "You haven't touched your breakfast. Can I warm it up for you?" Leo looked up at her but remained unresponsive. His eyes were dark and gloomy, and transmitted an unsettling melancholy. The cafeteria worker understood Leo's unspoken behavior. "I don't know how to help you. Can I find someone to help?" she asked. Leo nodded in agreement.

When Leo was brought to my office, he sat listlessly on the grey office couch. "It seems like you're having a difficult morning," I said. Leo did not respond, but I continued. "I imagine that so much has changed since your father's suicide." Saying the dreaded "s" word managed to get Leo to look my way, but he still did not speak. His family, the only people who shared his secret, never spoke of the suicide, and never spoke to Leo about how it made him feel. "I may not be able to change how your father died, or even why he took his life, but I can help you cope with how it feels," I said. "How have you been feeling?" An awkward silence ensued, and his eyes glazed over. "Leo, stay with me," I said, as I grabbed the Play-Doh that had been left out from a session with a kindergartener. Looking bewildered from his trance-like state, he took the Play-Doh. "Just keep pressing the Play-Doh in your hands as we talk. I'll take some, too," I said.

There was nothing magical about the Play-Doh I gave Leo, as it very well could have been a ball, a set of keys, or even water. The actual showstopper was the ability of the object to engage Leo's sense of touch, and keep him in the here and now. By taking part, and using the Play-Doh alongside Leo, I modeled a safe way to keep him from escaping to a dissociative state. I then used the cutouts on the "feelings" bulletin board in the office to help Leo identify his feelings. The cutouts provided visual representations of children's faces displaying various emotions. While making the office aesthetically pleasing, these objects of reference (Park, 1997) are part of my repertoire for working with children who are difficult to engage and who have difficulties communicating emotions. In their traditional use, such communication strategies are geared toward helping individuals who have visual, auditory, or learning disabilities. The cutouts worked for Leo because his dissociative self-state likely made it difficult to express emotion. Dissociative children need help identifying their feelings, and practice guidelines suggest that those who work with these children help them "to communicate feelings of anger, fear, and regressive needs . . . so that these are not enacted in dysfunctional ways" (Weber, 2009, p. 4). The picture cutouts on the bulletin board, therefore, helped Leo communicate and identify his own feelings within a safe environment.

"The wall behind you has different feelings that some people often feel. Can you find one that describes how you are feeling?" I asked. As Leo molded his Play-Doh into what seemed to be a string, he looked at the wall and responded, "I feel sad. I feel like I want to die the same way my father died." It was the response I dreaded from the moment I saw him waiting for me.

Leo's response showcased how complicated his grief had become. It gave way to a crisis moment that exposed the pervasive and relational nature of Leo's trauma. Because schools are only one part of a child's system of care, by involving family members, schools can also bear witness to the relational interactions of family systems. In Leo's elementary school, crisis situations were handled co-operatively with key school personnel who make up the crisis team, and wherein the "community is the primary agent of change" (NIDA, 2002). Each member of the team plays a critical role in stabilizing a child in crisis. And because crisis work can extend the roles of those involved, team members also share a collective responsibility for working with students and their families. Crisis work often entails frequent interactions with different members of the staff, so collective responsibility works toward the child's advantage as it allows for greater therapeutic reach.

The team determined that the initial point of contact would be the school's family worker. She would connect to Leo's family in the most personal way possible, using the home visit. Once at their home, the family worker encouraged and escorted his mother to the school. Making this initial connection is critical to building trust with families, and, with Leo's mother, trust building was an ongoing process. Dolores was a young woman in her twenties who preferred to speak in Spanish. She entered the office with hesitation, and her frightened appearance immediately triggered caution in me, as I wasn't sure how she would react to Leo's wish to die. Her numbness sparked my impulsive instinct to guard the door, as I feared she might flee. Attuned to the fear she elicited, I found myself speaking serenely so as not to startle her further. Dolores sat directly across from me, and I could tell by her empty gaze that she was disconnected from the encounter. She was also disconnected from Leo, who was sitting on the couch. There was no hug, no questioning, and no acknowledgment. As I described Leo's suicidal ideations, I noticed that the fearful expression she came in with faded, and she was gone to a dissociative state that I could not access but that I could recognize—Leo had produced the same blank stare earlier. Dolores was now emotionally unresponsive.

Though they sat in the same room, on opposite ends of the couch, Leo and his mother looked like complete strangers. They never exchanged eye contact, and remained physically distant from one another. As a matter of fact, throughout the entire encounter, Dolores never spoke to Leo, and he reciprocated the silence. Leo needed her to show emotion. I needed her to show emotion. I wanted Dolores to cry, to scream, to have an *ataque de nervios* (Guarnaccia et al., 2003). Anything would have sufficed. When she did not respond, I wanted to shake her, to wake her up from this comatose state of detachment, to grab a blow horn and scream in her ear, "DON'T DO THIS TO HIM!" But I did not. I did not because I sensed from her dissociative cues that she, too, had come into contact with trauma. I did not know what she was like before the suicide, what they were like before the suicide. I wanted to understand: what really happened to this family?

Behind an Imagined One-Way Mirror: Dolores

Understanding Leo's family involved positioning myself as an observer behind an imagined one-way mirror so as to construct a portrait of Leo and Dolores's lived experience before the suicide and in its wake. Through this imagined one-way mirror, I saw shame, cultural influences, and my own assumptions. To interpret what I saw, I first acknowledged that family structure, no matter the type (i.e. blended, adopted, foster), shares one central commonality: that it is shaped around a caregiving system (Edwards, 2009). I assumed that, for children especially, caregiver responses guide recovery efforts and promote healing in the aftermath of trauma. Actually, many clinicians and laypeople would share this assumption because of the qualities that are attributed to, and expected from, a mother or primary caregiving system. By virtue of this assumption, an insufficient or failed response from the caregiving system, such as when "a caregiver denies the child's [traumatic] experience" (Cook et al., 2007, p. 6), would have pigeonholed Dolores as failing to be what D. W. Winnicott termed the "good enough mother" (Traub and Lane, 2002, p. 3) or, more specifically, a mother who is emotionally accessible and supportive to her child (Traub and Lane, 2002). Society has overextended and confused the concepts of maternal care as postulated by Winnicott, resulting in "mother-blaming" (Jackson and Mannix, 2004, p. 150). The origin of this confusion, though, stems from Winnicott's own words, such as, "Mothers who do not have it in them to provide good enough care cannot be made good enough by mere instruction" (Winnicott, 1960, p. 592). I do not agree. Working with families *in vivo*, as we do in schools, requires frequent modeling. Even our tone of voice is an inconspicuous way of modeling appropriate communication. In time, modeling as a form of instruction does work. Even so, the notion of good enough mothering (Winnicott, 1960) has been so prolific that it has contributed to the social construction of what is considered normal or acceptable (Freud, 1999).

In constructing Dolores and Leo's lived experience, it was necessary to look beyond these expectations and judgments. So, what happened to Dolores? What got in the way of her instinctual mothering? Thinking back to the day I met Dolores in my office, I had longed for her to show me some kind of emotion that was readily recognized. Through the imagined one-way mirror, I can now see and understand that Dolores never failed to show me her emotions. Instead, I failed to see that her shame was always there.

Shame is an emotion that we all carry with us. But what differentiates shame from other emotions, such as anger and sadness, is the manner in which it is elicited, and what it evokes in the person being shamed. German psychiatrist and philosopher Thomas Fuchs has studied the phenomenology of shame, and tells us, "Typically, it [shame] arises in situations of disclosure or rejection" (Fuchs, 2002, p. 227). And while it may not be outwardly obvious, the person being shamed is left with a sense of "disapproval, even annihilation, by critical, contemptuous, and punishing gazes" (Fuchs, 2002, p. 229). I acknowledge that my therapeutic attempts to get to know Dolores roused shameful memories for her, and when her words could not identify the shame, her non-verbal cues did (Longhofer, 2013).

"He would hit me too much," disclosed Dolores, clenching and releasing her hands incessantly to control their sudden restlessness. "I didn't want to be with him anymore," she said in an apologetic tone as she offered me an incongruent smile. Then, with marked hesitation, she informed me of how she and Leo's father separated. Like a schoolgirl in love, she smiled and declared, "I met a guy at work who treated me well." I interrupted her happiness, and replied, "I imagine it felt good." She agreed, "Yes it did. We wanted to be together and that's why . . . I left." Not anticipating this response, I asked, "And what happened?"

Pausing with caution, she yet again offered me a nervous smile and responded, "I had a lot of problems with Leo's father because he wouldn't leave me alone . . . always calling and following me. But [she looked down and attempted to control the restlessness of her hands] after he found out, he started to forget about me." Confused, I asked, "What did he find out?" Turning her gaze away, she replied sheepishly, "My boyfriend and I were going to have a baby" (Translated conversation from Spanish).

This conversation helped me to understand that the death of Leo's father also meant that Dolores would need to attest to, and defend, the socially unacceptable act of infidelity. While I sympathized with the pain she felt, I must admit that it was never easy to be empathetic toward Dolores mainly because my empathy had been engrossed in Leo and, in some strange way, belonged to him. Could this have been an associated outcome of my socially constructed mother-blaming practices? If so, did I reproach her? Though it was never my intent, I discern that perhaps, to a certain degree, I must have. I can only hope that my gaze during Dolores's revelation was not perceived to be punishing, but this I can never really know.

My hesitation and uncertainty about our conversation emerges from my understanding of the Latino cultural value known as *simpatía*. *Simpatía* has no English equivalent, but has been understood to mean politeness, agreeableness, and respectful behavior toward others (Griffith et al., 1998). In Latino cultures, a person's worth is often measured by how others perceive this kindness. Where *simpatía* is highly regarded, an individual will respond positively, despite seemingly negative interactions (Guilamo-Ramos et al., 2007; Triandis et al., 1984). As a result, *simpatía* can encourage the suppression of feelings. Dolores's non-verbal cues were the only clues she gave me that perhaps I was shaming her. The incongruent smiles she offered me during this dialogue were the markers of *simpatía* at play. In being able to assume this role behind the imagined one-way mirror, wherein I had a panoramic view of Dolores, I continued to discover how shame took hold of her lived experience, and how everyday culture had influenced it.

Just two months after Dolores found out she would be a mother again, Leo's father completed suicide. The impact of the suicide for Dolores was surely capable of producing a sudden onset of shame (Loader, 1998). I believe this is how the grief Dolores and Leo experienced became disenfranchised (Doka, 1989), meaning, "The grief that persons experience when they incur a loss that is not or cannot be openly acknowledged, publicly mourned, or socially supported" (Kalich and Brabant, 2006, p. 230). In openly acknowledging the death, Dolores also ran the risk of making her infidelity public. With little regard for her reasons, Dolores would likely be marked with public stigma because, in contrast to other types of losses, death by suicide is often accompanied by shameful and guilt-laden responses.

Shame created a facade that overshadowed Dolores and Leo's grief experiences, and their relationship to the world around them and to each other (Trembley and Israel, 1998). Dolores distanced herself and Leo from the suicide by rejecting all recommendations for counseling. In an attempt to erase the shame brought on by the suicide, Dolores and Leo experienced marked isolation from each other. During individual encounters in her home, Dolores acknowledged that the death of Leo's father was never discussed. "¿No sé que decirle?" [I don't know what to say to him], she confessed. She avoided repeating the words suicide or death, replacing them with "lo que el hizo" [what he did]. In this context, Dolores felt safe communicating about the trauma, at least to me. Finding a way to talk to Leo was too difficult, and I surmise that, for this reason, Dolores chose silence.

Behind an Imagined One-Way Mirror: Leo

The silence fused Dolores and Leo to the trauma, and the silence protected Dolores from the stigma and shame associated with the suicide. Refraining to speak of the suicide also empowered Dolores, making it possible for her to handle the routine obligations of working and taking care of the children. In sharp contrast, the silence failed Leo because it disempowered him and promoted a sense of invisibility in him. He came in direct contact with the dead body, called for help, and protected his younger brother from the horrific sight, but was discouraged from remembering or speaking of what he saw. "My mother doesn't want there to be talk about that [suicide]," he once said. In essence, he was made invisible. Comprehending the phenomenon of invisibility with Leo also involved recognizing the cultural conditions that governed his family.

Dolores and Leo offered clues that alerted me to consider their responses through a cultural lens. My first clue was Leo's sense of allegiance to his family's country of origin. Though Leo was born and raised in the United States, he did not identify himself as American. In conversations, he frequently boasted about his proud heritage, often letting me know he was Dominican by saying, "Soy Dominicano" [I am Dominican] or "nosotros los Dominicanos" [us Dominicans]. This, however, was the extent of his spoken Spanish. Similar to many US-born children of immigrant parents, Leo spoke mostly Spanglish (Ardila, 2005), often overlapping the use of English with the bit of Spanish he knew. Leo's use of Spanglish, and his mother's maintenance of Spanish as her predominant language, served as a second cultural clue that they maintained close linkages with the customs and traditions of their Latino heritage. In Latino families, the constructs of *respeto, familismo*, and *simpatía* can be useful to understanding the intertwined features of trauma within the family. Understanding these constructs with Dolores and Leo proved crucial to building a therapeutic alliance with them, and enabled me to make sense of my own countertransference that was triggered during clinical encounters.

Keeping these constructs in mind, it is not surprising that Leo conformed to the silence Dolores initiated, given the high value that Latino families place on obedience. Obedience is equivalent to respect in Latino cultures and, as such, having *respeto* is a desirable trait in children of any age. Having *respeto* is also considered an integral component of the parent–child alliance because it signifies well-being within the relationship (Guilamo-Ramos et al., 2007). *Respeto* was a way for Leo to align with Dolores, and establish a sense of comfort and safety because, for a child, the death of a parent frequently involves negotiating assurances with the surviving parent about their own well-being (Trembley and Israel, 1998). Leo's use of *respeto* may also have been an unconscious attempt to mend the relationship with his mother, which was liable to have been severed when Leo chose to live with his father.

My later work with Leo revealed that he had not participated in funeral arrangements for his father. While seemingly cruel and heartless, excluding children from funerals is not uncommon in many cultures, and, in Latino families, is dictated by the cultural concept of *familismo*, which "emphasizes intergenerational solidarity, obligation, respect, and a duty to care for one's own" (Ruiz and Ransford, 2012, p. 50). The topic of death and dying is often bound to this strong sense of duty and obligation in Latino families. While there is an obligation and duty to care for those who are dying, there is also an obligation and duty to protect family, especially children, from death. It is not uncommon, therefore, for Latino families to "not discuss the family member's death among themselves because they didn't [do not] want to 'hurt' each other" (Kreling et al., 2010, p. 431). Excluding Leo, and refraining from speaking of the suicide, was his mother's way of shielding him from the emotionality of death. While this behavior may appear contradictory to a stereotypical definition of caring, it is not uncommon in families where *familismo* is highly regarded.

I understood his mother's decision, and her discomfort with death, because my own mother had shielded me from death, too. I was expecting my first child when my family became secretive about a funeral they were attending. I did not give the secrecy much thought until I realized that the family was diverting my innocent questioning. After my baby was born, I learned the truth: my out-of-state cousin had suffered a sudden traumatic death. I was bothered at first, but I came to understand that my family had been protecting my unborn child and me. Their actions were not intended to cause harm. But I was an adult. Leo was a child, and likely did not pick up on or understand these cultural values, so they further maintained his invisibility. Behind the imagined one-way mirror, I came to see how these cultural constructs impact the understanding of traumatic responses, and it has led me to contend that responses to trauma can be culturally constructed. Left to struggle alone, dissociation became part of how Leo coped.

The Self-Inflicted Magic Act: Dissociation

Leo referred to his disconnection from reality as "blacking out," and it typically happened during moments of rage. Leo recounted his experience once, and said, "I get so mad, so mad that I punch the walls and I black out. I can't control it, and I can't remember much else when it happens." Of course, the dissociation was not readily visible. As many children of trauma often do, "They can dissociate – fragment their experience in a way that protects them against the very real danger of physiological overload" (Bloom, 2000, p. 11). Now add a child's natural propensity for play, and the layered impact creates responses that are compromised. Because children's behaviors, such as laughing and playing, can be seemingly unaffected following adversity, these can be misinterpreted to mean contentment or peace. What must it have been like for Leo? There is a disparity between how an adult and a child understand and express loss. Children generally are unable to formulate succinct expressions due to their own lack of understanding about loss, and they respond in a disorganized manner that adults can disregard or misinterpret at times. One response can look like anger, for instance when Leo overturned his desk in school, or picked fights with others. Dissociation is another response and it predisposes children to invisibility and affect dysregulation. I speculate, however, that Leo's dissociative coping began when his family was still intact, before the suicide. It was clear from the interactions between Leo and his mother that they bore relational trauma. For example, the day I met Dolores in my office with Leo there, they behaved like strangers. Dolores had been unable to guide Leo toward restorative transformation, and Leo was left alone to deal with the physical loss of his father and the ambiguous loss of his mother (Boss, 2010). The crisis moment at school that day launched a therapeutic momentum that dared not be hindered, and that highlighted the critical need for constructing a therapeutic alliance between the school, Leo, and Dolores.

An Alliance with Home

I recall reaching out to Dolores to take a family history, but I had great difficulty building a therapeutic relationship with her in the confines of my office at school, so our sessions often felt detached. While she was always compliant, her answers were very brief, and she required a lot of probing. Her answers gave the impression of being scripted and inauthentic. I had seen this behavior quite often in other encounters with Latino families, and I understood it to be part of a cultural script known as *simpatía*. In providing seemingly scripted responses to my questions, Dolores maintained a high level of respect. She gave me the answers that she thought I wanted to hear. In a clinical encounter, "individuals demonstrating high levels of simpatía may appear to agree and understand a message, when, in fact, they may not have understood or have no intention of following the message" (Griffith et al., 1998, p. 469). The in-school encounters seemed ineffective at building an alliance with Dolores, so I decided to meet with her in their home. I offered her this non-traditional approach in an attempt to break the impasse.

It was evident that she took great care in ensuring the one-bedroom apartment was tidy. It was small, but comfortable. All at once, she did not seem so cold and distant. She offered me a seat at the kitchen table, but I wanted to avoid the stale dynamic that such an arrangement would provide. Instead, I asked her permission to sit on the couch. She seemed much more relaxed about talking, and I felt less anxious about asking the right questions. Dolores was a good host: she offered a refreshing drink, and lowered the volume on the television during our conversation. Culturally, I knew this was her way of showing me that I was welcome. I also had the opportunity to meet Leo's baby sister, and witnessed warm mother-child exchanges. Home visits proved to be the most fundamental component to building rapport and trust with Dolores.

Indeed, the home visit has been the basic foundational element of the social work profession. "Friendly visiting" (Woods, 1988), particularly among marginalized populations, not only complements, but also strengthens clinical approaches to non-traditional work with families. In this case, the use of home visits anchored the therapeutic alliance with Dolores, which, in turn, enabled her to trust the role of the school with her family. It was subtle at first, when she would sheepishly call the school to say, "Necesito ayuda para pagar la luz" [I need help paying the electricity]. The school met her concrete needs through case management, confirming for Dolores that it was a source of assistance. Providing Dolores a "direct benefit" (Celano and Kaslow, 2000, p. 222) may be seen as controversial, and call into question ethical concerns. However, when working with culturally diverse groups, this sort of "giving" (Celano and Kaslow, 2000, p. 222) serves to mitigate uncertainty. For Dolores, this meant trusting the school, and trusting me with her secrets, her shame, and her son. To my surprise, Dolores soon began making regular calls with the same intentional, yet unspoken, message: I need help. Now, her intent was no longer about her concrete needs, but rather about her relational shortcomings with Leo.

On Their Turf

One day, Dolores found it difficult to rouse Leo for school. For me, that morning began quite routinely, with the second grade morning greeters making their usual welcoming remarks: "¡Hola Miss . . .buenos días!" I unloaded my belongings into my desk drawer, and as I savored my first sip of coffee, the red message light on my office phone caught my eye. I had missed nine incoming calls. I scrolled through the caller ID, and realized all the calls were from the same number: Dolores's phone. I paused for a minute before calling her back and wondered, or rather hoped, that Leo was well. When Dolores answered the phone, her voice was wobbly. She recounted her conversation with Leo, and his refusal to attend school that day. "He doesn't want to open his bedroom door. He says he's too tired, he says he wants to die," she told me in Spanish. I suspected that mornings evoked memories that transported Leo back in time to his father's suicide.

His sleeplessness and restlessness typically began around midnight, but Leo made the best of it by playing video games. At first, it was not all bad, as the insomnia helped Leo become the best gamer in his grade. "Yo, you're so lucky! You get to play all night," his friends would say. But Leo didn't feel so lucky.

If only they knew how much he dreaded sleep. If only they knew how much it hurt. It seemed the last time he had a good night's rest was when he was seven years old. Dolores was unable to associate Leo's difficulty with waking up as a recurrence and reminder of waking up to find his father's dead body. Dolores seemed to be in a constant state of hyper-vigilance, severed from her own emotions and the emotions of her son. In calling upon the school for help, though, I sensed that her awareness of Leo's internal struggle was surfacing. Working with them from their home, therefore, was an opportunity I could not disregard.

Dolores never asked, "Can you come to my house?" but I felt manipulated by her tone of despair on the phone that day. It became an opportunity to see Leo and Dolores interact in their moment. The "value of seeing the client in his/her environment" (Beder, 1998, p. 514) could expand and evolve the clinical landscape for formulating Leo's lived reality. Together with the school's family worker, I responded to Dolores's unspoken request for help with a home visit. It was the first time I had been to the apartment while both Leo and Dolores were home. Dolores's nervousness infused the small apartment and, admittedly, it felt awkward. This felt difference is brought about when doing home-based therapy, and can unfold in an unpredictable manner because:

> The therapy process is altered when it is moved into the home setting because the therapy occurs in a heightened reality context that includes the possible participant observer role of the therapist, more active involvement of family members, and the opportunity for immediate analysis of family members' actual behavior.
>
> *Woods, 1988, p. 212*

By entering their lived space, the emotional distance between Leo and Dolores was alarmingly magnified. She granted me permission to enter their shared bedroom and, without warning, Dolores withdrew from the moment and hid in another room. No longer was I an observer who was meant to "stay out of the way of family patterns" (Woods, 1988, p. 212). Instead, I now had an active role in their family system as Dolores left us unaccompanied in their home. That phone call, her toneless voice, how did I get caught up in this? Had Dolores found another way to avoid confronting Leo and his emotions? These thoughts flooded my mind as the feeling of déja vu filled the air and I thought, here we are again. Leo needed Dolores, and she was emotionally unavailable to help him. I was challenged by the decision whether or not to help Dolores work through this dissociated pattern of behavior because I felt disappointed in her. She seemed to not even try. I was disappointed in myself as well, because maybe I hadn't done enough to help Dolores. I reminded myself that I was on the front line, and I had to offer myself once again because dissociation was a coping mechanism overused by Dolores and Leo to live in their world. The dissociation provided them with sanctuary from a restricted reality and so, with a few non-verbal nods of understanding, the family worker and I dispersed on separate agendas: she to comfort Dolores, and I to find Leo.

As I entered the bedroom, my immediate view was of the family bed, a queen-size mattress on the floor. Leo's baby sister lay on it, peacefully asleep. But where was Leo? I looked to the other side of the room, and found a large opening midway up the wall. It resembled a storage area, but by adding a mattress and some sheets, it was converted into a built-in bunker. I found the sleeping arrangement to be symbolic of Leo's relationship to his mother. It was distant, as if Leo was on the outside of the family looking in. Yet, there was a sense of protectiveness in this sleeping arrangement that resembled the secret Dolores guarded from the world about the suicide of Leo's father.

To reach this odd sleeping quarter, I had to climb on top of a chair and a dresser. When I got to the top, I found Leo covered from head to toe in his blankets. I called his name, and he uncovered his head. He looked surprised. I smiled and said, "What, you didn't think I could climb up here?" He smiled back. This simple dialogue and rudimentary approach was part of an ongoing affirmation of trust that Leo needed. Creating a sense of safety is a common goal in therapeutic communities, and in interventions for children of trauma. The home visit extended the school's therapeutic purview, and functioned as a vehicle from which to capture Leo's reality. Although we intentionally entered Leo's home to ameliorate truancy, the unintended outcome of being "friendly visitors" (Woods, 1988, p. 211) was that Leo's home life was rendered palpable.

By being able to connect to his home environment, the school as a therapeutic community served to enhance Leo's own sense of connectedness to a positive attachment. Because the school environment mimicked qualities of a therapeutic community, it greatly influenced Leo's emotional stabilization, and evoked what researchers Tedeschi and Calhoun termed post-traumatic growth. Essentially, post-traumatic growth is the positive transformational outcome following traumatic adversities (Calhoun and Tedeschi, 1999) but it is "not simply a return to baseline – it is an experience of improvement that for some persons is deeply profound" (Tedeschi and Calhoun, 2004, p. 4). This change experience is demonstrated through an individual's outlook about new possibilities, improved relationships with others, increased sense of personal strengths, increased appreciation for life, and, for some, spiritual transformation (Tedeschi and Calhoun, 2008). Despite limited research on post-traumatic growth and children, I strongly contend that because of the clear-cut opportunity to establish meaningful relationships and trust bonds in a school setting, the likelihood for eliciting post-traumatic growth through social competence is great (Tedeschi and Calhoun, 2008). Utilizing a therapeutic community modality increases this likelihood because the fundamental characteristic of therapeutic communities is a communal commitment to others. Similarly, collaboration is a fundamental characteristic of schools. In both schools and therapeutic communities, caring develops to be more than a task or a charge that belongs to one or two people, and instead becomes a way of being that belongs to everyone (Battistich et al., 1997). By engaging whole-school personnel to be cognizant of all children, school personnel become active observers who can gauge changes in a child's baseline behaviors, be they emotional and/or academic. These observatory baseline measures can thus significantly improve the identification of children in need, and the onset of interventions for them. This then facilitates a sense of connection to others, the post-traumatic growth, and can, in turn, become the cornerstone for disclosure. Disclosure, if and when it takes place, tends to more easily occur when children feel safe. This is due in part because "disclosure is not a single event but a process that is highly dependent on the reactions of others" (Freyd, 2010). This process is often enacted in schools as teachers navigate the mystic qualities that surround traumatic experiences on a day-to-day basis. In doing so, opportunities for disclosure and healing are created. The culture of Leo's school allowed a therapeutic community environment to form. By incorporating multiple members of Leo's school, in addition to my role, to aid him, the school as a whole became the primary host for healing when his mother was unable to. Even so, some will question whether therapeutic communities in a public school are possible.

The Making of a School-Based Therapeutic Community

To answer this question, I must first acknowledge my own journey into the field of social work. Long before I worked in the field of school social work, I had the unique opportunity to work in a residential therapeutic community for persons wanting to overcome addictions. Here, I gained first-hand knowledge about therapeutic communities, the role of attachment in treatment, and its impact on healing. But above all, I learned that a therapeutic community is much more than a treatment modality. It is a highly specialized created environment where everyone assumes responsibility for healing, and whereby an identity is formed and guided by the notion of a family.

Family is shaped and formed around groups of caring individuals who not only exist within family systems, but also co-exist around family systems, such as schools. It is precisely these kinds of groups that, in turn, shape healthy relationships that become restorative and enhance the functioning of a person. Consequently, I realized that schools, like the therapeutic community I once worked in, are able to take on attributes such as trust, respect, and encouragement, all of which are essential to well-being and akin to healthy families. These features offer protection, and can cultivate a sense of safe haven or "holding" (Winnicott, 1965, p. 43). As theorized by D. W. Winnicott (1965), the term holding is used to describe not only the physical needs of a child, but also the psychological environment necessary to achieve the overall healthy development of the child. In schools, the use of a therapeutic community approach can develop trust bonds. A trust bond is critical to a holding environment, and the essence of a therapeutic community. In this way, the helping milieu of attuned schools can create a pseudo-family, which can then serve as a vehicle for restructuring trust bonds (Soyez and Broekaert, 2005), in particular for children impacted by relational trauma.

Healing from trauma is intricately associated with, and dependent on, healthy attachment. The already inherent sense of trust in schools, and the fact that children spend the majority of their day—at least six hours—in school systems, makes them ideal settings to establish pseudo-families. "School bonding is akin to attachment" (Bergin and Bergin, 2009, p. 141) and can thereby serve to empower and accompany children through their traumatic experiences so that they will not need to suffer alone. With this perspective in mind, schools can have the potential to build attachment relationships and also to rebuild disrupted attachments (Pearlman and Courtois, 2005). Studies have found that "seriously disrupted attachment without repair or intervention for the child can, in and of itself, be traumatic, as the child is left psychologically alone to cope with his or her heightened and dysregulated emotional states, thus creating additional trauma" (Pearlman and Courtois, 2005, p. 451). The suicide of a parent is the greatest attachment breach a child can experience. Having knowledge that a child has suffered alone is the greatest opportunity to repair attachment, and constructing pseudo-families for children is a means to intervene.

Guided by the *in loco parentis* premise, schools naturally incorporate parenting. As therapeutic communities, schools can transform this naturally occurring parenting relationship to one of clinical parenting. Commonly referred to as "therapeutic parenting" in available literature on trauma and looked-after children, this form of healing approach is an essential component of highly specialized residential facilities that work with severely traumatized children. The idea is that "therapeutic parenting provides a structured means for a severely traumatized child to move from insecure to secure attachment, to fill gaps in their formative experiences, and to work through feelings associated with their trauma" (Tomlinson, 2008, p. 360). The formidable relationships that can be formed in schools make it possible to be the source of such transfer. Most people, for example, can easily recall their favorite teacher or the most helpful adult in school. This serves as a straightforward demonstration of the everlasting influence of attachments in the school setting.

In hindsight, there were rich indicators that the culture of Leo's school contributed to the development of therapeutic parenting. The school coordinated shoe drives, coat drives, and numerous other drives. Doctors, nurses, and dentists are accessible within the school to meet a child's basic medical needs. Combine these with parent clinics and an open-door policy, and the lived experience of the school itself begins to take shape. Is this unique to Leo's school? I do not think so. Many school systems, in an effort to eliminate barriers to learning, particularly in urban areas, have assumed a one-stop shopping approach within education. They offer students comprehensive medical, social, and psychological school-based services, thereby helping to meet the students' physical and emotional needs. The outcome of such collaborative school systems thus can yield consistency, structure, and nurturance. It can also spread beyond school children, as their families also seek emotional asylum within the corridors of the school.

Such environments can also be favorable for other students who have suffered trauma, or are living through their own traumatic experiences. Consider Jose, who was raised transnationally in Mexico for ten years while his parents lived in the United States. When he reunites with his parents, they are virtual strangers. Could this attachment breach manifest relational trauma later? His 5-year-old sister Lila reunites with them one year later, but to do so, she must spend one month in the care of a coyoté, a paid stranger who is charged with smuggling her across the Mexico/US border. How might she manifest trauma? Think about Maria, age nine, whose role was reversed from child to respite worker as a result of her mother's terminal illness. How will this experience change Maria? And when her mother dies? There is also Pilar, a fourth grader, who endured years of sexual abuse by a family member, and later witnessed a gruesome physical assault on her mother and sister as they were left for dead by this same family member. Who will notice her pain? Schools, as therapeutic communities, can.

So, are therapeutic communities in public schools possible? The answer is yes, and this case study makes the argument for how it can be done. By reinterpreting the pre-existing notion of *in loco parentis*, and by cultivating a school's natural capacity to create and actualize formidable attachments for children, schools can be transformed into therapeutic communities. As this case study demonstrates, attuned environments enable all members of that environment to participate in healing. We must take advantage of a school's unique ability to do this, and build on the trust that is inherently attributed to schools. Doing so can be an effective intervention to trauma, and a crucial component for healing. It was for Leo.

CLOSE READING QUESTIONS

1. Sandoval-Arocho says that schools as therapeutic communities do not "overextend the role of school personnel." Why does she make this claim? Do you agree? What kinds of emotional investment do we see Sandoval-Arocho make? Give specific examples of how she processes secondary trauma. Bonus: In "Mindfulness Group Work in the School Setting," how does Cuseglio negotiate his burnout? What do you learn about the importance of self-care from these two case studies?

2. Sandoval-Arocho writes, "School systems are microcosms of society, and must therefore respond accordingly to society." Think about the context of her assertions. What do you think she means? Does her school respond accordingly to society?

3. What do you learn from Sandoval-Arocho about treating trauma and grief in children?

Prompts for Writing

1. Both Sandoval-Arocho and Kaliades discuss zero-tolerance discipline models in conjunction with their ideas on shame among the students and families that they serve. Juxtapose these two case studies and establish the central connections between them. What do you learn about how shame manifests and is treated in the school setting?

2. When Leo says that he is contemplating suicide, his school truly mobilizes into action. Part of the reason, as Healy suggests in his case study on the "Sexual and Gender Minority Student," is that schools want to protect themselves against liability. Research suicide in the school setting. How do your findings relate to Sandoval-Arocho's and Healy's case studies?

3. Sandoval-Arocho mentions the "Sanctuary Model" and "Planned Environment Therapy." Research these models in depth and offer examples from Sandoval-Arocho's case study to discuss how these models work in action to shape schools into therapeutic communities.

References

Ardila, A. (2005). Spanglish: An anglicized Spanish dialect. *Hispanic Journal of Behavioral Sciences*, 27(1), 60–81.

Battistich, V., Solomon, D., Watson, M., and Schaps, E. (1997). Caring school communities. *Educational Psychologist*, 32(3), 137–151. Accessed online February 28, 2017 at http://dx.doi.org/10.1207/s15326985ep3203_1.

Beder, J. (1998). The home visit, revisited. *Families in Society*, 79(5), 514–522. Accessed online February 28, 2017 at http://search.proquest.com/docview/230198775?accountid=13626.

Bergin, C., and Bergin, D. (2009). Attachment in the classroom. *Educational Psychology Review*, 21(2), 141–170. DOI: 10.1007/s10648-009-9104-0.

Bernhard, J., Freire, M., Bascunan, L., Arenas, R., Verga, N., and Gana, D. (2004). Behavior and misbehavior in Latino children in a time of zero tolerance: Mother's views. *Early Childhood Education Publications and Research*. Paper 20.

Blackstone, W. (1765–1769). Of parent and child. In *Commentaries on the laws of England 1765–1769* (Book 1, Chapter 16). Accessed online April 25, 2017 at http://lonang.com/library/reference/blackstone-commentaries-law-england/bla-116/.

Bloom, S. L. (2000). The grief that dare not speak its name Part II: Dealing with the ravages of childhood abuse. *Psychotherapy Review*, 2(10), 1–22.

Boss, P. (2010). The trauma and complicated grief of ambiguous loss. *Pastoral Psychology*, 59(2), 137–145.

Bowden, R. (2007). Evolution of responsibility: From in loco parentis to ad meliora vertamur. *Education*, 127(4), 480–489.

Cain, A. C. (2002). Children of suicide: The telling and the knowing. *Psychiatry*, 65(2), 124–136.

Calhoun, L. G., and Tedeschi, R. G. (Eds.) (1999). *Facilitating posttraumatic growth: A clinician's guide*. New York: Routledge.

Celano, M. P., and Kaslow, N. J. (2000). Culturally competent family interventions: Review and case illustrations. *The American Journal of Family Therapy*, *28*(3), 217–228. DOI: 10.1080/01926180050081658.

Cook, A., Spinazzola, J., Ford, J., Lanktree, C., and Blaustein, M. (2007). Complex trauma in children and adolescents. *Focal Point*, 21, 4–8.

Costello, E. J., Erkanli, A., Fairbank, J. A., and Angold, A. (2002). The prevalence of potentially traumatic events in childhood and adolescence. *Journal of Traumatic Stress*, *15*(2), 99–112.

Doka, K. J. (1989). *Disenfranchised grief: Recognizing hidden sorrow*. Lexington, MA: Lexington Books.

Edwards, J. O. (2009). The many kinds of family structures in our communities. Sonoma County Office of Education. Accessed online February 28, 2017 at www.scoe.org/files/ccpc-family-structures.pdf.

Epstein, M. (2013, August 4). The trauma of being alive. *New York Times*. Accessed online August 4, 2013 at www.nytimes.com/2013/08/04/opinion/sunday/the-trauma-of-being-alive.html?pagewanted=all&_r=2&.

Fairbank, J. A. (2008). The epidemiology of trauma and trauma related disorders in children and youth. *PTSD Research Quarterly*, *19*(1), 1–8.

Freud, S. (1999). The social construction of normality. *Families in Society*, *80*(4), 333–339.

Freyd, J. J. (2010). Disclosing trauma: Research and implications. Invited address for the 118th Annual Convention of the American Psychological Association, San Diego, California, 12–15 August.

Fuchs, T. (2002). The phenomenology of shame, guilt and the body in body dysmorphic disorder and depression. *Journal of Phenomenological Psychology*, *33*(2), 223–243.

Gerrity, E., and Folcarelli, C. (2008). *Child traumatic stress: What every policymaker should know*. Durham, NC and Los Angeles, CA: National Center for Child Traumatic Stress.

Griffith, J. D., Joe, G. W., Chatham, L. R., and Simpson, D. D. (1998). The development and validation of the Simpatia scale for Hispanics entering drug treatment. *Hispanic Journal of Behavioral Sciences*, 20, 468–482.

Guarnaccia, P., Lewis-Fernandez, R., and Rivera Marano, M. (2003). Toward a Puerto Rican popular nosology: Nervios and ataques de nervios. *Culture, Medicine, and Psychiatry*, *27*(3), 339–366.

Guilamo-Ramos, V., Dittus, P., Jaccard, J., Johansson, M., Bouris, A., and Acosta, N. (2007). Parenting practices among Dominican and Puerto Rican mothers. *Social Work*, *52*(1), 17–30.

Hargreaves, A. (1998). The emotional practice of teaching. *Teaching and Teacher Education*, *14*(8), 835–854.

Imber-Black, E. (2009). *The secret life of families*. New York: Bantam Books.

Jackson, D., and Mannix, J. (2004). Giving voice to the burden of blame: A feminist study of mothers' experiences of mother blaming. *International Journal of Nursing Practice*, *10*(4), 150–158.

Kalich, D., and Brabant, S. (2006). A continued look at Doka's grieving rules: Deviance and anomie as clinical tools. *Omega*, *53*(3), 227–241.

Kennard, D. (2004). The therapeutic community as an adaptable treatment modality across different settings. *Psychiatric Quarterly*, *75*(3), 295–307.

Kreling, B., Selsky, C., Perret-Gentil, M., Huerta, E. E., and Mandelblatt, J. S. (2010). "The worst thing about hospice is that they talk about death": Contrasting hospice decisions and experience among immigrant Central and South American Latinos with US-born White, non-Latino cancer caregivers. *Palliative Medicine, 24*(4), 427–434.

Loader, P. (1998). Such a shame: Consideration of shame and shaming mechanisms in families. *Child Abuse Review*, 7, 44–57.

Longhofer, J. (2013). Shame in the clinical process with LGBTQ clients. *Clinical Social Work Journal, 41*(3), 297–301.

Mathews, T., Dempsey, M., and Overstreet, S. (2009). Effects of exposure to community violence on school functioning: The mediating role of posttraumatic stress symptoms. *Behaviour Research and Therapy, 47*(7), 586–591.

National Institute of Drug Abuse (NIDA) (2002). Therapeutic community. Research Report Series. 1–12. Accessed online February 28, 2017 at www.drugabuse.gov/publications/research-reports/therapeutic-community.

Overstreet, S., and Mathews, T. (2011). Challenges associated with exposure to chronic trauma: Using a public health framework to foster resilient outcomes among youth. *Psychology In The Schools, 48*(7), 738–754.

Park, K. (1997). How do objects become objects of reference? *British Journal of Special Education*, 24, 108–114. DOI: 10.1111/1467-8527.00025.

Pearlman, L., and Courtois, C. A. (2005). Clinical applications of the attachment framework: Relational treatment of complex trauma. *Journal of Traumatic Stress, 18*(5), 449–459.

Rodden, J. (2000). The TEACHER as HERO. *The American Enterprise, 11*(6), 40–41.

Rollins, J. A. (2012). Revisiting the issue of corporal punishment in our nation's schools. *Pediatric Nursing, 38*(5), 248–269.

Ruiz, M., and Ransford, H. (2012). Latino elders reframing familismo: Implications for health and caregiving support. *Journal of Cultural Diversity, 19*(2), 50–57.

Shengold, L. (1989). *Soul murder: The effects of childhood abuse and deprivation.* New York: Fawcett Columbine.

Smrekar, C., and Cohen-Vogel, L. (2001). The voices of parents: Rethinking the intersection of family and school. *Peabody Journal of Education, 76*(2), 75–100.

Soyez, V., and Broekaert, E. (2005). Therapeutic communities, family therapy, and humanistic psychology: History and current examples. *Journal of Humanistic Psychology*, summer (45), 302–332.

Stuart, S. (2010). In loco parentis in the public schools: Abused, confused and in need of change. *University of Cincinnati Law Review, 10*(03), 1–48. DOI: http://ssrn.com/abstract=1548675.

Tedeschi, R. G., and Calhoun, L. G. (2004). Posttraumatic growth: Conceptual foundations and empirical evidence. *Psychological Inquiry, 15*(1), 1–18.

Tedeschi, R., and Calhoun, L. (2008). Beyond the concept of recovery: Growth and the experience of loss. *Death Studies, 32*(1), 27–39.

The Consortium for Therapeutic Communities (2013). What is a TC? Accessed online February 28, 2017 at www.therapeuticcommunities.org/what-is-a-tc/.

Tomlinson, P. (2008). Assessing the needs of traumatized children to improve outcomes. *Journal of Social Work Practice, 22*(3), 359–374.

Traub, H., and Lane, R. (2002). The case of Ms. A. *Clinical Case Studies, 1*(1), 49–66.

Trembley, G., and Israel, A. (1998). Children's adjustment to parental death. *Clinical Psychology: Science and Practice, 5*(4), 424–438.

Triandis, H. C., Marin, G., Lisansky, J., and Betancourt, H. (1984). Simpatia as a cultural script of Hispanics. *Journal of Personality & Social Psychology, 47*(6), 1363–1375.

Wayland, F. (1860). *Elements of moral science*. Boston, MA: Gould and Lincoln.

Weber, S. (2009) Treatment of trauma- and abuse-related dissociative symptom disorders in children and adolescents. *Journal of Child and Adolescent Psychiatric Nursing, 22*(1), 2–6.

Willis, C. A. (2002). The grieving process in children: Strategies for understanding, educating, and reconciling children's perceptions of death. *Early Childhood Education Journal, 29*(4), 221.

Winnicott, D. W. (1960). The theory of the parent-infant relationship. *The International Journal of Psycho-Analysis*, 41, 585–595.

Winnicott, D. W. (1965). *The maturational processes and the facilitating environment: Studies in the theory of emotional development*. New York: International Universities Press.

Woods, L. J. (1988). Home based family therapy. *Social Work, 33*(3), 211–214.

Yale Center in Child Development and Social Policy (2003). *Portrait of four schools: Meeting the needs of immigrant students and their families*. New Haven, CT. Accessed online February 28, 2017 at medicine.yale.edu/childstudy/zigler/21c/.../immigrantprojects.aspx.

6

SCHOOL SOCIAL WORK REDEFINED

Alternative Education Program Design

Eric K. Williams

Pre-Reading Questions

1. Look at the first line of Williams's case study. What do you imagine is the lived experience of a student in an alternative school setting? And what about the staff?
2. What do you know about systems theory? How might it be applicable in a school setting? In what other social work contexts is systems theory useful?
3. In which ways might a school social worker be particularly suited to rethink a school environment? If you could redesign a school to promote the best outcomes for non-traditional students, what is the first change you would make? How does your thinking about the person-in-environment concept affect your choice?

Introduction

An alternative school is designed to accommodate educational, behavioral, and/or medical needs of students that cannot be addressed in a traditional school environment. It falls outside the familiar categories of regular, special, or vocational education (US Department of Education, 2002). The alternative high school where I work as a school social worker—which I will herein refer to as United Alternative Academy—is defined largely by flexibility in how education is delivered and what supports are available to the student. A more nuanced description that fits with the frame of United's "alternative program" comes from Gann (2011):

> In theory, Alternative Education Programs exist to provide students who have experienced personal, social, and academic failure a second opportunity at success. Creating an educational environment which allows a student a voice in determining outcomes and is challenged by the staff to change those things that led to previous school-related failure is the foundation of such a program.
>
> *p. ix*

Aron (2003) suggests that the lack of a commonly accepted definition of "alternative education" indicates the fluidity of related policies and legislation, the diversity of contexts and settings, and the various groups of at-risk youth who may benefit from alternative education options. Unfortunately, the environment I encountered when I arrived at United showed that this "fluidity" sometimes resulted in disorganization; the school was far from Gann's theoretical ideal.

Physically, United Alternative Academy is set separate from the city's general secondary school building, but students attending United are integrated in all other aspects of the high school's programs. They are able to participate in all extra-curricular activities and are eligible for all resources offered at the school's main campus. The population at United—urban youth from mostly African-American and Latino backgrounds—is capped at 125 students. The enrollment is kept capped at this number to ensure the appropriate student-teacher ratio as well as to comply with the occupancy regulations of a smaller, satellite school within the overall campus. These students have historically displayed school behaviors that are inappropriate for a school setting: some are returning drop-outs, others have interacted in some way with the juvenile justice system. Fuller and Sabatino (1996) find that by and large, these students are defensive, hopeless, attention seeking, drug-using, and often from troubled families; they outline nine attributes of alternative school students:

> 1) records of poor academic achievement, 2) family backgrounds of low socioeconomic and cultural status, 3) poor school achievement after several social promotions, 4) truancy, 5) no membership in school extracurricular activities, 6) verbal abilities inferior to nonverbal abilities, 7) records of repeated norm-violating disruptive behaviors, 8) a peer group composed of similar students, and 9) a negative attitude toward school.
>
> *pp. 293–294*

These students represent approximately 5% of the overall secondary education population in this school district. The practice of suspension or expulsion for 5% of the population is discriminatory, punitive, and only fosters further opportunities for delinquent behavior.

The school sits inconspicuously in an unremarkable neighborhood in the heart of a hardscrabble urban city. Among the dull grey brick apartment buildings, with their network of black iron fire escapes, winding and interconnecting, United is hardly distinguishable as an actual school, save for the bright silver letters emblazoned on the pale yellow stucco facade of the one-level building, simply reading: "United Alternative Academy." The structure had once served the city as a factory, and it was easy to imagine the systems that had been in place there: the efficiency of assembly lines, the order in chains of command, the mechanisms for quality production.

My job as a school social worker within these walls would require me to go beyond the roles of clinical intervention and student evaluation as I had formerly known them. I was tasked with creating and implementing a new system that would change the whole feeling of the place. I needed to design a comprehensive program for at-risk youth that would transform the factory-like aspects of American education into a system that respected the modern-day concept of person-in-environment. The effectiveness of my program could literally make or break the school environment and the students' success—and perhaps even their survival—at large. After all, this student population was as vulnerable as the lower class of factory workers; just as laws and unions had to be put in place to protect the workers' rights, it was a rather recent awareness of legal responsibility that had made United's mission possible: to protect the human rights of students outside the mainstream. Moreover, I had a personal stake in this mission: I had been a lifelong resident of this particular community. Although I do not come from a minority group, I was born and raised in an urban, multicultural environment. Over many years, my experiences afforded me numerous opportunities to become personally familiar with the customs, values, language, and norms of this diverse community. This greatly influenced my understanding of systems and the impact they can have on the individual. It also taught me how to be responsive in ways that are aligned with the unique sociocultural needs of particular populations.

In this chapter, I chronicle my role as a school social worker beyond assessment and therapeutic intervention. Using a phenomenological approach, an account of my lived experience, I demonstrate how, as a school social worker, I changed United's structure, routine, and rituals to facilitate a re-orientation of the disenfranchised student's sense of self, drawing them closer to staff, one another, and, ultimately, themselves. But truly, this is a case study of my experience, that of a traditional school social worker who came to a non-traditional school, and how I used systems theory to rethink the possibilities of school social work.

Systems Theory

In order to effectively understand an individual's particular dilemma and consequently facilitate change, the social worker must be able to grasp how all of the complex components interact with and impact the individual. Streeter and Franklin (2002) maintain that school social workers possess a unique perspective about how different systems affect the individual. Teasley (2004) furthers that social workers hold high value in the school setting because the profession is rooted in the generalist perspective, which promulgates strategies for change at the macro, mezzo, and micro levels. This analysis of how systems impact the individual, more commonly referred to as the person-in-environment, person-in-environment perspective, or person-in-situation, is a tenet of social work practice. Kondrat (2011) maintains that the person-in-environment perspective in social work is a guiding principle that stresses the importance of understanding an individual and individual behavior, taking full consideration of the environmental contexts in which that person lives and acts. This view holds the individual as part of a system of interacting components, heavily influenced by all parts.

This orientation, practiced by social workers in virtually all settings, is rooted in the more complex sociological theory called "systems theory." Anderson et al. (1999) point out that systems theory is a way of understanding the complexity across a continuum that encompasses the person-in-environment. It undertakes a broad examination of the individual in the environment and is best applied in situations where multiple systems are inextricably connected and influence one another. This process is a way of thinking about how the whole is arranged, how its parts interact, and how the relationships between the parts produce something new. It highlights that people and their life circumstances stand in relationship to something, with all parts of the system affecting each other. Behaviors are reciprocal to one another and mutually reinforcing. Change in one part produces change in another part and the whole: there is a ripple through the system. And because no problem can be seen in isolation, we must view the system as the locus of the problem. The problem is in the interaction between the parts and correspondingly, the same is true for solutions and corrections.

As an organizing framework for social work practice, systems theory draws from various disciplines, including the physical sciences, but it is most noted for its application in the social sciences. In their work on systems theory in social work, Friedman and Allen (2011) cite Robbins et al. (2006) who note that the term "systems" emerged from well-known sociologist Emile Durkheim's early study of social systems. Durkheim's work focused on how traditional and modern societies evolved and function through the interaction of various systems.

Talcott Parsons, a follower of Durkheim, is also credited with the development of systems thinking and, much like his predecessor, was concerned with how humans organize themselves and behave. Parsons took a specific interest in and wrote about youth and societal structure. As quoted in Knapp (1994), Parsons states: "people act on the basis of their values; their actions are oriented and constrained by the values and norms of people around them; and these norms and values are the basis of social order" (pp. 191–192). As I will describe, this idea, that actions can be influenced by systematic implementation of particular norms and values, was essential to how I re-conceptualized my role as a school social worker.

While Durkheim and Parsons provided the initial frame for systems thinking, it was an individual from the world of science who is credited with bringing it to the fore of social work practice. Friedman and Allen (2011) point out that it was biologist Ludwig Von Bertalanffy who has had the most influence on systems thinking and is widely credited with being the originator of the form of systems theory utilized in social work. Von Bertalanffy's general systems theory is essentially a science of wholeness. His unique contribution lies in the notion that "the whole is more than the sum of its parts" (1968, p. 18). Previous cause-and-effect theories concerning change in living organisms were reductionist, meaning that they sought to understand the whole by breaking down its parts. Von Bertalanffy's dissatisfaction with such views led him to change the framework by looking at the system as a whole, with its complex relationships and interactions with other systems, as an important mechanism for growth and change. This shift from observing and explaining how an organism develops in a systems context, to viewing how the system can effect change is critical to our understanding of the role of school social worker, especially in terms of designing programs that take into account the influence of systems and how to modify them to bring about change not only for the individual, but for the various systems involved as well.

Arriving at United: Redesigning the System

It was two days before school officially began, but I needed to bring my assortment of social work wares—my books, posters, and various motivational objects—to set up my office. As I stood for a moment to take in my surroundings, there was an odd feeling that grabbed me, a coldness of sorts. United Alternative Academy seemed sterile, lifeless. I proceeded up the steps and rang the security bell. I was buzzed in, and as I stepped through the double glass doors, I could smell fresh paint and the scent of pine oil, the familiar smells of a school that had gone through its annual summer ritual preparation for opening day. As I walked through the glistening hallways, speckled with live green plants and potted small trees, I admired the school's decor, walls adorned with student art from the previous school year, some quite impressive. I peeked into a few classrooms and saw they were prepared; a poster of Martin Luther King Jr. in a striking contemplative pose, a giant periodic table covering an entire wall, a bust of William Shakespeare awaiting the company of young minds to engage. By all initial impressions, United appeared to be a fully functional school. All that was needed now, it seemed, were students to fill halls and classrooms and bring the building to life.

I had been a school social worker in the school district for fifteen years prior to my arrival at United. In each of the schools I served, there was a loose but organized structure in place for social workers: deal with any emotional and/or behavioral problems that students exhibit, work with the families when needed, make referrals to outside agencies, and, above all, make sure teachers were able to do their job and teach students. Each of the school administrators I served under didn't seem overly concerned with methodology, just results. Upon arriving at United, I met with the principal, and she briefed me on how social work had been conducted for the first two years the school had been in existence. It was immediately apparent that supportive services, especially for this type of school, were severely lacking. The principal explained that a social worker was assigned to United part-time, usually two days a week, and thus, had not been a regular fixture of the school community. The social worker would review any emergencies that occurred, conduct a student interview, provide basic counseling, and refer out any cases that needed more specific, intensive services. In this crisis management mode, absent was any approach that sought to connect issues or identify root causes of problems. The person-in-environment approach was essentially *non esse*. The strategy of simply completing each school day and "staying afloat" resulted in an increasingly disconnected student body and a faculty overwhelmed by serving quasi-functions of educator, behavioral specialist, and crisis manager.

The principal admitted that this lack of any coherent social work structure within the school was impairing the overall ability to deliver effective educational services. As Teasley (2004) notes, structural inadequacies must be addressed if there is to be success when addressing the social and emotional needs of students in at-risk urban communities. Following my meeting with the principal, the inadequacy of social work at United was glaringly clear: the needs of students were barely being met because there was little to no structure to how social work was being conducted. The paucity of regular supportive services and, by extension, the lack of important social and emotional engagement, left the students at United, in my estimation, even more at-risk than they were prior to enrollment. School had not yet started, and before I had even met one student, I was presented with the information that would make my purpose clear: the first course of action was to move away from a program that operated primarily in crisis response mode and replace it with a more proactive approach to problem-solving, one rooted in analyzing systems and their impact on the individual.

Day 1

7.45a.m. I arrived early to stake out a spot at the entrance of the school to observe the morning routine. I planned to be a participant-observer on my first day. Inside United, there was little life besides the sound of a single copy machine rattling off pages, a few teachers doing last-minute prep, and a couple of janitors making their rounds. That was it. The bus pulled up to the curb at 8.00a.m. sharp and opened its folding doors. Students began to ooze out slowly, none too eagerly. I watched as they filed into the building, some making eye contact, most not. I heard a half hearted "whatssup man" uttered by a tall lanky boy as he passed me. In a more lively moment, a female student with thick long dreadlocks wearing a neon sweatshirt with the words "The One" splashed in graffiti paint across the front proudly announced her arrival by proclaiming "I'm here everybody!" A few other students chattered on in small cliques or laughed with each other, but only amongst themselves. It was evident that the lines were clearly drawn between students and staff, and there was little crossover. As I watched the students move in a steady, somewhat sullen procession to their classes, I was struck by the juxtaposition of the scene: amidst the movement of these young bodies, through colorful hallways, dotted with plants, art, and emblems of inspiration, the overall environment lacked energy. A kind of apathy pervaded. Teachers were doing their jobs and lessons were taking place, but there was an almost rote, mechanical quality to it all. There was something essential missing: real interaction. I felt both profound disappointment at the lost opportunity for connection, and yet, at the same time, I was inspired to immerse myself in the work ahead: to engage with the students in their environment so as to alter the system.

   To gain a deeper understanding of this challenge necessitates a return to Parsons's (1950) examination of adolescent stage development and social structure. His major contribution is the articulation of patterns of attitudes and behavior he observed in youth, highlighted by the following observations:

> a compulsive independence of and antagonism to adult expectations and authority which involves recalcitrance to adult standards of responsibility and as a result, attempts isolation from them. Also, a compulsive conformity within the peer group underscored by an intense fear of being excluded, a corresponding competitiveness for acceptance to be part of the accepted groups, and a ruthless rejection of those who don't fit in.
>
> *p. 378*

Parsons also notes the propensity of youth to engage in "romanticism," which he describes as "an unrealistic idealization of emotionally significant objects. There is a general tendency to see the world in sharply black and white terms; identifications with one's gang, or team, or school tend to be very intense and involve highly immature disparagements of other groups" (p. 378). Using Parsons's observations as a framework, the challenge before me as the social worker in this circumstance was complex: it involved a configuration to the daily routine of students that provided structure yet allowed for personal choice and expression. It meant walking a delicate line between courting adolescents' developmental need for idealization and identification while also remaining cognizant of their propensity to reject authority and the associated demands and expectations of the adult world.

   To its credit, this particular school district, one that has received much recognition for urban public education reform, is a proactive organization that is engaged with staff about the day-to-day challenges they face. The Board of Education evaluated my initial assessment about the lack of a formal social work program and immediately expressed support to remedy the problem. They understood that fundamental changes were necessary and that social work would be the key ingredient in any successful intervention. In establishing United two years prior, the district had already made important staffing decisions, such as placing an executive director, who had authority beyond that of just a principal, at the helm of the school. This move was significant because the decisions regarding school programming could be made at the school level and in response to the unique needs of the school, sometimes on a daily basis. Normally, decisions about the programmatic aspects of school functioning need to be submitted to the Board of Education for review, and the in-house executive directorship streamlined the decision-making process, allowing United to be more flexible and responsive to the immediate needs of students. This also made it possible for me as the social worker to work freely, unimpeded by the normal bureaucracy of a public education system. The executive director provided full support and gave sanction and authority for me to develop specific programming, as well as modify the structure of the daily routine at United Academy.

My first task at United was to implement an actual program with a clearly stated objective for school social workers. The ad hoc nature of previous years' approach resulted in an absence of any real structure or goals. Many of the students had had negative interactions with different types of social workers throughout their lives, and they needed a redefinition of how we could be helpful. Therefore, the first step was to create a mission statement for the social work department. In simple, straightforward language, I devised the following:

> Schools and families are environments in which children should develop socially, emotionally, and academically to realize their own intrinsic worth and potential. United Alternative Academy's multi-dimensional and comprehensive School Social Work Department seeks to ensure social, emotional, and academic success through collaboration with our students, their families, and their communities.

Inherent in this statement is the social work program's explicit intent to make a philosophical and operational commitment to view student needs and potential resources through the person-in-environment perspective, utilizing a systems approach. In his assertion that a systems approach is particularly useful when developing alternative programs, Kellmayer (1995) highlights how the school can serve as a process model in which staff, parents, and support staff work collaboratively in a modifiable social system. The document was approved, adopted for official use, and distributed by the social worker to all stakeholders: staff, students, and parents, as well as the school district administrators. Each group individually received a formal presentation of the statement along with a detailed explanation of its theoretical foundations. The immediate goals were to introduce this new paradigm in which students' social and emotional issues would be viewed, and also to have each group identify themselves as an integral part of the overall process. From an understanding of how, in a systems framework, particular challenges develop, to identifying elements within the system that can be harnessed for change, the presentation and ensuing dialogue served as both tutorial and indoctrination to the idea of the person-in-environment as well as how a systems theory approach would be implemented at United.

Day 18

8.15a.m. Mr. Davis, the school security guard, was at his newly assigned post: holding the door open and greeting students as they filed into the building. Lining the corridor of the entrance were the entire teaching staff, greeting every student by first name. It was now part of the new morning routine that I had established; welcoming students involved interacting with them. Teachers were required to have a brief exchange, even just "hello," to get a sense of the students' mood and temperament. I stood at the end. This was my post, where I was available to students who had come to understand that this was their "check-in" time with me. They had the opportunity each day to either speak with me briefly or could make an appointment to speak with me for an extended period in private about anything that concerned them. This first point of contact was critical in engaging students right away in the morning. It also proved to be a valuable screening tool. This experience allowed me to observe the students, make note of any irregularities in their mood or behavior, and to intervene immediately if necessary. This morning once again proved our new system was working. Mrs. C, the math teacher encountered Marcus at the entrance, and after a few words, she sent him directly down the hallway to schedule an early morning appointment with me. Head down, lips locked, something was clearly wrong with Marcus. He had usually been enthusiastic and talkative, one of United's more vocal "family members." (Since day 2, in an appeal to adolescent need for identification and unity, we had been referring to the student body and entire school staff as the "United Academy Family." Students warmed very quickly to this concept.)

I redesigned the social work program at United Academy with the specific intent of using *all* relationships, not only the social worker/student relationship, as a means to identify potential student problems. In order to take full advantage of this intention, the executive director made it a mandatory assignment for teachers to gather each morning to greet students in the entry hallway. The benefits of this structural change of environment were immediately realized: students were benefiting from the more personalized relationships with staff and a true sense of community was being developed among students and teachers. This place was no longer a factory. This place was a home.

Day 30

9.00a.m. Something amazing occurred this morning at United. Joining staff members in the hallway were several students of the recently constituted "Welcoming and Hospitality Committee." The idea of student committees had developed during the newly established weekly "Community Meeting," where students were able to voice their concerns about any aspect of the school environment that concerned them. What began as gripe sessions, and at times, plain nonsense and fooling around, evolved into meaningful discussions that revealed students' desire and capacity for self-determination. The idea of a welcoming committee came from a quiet, sullen 15-year-old girl named Sasha. She was once described by a teacher as "brooding" and "difficult to engage." However, during the community meeting held last week, Sasha suddenly came alive. Opening the meeting in my normal manner, I asked if there were any students who had suggestions for improving things at United. I scanned the room and took notice of Sasha. Her eyes darted nervously around the room at her peers. I let the silence continue for a few moments as I had come to learn that the students did not need rescuing from the anxiety that develops in silence. In fact, it was the presence of that anxiety that often propelled a student in the crowd to break the silence with a spontaneous offering to the group. In an act that I can only assume took a leap of courage and faith, Sasha took a deep breath, confidently pushed herself off of the arms of her chair and gracefully strode to the front of the classroom. She took a long look around the room, cleared her throat and in dramatic fashion proclaimed: "If this is really a family then we should be in the front of the school saying good morning to each other, too!" What I came to learn about Sasha was that she was an only child from a single parent family. Her mother worked the night shift at a factory and often did not get home in time to wake her up or even say "good morning."

On this morning, Sasha and four other students arrived several minutes early for school and took their place alongside staff members to greet their peers as they arrived. I was struck by the manner in which students approached their new roles. There was a seriousness about them; they appeared almost nervous as they stood fidgeting with their clothing, hair, and posture. When the students came through the front entrance and it was time to engage, a playful sensitivity emerged from the group, and to my surprise, even Sasha. As the procession of students continued, Sasha and the committee worked their way through the hallway, greeting their peers by first name (or personal nicknames), inquiring how they felt and even directing a few students to me for further support. The powerful effect the morning routine had on the students was immediately noticeable. The specific manner in which Sasha and the other students behaved suggested that they had been strongly influenced by their experiences and were identifying with the adult staff. They had integrated their regular morning experiences with them, some using similar greetings and body language, none of which was rehearsed or coached.

Real change is a process that requires, among other things, patience as well as the successful combination of different elements. It would take some time before the changes made at United would begin to have their full effect on the environment. Structural alterations, such as the manner in which students were greeted by name everyday when entering the school, immediately had a positive impact. But if the program had any chance of real, lasting success, something more than structural change was needed. That was the human element: living, breathing beings in the form of students and staff. In his seminal work *On Adolescence* (1966),

Peter Blos writes that "The child's environment always and everywhere is represented by the specific practices and attitudes with which significant persons meet his physical and emotional needs. Reality resides in the mental representations of the outer world, the environment, which contains meaningful objects, values and ideas with which the child becomes familiar" (p. 199). The program would rise or fall based upon the students' response to change, and more importantly, whether they felt personally connected to the systems being modified and created. The collective expectation was that students would experience the shift in our approach, that they would incorporate the changes not only in structure but in the way that it was being delivered, through more connective relationships with staff and that that would increase the personal value of what was occurring in this new paradigm. In doing so, we hoped that they would begin to assume ownership and become a healthy system for one another and, by extension, influence the environment of the school as a system as well. Over the course of the next few weeks, a series of events suggested that was beginning to materialize.

Day 45

1.30p.m. There was an incident today in the cafeteria. Michael and Carlos got into a heated argument and began insulting one another, and it led to a brief physical exchange. After things calmed down, one of the students who witnessed the entire event, a girl name Marie, asked to speak to me. She said she had an idea to prevent such things from happening and that was to have the entire student body create a pledge to conduct themselves a certain way. I have been ruminating about the idea of having students write their own social contract, and Marie's suggestion offers the perfect opportunity for me to put this idea at the top of the agenda for the next community meeting.

Day 52

10.00a.m. In our community meeting this morning, the students drafted their "Code of Conduct" for United Academy. With minimal facilitation from staff, the students articulated their beliefs on acceptable student conduct. Students wrote out the specific behaviors they would engage in to promote an environment of respect. The contract was written on a large poster board, signed by all students, and placed on a bulletin board near the main entrance of the school.

Day 65

2.00p.m. Student members of the newly constituted Community Service Committee just returned from the local homeless shelter/soup kitchen where they completed their first day of volunteer work preparing care packages for needy families. As part of a service learning project, I had recently arranged a visit to the shelter, and students were so moved by their experience that they requested to set up a committee to make weekly volunteer visits. Through this activity, I came to learn that one of our students named James, along with his family, frequented the soup kitchen for the weekly care packages. James delivered a passionate speech during our regular community meeting, speaking of the importance of volunteering and giving back to the community. Following his lead, over twenty students signed up for the committee. Impromptu, they elected James as their student leader. James proposed the first ever "United Academy Family Thanksgiving Dinner," where the school hallway would be transformed into a huge dining table for over 100 students and staff.

Day 80

9.00a.m. Today marked an important milestone for United Academy. This morning, the students took full responsibility for the entire morning routine. Not only did they facilitate the morning welcome, they also conducted the morning announcements over the PA system, an important function that helps structure the school day. Students representing the recently constituted Motivation and Inspiration Committee led the student body in the pledge of allegiance, disseminated important information, recognized specific student achievements and milestones, and they culminated with personal thoughts to motivate and inspire others. This specific activity required students on the committee to either research a famous quote or write a passage of their own and explain its wider meaning to their peers. What I observed this morning was a full expression of self-determination by the students of United.

The changes that were occurring at United were the culmination of many factors and through the work of many people, and in my role as a school social worker, I had organized this massive collaboration. Over the course of the year new elements were introduced to the program, further modifying systems, creating a new environment to empower students. The community meeting proved to be the most influential of all systems because this is where ideas were discussed, feelings exchanged, and relationships deepened. Out of the community meeting, three service committees were established, and they came to represent the school's core philosophy, "service to self, school, and community." The manner in which changes occurred at United exemplified the concepts of the person-in-environment and systems theory. I inspired this change by looking at the students and identifying their needs through observation and active engagement: Marcus needed someone to open up to, Sasha needed a familial greeting, and James needed a space for himself and his family to give back so as not to feel shame. The students needed opportunities for leadership, ways to take ownership, and stable adult support systems to help them grow on their own. Reflecting back, the initial feeling of coldness I had encountered walking through the doors at United had been replaced by warmth and a sense of human fullness that can only be created through the experience of relationship with others. It was clear that the change occurring at United was mutual among students, staff, and faculty.

By the end of the year the Board of Education wanted the changes at United to be formalized into an official program, with the specific functions of school social worker to be detailed. I decided to name the program Project UNITE, which stands for "Using New Integrative Techniques in Education." The role of the social work department remained consistent with the mission statement, focusing on supporting the students' emotional and social development. I wrote up my less "traditional" school social work roles, which included facilitating and engaging in the morning welcome process and conducting a class on social emotional learning. The class included psycho-education, supportive counseling, character education, social skills training, and service learning. I also ran a community meeting, and student feedback revealed that this was the place that students most felt able to express themselves, sharing concerns as well as needs, which proved to be a vital component of this new culture. In the community meeting, students developed their own social contract: the "code of conduct." And to address infractions to that code, I set up a peer mediation group. The morning announcements and inspirational speeches were under my aegis, as was serving the wider community through volunteering at the homeless shelter.

All of these activities had a proactive effect on the school environment, reducing the overall number of crisis incidents and student conflict. For those situations that required more traditional intervention, I provided crisis intervention, and individual, group, and family counseling. I also provided brokering and advocacy for students and their families with outside agencies. Fulfilling my duties at United was as diverse as it was demanding. There was never a shortage of work for me, and the decision to assign a social worker full time at United was probably one of the most important decisions the Board of Education made. This experience led to the conditions that forced me to reconceptualize my role as a social worker in the educational setting. It provided me with an opportunity to think beyond the traditional view and define a new role for the school social worker: program designer.

Conclusion

My time at United offered a unique opportunity to truly apply and integrate "systems theory" in the structure of an inner city school setting. The application of a "systems" approach is not without its pitfalls and difficulties. In fact, systems theory teaches us that systems, from the micro of the individual to the macro of a country, are often resistant to change and innovation. So it is important to recognize the vital factor of the role of the administrative staff and educators to energize and participate with the innovative programs and techniques mentioned in this chapter if they are to prove effective. It would give a false expectation that all schools would happily comply with these changes, and much more could be said about the manner of approaching the personnel of a school to engender their cooperation. Further, it is often the case that schools along with the student population and parents, whether they are in an inner city, alternative, or suburban system, are entrenched in their approaches and often, cultural change takes incremental steps over long periods of time. This reality speaks directly to the opportunity for school social workers to offer their unique orientation toward the person-in-environment to create programs designed to harness the power of systems to influence change.

CLOSE READING QUESTIONS

1. Carefully read the mission statement that Williams devises for his social work department and interpret the thinking behind this statement. Do you think that he realized his mission? If so, how? What would you have done differently, and what more could be done to realize the potential Williams projects here?

2. Williams writes that "actions can be influenced by systematic implementation of particular norms and values." Use the context of this statement to interpret what he means here, and then explain the broader implications of this statement in relation to social work values. How do values influence student and staff behaviors in this case study?

3. Which aspects of Williams's lived experience as a school social worker do you connect to most and why? Give examples from the case study to think about the elements of school social work that matter most to Williams.

Prompts for Writing

1. Zoom out from what happens inside the walls of United Alternative Academy to describe some overarching systems that create the need for and possibility of an alternative school. Then zoom back in to describe the systems specific to Williams's school that make his project successful. How might the smaller system of the school now that it has changed work to affect the system that created the need for and possibility of alternative education design in the first place?

2. Juxtapose Williams's case study and Kaliades's case study to think about a social worker's role in creating order and discipline in the school setting. How does Williams's design answer the call for change in Kaliades's critique? How does the system that Kaliades describes create many of the problems that Williams is tasked to solve? When would crisis management be appropriate in school social work?

3. Reflect on a problem that needs solving in your school setting. Using systems theory and the person-in-environment concept, design an alternative program to solve the problem. Be sure to discuss the way all the moving parts in your plan will work together. You can use Williams's reference list as a start to gathering more information about systems theory and the person-in-environment concept.

References

Anderson, R. E., Carter, I., and Lowe, G. R. (1999). *Human behavior in the social environment* (5th edn). New York: Aldine de Gruyter.

Aron, L. Y. (2003). *Towards a typology of alternative education programs: A compilation of elements from the literature*. Washington, DC: Urban Institute.

Blos, P. (1966). *On adolescence*. New York: The Free Press.

Friedman, B., and Allen, K. (2011). Systems theory. In J. Brandell (Ed.), *Theory and practice in clinical social work* (pp. 3–20). Thousand Oaks, CA: Sage.

Fuller, C., and Sabatino, D. (1996). Who attends alternative high schools? *The High School Journal, 79*(4), 293–297.

Gann, F. M. (2011). *Groundwork: A practitioner's guide to building alternative education programs*. Bloomington, IN: IUniverse Press.

Kellmayer, J. (1995). *How to establish an alternative school*. Thousand Oaks, CA: Sage.

Knapp, P. (1994). *One world – many worlds: Contemporary sociological theory*. New York: Harper-Collins.

Kondrat, M. E. (2008). Person-in-environment. In *Encyclopedia of Social Work*. New York: Oxford University Press.

Parsons, T. (1950). Psychoanalysis and the social structure. *Psychoanalytic Quarterly, 19*, 371–384.

Robbins, S. P., Chatterjee, P., and Canda, E. R. (2006). *Contemporary human behavior theory: A critical perspective for social work* (2nd edn). Boston: Allyn and Bacon.

Streeter, C. L., and Franklin, C. (2002). Standards for school social work in the 21st century. In A. Roberts and G. Greene (Eds.), *Social workers' desk reference* (pp. 612–618). New York: Oxford University Press.

Teasley, M. (2004). School social workers and urban education reform: Realities, advocacy, and strategies for change. *The School Community Journal, 14*(2), 19–39.

US Department of Education, National Center for Education Statistics (2002). Characteristics of the 100 largest public elementary and secondary school districts in the United States: 2000- 01, NCES 2002-351, Washington, DC: Author. Accessed online September 3, 2016 at http://nces.ed.gov/pubs2002/2002351.pdf.

Von Bertalanffy, L. (1968). *General system theory: Foundation, development, application*. New York: George Braziller.

7

SCHOOL SOCIAL WORK AND THE SEXUAL AND GENDER MINORITY STUDENT IN THE TWENTY-FIRST CENTURY

Russell Healy

Pre-Reading Questions

1. What specialized knowledge might be required of a school social worker when engaging with students from the LGBT population? What are a school social worker's options for gaining specialized knowledge and skills in situations that are unfamiliar?
2. What do you know about the transgender population? How might the experience of a transgender student be different than a lesbian, gay, or bisexual student?
3. How would you define the key term "gender"? How is a person's "gender" different from a person's "sex"?

Introduction

Much data exists that suggests that lesbian, gay, bisexual, or transgender (LGBT) students are a population at risk for suicide, stress–related mental health problems, bullying, and harassment. While it is important to know the current research and to understand the relationship between school climate and the LGBT student's overall health and educational experience, it is equally important for school social workers to evaluate every LGBT student based on the student's lived experience. Sexual and gender minority students are not monolithic. Survey data can fill in some blanks in the LGBT student narrative, but LGBT students come from the same variety of cultural, socioeconomic, and family backgrounds, as do non–LGBT students. Having a known, or not yet known, sexual or gender minority status may complicate an already confusing period in the life of a child or adolescent.

Although the subject of the case study is named Jay, a female to male (FtM) transgender high school student, attention will be paid to the risks lesbian, gay, and bisexual students encounter as well. Our society considers sexual and gender minorities as one cohort, but the needs of transgender students differ in many aspects from those of lesbian, gay, or bisexual students. In the socio-political realm, the movement for equality includes transgender activists, working with gay activists under the acronym LGBT, with the "T" representing transgender rights. *In vivo*, however, the lived experience of transgender youth is very different from that of sexual minority youth. They are still subjected to a mental health diagnosis, *gender dysphoria* (American Psychiatric Association, 2013), and require medical treatment, legal assistance, and social adjustment in order to confirm their gender and alleviate the dysphoria they often experience. They cannot simply come out of the closet.

The reader will have the opportunity to explore the case through the experience of both Jay and his social worker Carmen. I became involved as a consultant to the school district when Carmen requested some transgender-specific consultation. Carmen attended a continuing education seminar I taught on transgender-affirming assessment and treatment. I was happy to get to know this very gifted social worker better.

At first, the school administrator wanted Carmen to refer Jay to me. I work with transgender youth and their families in my private practice. Carmen thought the school might have had liability concerns, because transgender youth are believed to be at greater risk for suicide and self-harm. I thought that the school should have someone in their counseling department who could understand gender diverse and transgender-identified students. To me, that seemed like a just distribution of health care resources, as long as there were no other co-occurring conditions that would be beyond the scope of a clinical school social worker. There are no gender clinics in the region where we work, so families have to see an array of costly private practitioners if they want quality healthcare for their transgender children and teenagers. Jay came from a single-parent household with scarce resources. He needed specialized care, and with my help, he could get that from Carmen. Since liability is a medical concern in transgender healthcare, I agreed to formally evaluate Jay and write his letter of referral if and when hormone replacement therapy (HRT) or other medical care was needed.

Meet Jay

Based on my consultations with Carmen, I believe that it took a lot of courage for Jay to talk to the school social worker. He had not told his parents or family about his authentic self. He was fourteen. He knew since he was twelve that there was something terribly wrong with his body. Throughout his childhood,

Jay always assumed that his chest would stay flat and that he would develop a muscular, male physique. Many gender diverse children have this experience. They take it as given that they are the gender they experience. Some are gender creative (Ehrensaft, 2016) and have little to no awareness that they are thinking, feeling, or behaving in an atypical manner. Jay was like that in his childhood, but things changed when he turned twelve. Jay loved being outdoors as much as possible. He loved the freedom of running around his backyard without a shirt on. One day, two years earlier during summer break, his mother came out and told him to put his shirt back on. Jay felt something like shame, but more so. His nipples had been hurting for a few weeks, and he noticed that his chest was developing buds, like breasts. Did his mother notice? And, was his body somehow wrong?

Always compliant, Jay did as his mother told him. He never thought that his brother, who he always had fun with during the summer months, had told their mother that Jay made him feel weird when he ran around shirtless. For Jay, he always thought that his body and his anatomy would be like his brother's was. Jay simply thought that he was slow to develop. Things got worse for Jay when he experienced his first period.

"All girls hate their periods," Jay's mother told him. But, he felt horror and helplessness. Jay doubted that girls felt that upset when they had their periods. He wasn't stupid. He knew that kids assigned as girls had a menses cycle. He learned that in health class. What Jay did not fully grasp, for whatever reason, was that his anatomy was what doctors called female. He would never grow male genitals, in spite of his intense wish to be a boy. Slowly, Jay was unpacking the compartments in his mind that were trying to soothe him by telling him that he was a boy. As reality encroached, Jay began to feel a kind of fearful dread.

Jay had an agenda that was not immediately obvious to Carmen or me. Jay thought that by seeing Carmen he could get out of gym class. He hated gym. His fears about the upcoming marking period's physical education cycle were a constant preoccupation. Jay had never given himself the chance to discover whether or not he enjoyed games, team sports, or any kind of physical activity. What he dreaded now that puberty had begun were the locker rooms and having to undress in front of his peers.

From IPLGY to GSA: A Brief History of Gay Youth, Social Service, and Education

LGBT students were not always visible in schools. In fact, their presence is a fairly recent phenomenon. The movement to focus on the needs of gay youth arguably began in 1979, when Psychiatrist Emery Hetrick, and his partner, NYU Professor Damien Martin, organized the Institute for the Protection of Lesbian and Gay Youth (IPLGY) in New York City. In 1987 and 1988, they published several articles in the *Journal of Homosexuality*. These articles were among the earliest efforts to recognize gay youth as a population with specific social and mental health needs. Their thesis was that the socialization of the lesbian or gay adolescent involved hiding, which was damaging to their development. They believed adults in mental health care and social service had an obligation to protect gay youth and make the world safe for them to be able to live openly and express their true selves. They were angered by the suicide of a 15-year-old, gay identified, runaway boy who had been beaten and cast out of a group home. At that time in history, the gay world was largely an adult realm that was found in major cities. When teenagers came out as lesbian or gay, they faced being rejected by their families to a much greater degree than they would today. Homelessness was a very real problem. They either lived on the street or in social service or foster care settings ill equipped to manage them and provide for their needs. In the laissez-faire years of the 1970s, many gay youth risked exploitation if they found themselves in certain parts of the urban gay sub-culture (Hetrick and Martin, 1987; Martin and Hetrick, 1988).

Hetrick and Martin created a new paradigm for social work with lesbian, gay, and bisexual youth. Sadly, both men died before they could realize the full scope of their achievements. After Dr. Hetrick died of complications related to AIDS in 1988, IPLGY was renamed the Hetrick-Martin Institute (HMI) in honor of his work. Professor Martin died in 1991, also of complications due to AIDS. Perhaps their most important contribution began in 1985, when HMI collaborated with the New York City Department of Education to form The Harvey Milk High School (HMHS), an alternative school for LGBT youth at risk of failing in the New York City public school system.

The students who attended HMHS in its early years were adolescents who simply could not attend regular public schools. They were at risk of assaults that went far beyond what we understand as bullying today. The issue was one of safety. Most of the students presented with gender non-conforming behavior. Many were cross dressers. Some were young drag queens, some were transgender; regardless, they could not survive in the public schools in their communities. The only social service agency in New York City for LGBT youth was HMI, so the city created a solution to the danger faced by this particular group of LGBT teenagers.

In 2002, HMHS became a fully accredited public school in the New York City public school system. As word of the school spread, detractors of HMHS emerged, claiming that the school represented a form of segregation. In 2003, the school was sued because its proposed $3.2 million taxpayer-funded budget was seen as a waste of the city's money and an unfair, perhaps illegal advantage to a small number (100) of students. A New York State Senator brought the suit forth: the argument was that HMHS was providing what appeared to be special treatment based on sexual orientation. The suit was settled in 2006 when HMHS agreed to evaluate non-LGBT students for admission to the school, as long as those potential students were equally at risk as their LGBT counterparts (Colapinto, 2005).

The HMHS has become a model for other cities and school districts across the country. The most recent such school is Pride School Atlanta (PSA), which opened in 2016 in Georgia. This private, nonprofit school's mission is the same as HMHS: to educate LGBT students in an environment that is free from bullying and social homophobia. Its website clarifies that the school will not discriminate against any student because of sexual orientation, implying that non-LGBT students will be considered for admission. Since students must apply to HMHS and PSA, segregation is voluntary, raising the question of whether voluntary segregation of a minority for reasons of safety is the best educational approach. If so, what are the implications?

Schools that function to educate only certain LGBT students are taking a position that education for those students must be "separate but equal," the notion that was dispelled by the Supreme Court's *Brown vs. Board of Education* decision in 1954 (Ford, 2004). In education law, two perspectives may be found. The first is that of "formal equality," the notion that public education must equally accommodate, without segregation, all students in a given region. Formal equality acknowledges that certain disabilities may require special accommodations, but without segregation based on ethnicity, gender, or other factors. The second notion, "anti-subordination," argues that it "is perfectly acceptable, even desirable, to treat children differently on the basis of their group membership if it will help them overcome the special obstacles they face" (Brittenham, 2004, p. 870).

The strength of the anti-subordination approach is that it meets the needs of at-risk students in the short term by voluntarily placing them in safer educational settings. W. E. B. DuBois is quoted as having said, "children need education, not integrated education or segregated education" (as cited in Brittenham, 2004, p. 878). The pragmatic reading of this quote is that education itself comes first, before any other concerns. DuBois is making a utilitarian, consequentialist argument: the ends justify the means, as long as education is provided and received. Thus, as an issue of justice, anti-subordination in education would offer both safety and a quality education. There is no reason why both cannot exist simultaneously. However successful the anti-subordination approach may be in the short term in addressing issues such as bullying, the underlying sources of prejudice and bias remain unaddressed.

The formal equality stance is concerned with consequences. If children and adolescents are voluntarily segregated, educators run the risk of reinforcing the very hostility and stigma they are trying to avoid *prima facie*. In fact, segregation, even if safety is the objective, creates a category that itself may be stigmatizing (Brittenham, 2004, pp. 880–881). Advocates of this approach argue that high school is the most important stage of an individual's socialization. In high school, adolescents discover and define who they are. Graduating from high school is when their participation in society begins. Interactions between gay and lesbian and straight students are desirable in a pluralistic society. High school is an opportunity for educators to shape behavior and to teach the values of our society before adolescents enter the community. For many teenagers, high school will be the last opportunity for society's agents to teach tolerance.

Most adherents of the formal equality perspective would likely agree that LGBT and other at-risk student groups often face violence and discrimination in public schools. Bullying must be addressed, and bullies must learn to adhere to a standard of conformity that insists that harassment of any form is unacceptable. As school social workers are well aware, true change from within a school system is challenging at best. Making it normative that phenomena like bullying, harassment, and discrimination are intolerable offenses takes time. When a child or teenager is subjected to the stress of bullying, time is another adversary.

In the 1990s, another approach to assisting LGBT students in high schools came about: the Gay/Straight Alliance (GSA). The Gay, Lesbian, and Straight Education Network (GLSEN) define the GSA as, "student-led, school-based clubs open to all members of the student body regardless of sexual orientation" (GLSEN, 2007, p. 1). According to GLSEN, there are many benefits to having a GSA in high schools. First, the presence of a GSA may enhance the safety of LGBT students. GSAs serve to remind students, staff, and faculty that harassment and homophobic bias is inexcusable. Second, GSAs make schools more accessible to LGBT students. According to a finding by GLSEN, LGBT students are more likely to attend school and to feel safer at school if their school has a GSA. Finally, schools with GSAs help students identify faculty and staff members who can be allies (GLSEN, 2007). It makes sense that an alliance of gay and non-gay students and adults would be beneficial for LGBT youth, because it mirrors our society at its best: when everyone in a diverse culture works together to create safe and vital communities.

The activities of a GSA are no different than any other club based in a school. Students engage in discussions, view films, do fundraisers, and organize educational presentations. Typically, there is a faculty or staff member who acts as an advisor for the GSA and is present at meetings. Membership waxes and wanes, a core group forms, and cliques develop. Sexual and gender minority youth and their allies are, after all, adolescent. They are no different in that sense from their non-LGBT peers, but in my experience, the adolescents in this group intuit that something or someone outside their own lives is at stake.

In 1989, the National Institute of Mental Health (NIMH) and the Centers for Disease Control (CDC) prepared a study, "Gay Male and Lesbian Youth Suicide," by Paul Gibson, for the US Department of Health and Human Services (USDHHS) (Gibson, 1989). Early versions of Gibson's paper made it to publication, but it was not included in the official report. The USDHHS claimed that the report was a meta-analysis of existing data with sampling flaws and not original research. At present, the USDHHS does gather and analyze statistics about the health and well-being of LGBT adolescents. The notion that LGBT youth are more at risk for suicide than their non-LGBT peers has continued to challenge researchers and suicidologists since the 1990s. In the decades since

Gibson's report was written, researchers have produced evidence that LGBT youth are more at risk for suicide (Russell, 2003; Grossman and D'Augelli, 2007; Remafedi et al., 1991). Initially, the research was plagued by problems with sampling and poorly constructed questionnaires (Savin-Williams, 2006). As schools became more concerned with questions of youth suicide in general, researchers obtained access to random samples of high school students throughout the country. This has yielded better data and better results.

Jay and Carmen, First Visit

"No one knows what it is like to be *me*," Jay said emphatically. "I tried to pass myself off as a tomboy, but nobody likes a tomboy who hates sports." Jay glared at Carmen, waiting for a reply. Carmen was in her fifth year as a school social worker. A Latina, whose parents were born in Puerto Rico, she worked in a socioeconomically diverse middle-class school system in a metropolitan suburb. She knew diversity first-hand, having gone to urban schools herself. But, Jay was a first. Carmen had worked with gay students before. In fact, gay students were fairly unremarkable in her school. The high school where she worked was among the first to have a GSA, and it was very supportive of sexual minority students. Jay was the first transgender student she worked with, and she wasn't certain what he wanted.

Jay continued, "most kids like tomboys. But once they find out that the tomboy doesn't play sports, things change. They become mean. It's called transphobic, which is like homophobia, but aimed at transgender people. I am not a tomboy, I am a *boy*."

There was so much Carmen wanted, and needed, to know about her new client. How did he come to understand his gender identity? How did he piece it together at what seemed to be a young age? If Jay used the internet to learn about his gender identity, what kinds of sites did he use? Were they safe? Finally, how much did his mother know about her son? Carmen had only met his mother once, when Jay's brother had gotten into a scrape. She seemed reasonable. Like many single parents, she embodied a mix of exhaustion and fierce protectiveness. Little mention was made of Jay's father in his file.

"I can't help but be curious, Jay. How did you come to realize that you are a boy? You seem kind of young to me to make this kind of claim. I believe that you believe you are a boy, but it would help me to understand how you got there." Jay hid his disappointment. One of his gay friends told him that this social worker would be a good ally, but she didn't seem to know much about transgender youth. He told himself that it was only the first session. He had come this far, he might as well try to answer her question.

"I used scientific method," Jay answered, with a kind of sincerity that did not belie his actual feelings at that moment. "I mean, I did research. On the internet. I thought maybe I was gay, because I sort of like girls. I went to reddit and tumblr, but I couldn't relate to most of the blogs and posts about teenage lesbians. So, that hypothesis didn't bear any fruit." Jay wondered if he was being too sarcastic. How could he explain that he simply *knows*? He just knew. Having to prove it made him feel suspicious, and sad.

"Jay, I probably shouldn't have implied that I don't believe you. I'm sort of feeling my way through this. Some of the gay students I know have used the internet to *confirm* what they were feeling. Does that make any sense? I'm cisgender. It's hard for me to imagine what it's like to have a body that doesn't reflect who I know I am. I can't help being curious about the how of you as much as I am the who of you." Jay was confused—how? Who? All he knew is that he felt like he should be a boy. He used to think nature made some kind of error, but now he thought that people are the problem, not nature. Transphobia happens because of ignorance, Jay thought.

But, the social worker did seem genuinely curious. After all, Jay did decide to make this appointment. He had to start talking about his gender with someone other than his online friends. Jay recalls clearly the moment when the word transgender made sense to him. Yes, he was online when it happened. He was chatting with one of his online friends, also a transgender boy. This boy had already started hormones and was feeling better. He knew how to word the questions that helped Jay have his breakthrough. He simply asked Jay if he ever put a towel over the mirror when he showered, or if Jay ever went someplace else in his mind when he had his periods.

Jay told Carmen about Trey and about his breakthrough. Jay no longer could keep his feelings about his body and his gender in compartments in the back of his mind. Carmen conceptualized from a family systems perspective, so she believed in the "ah-hah" moment. I explained to Carmen during one of our meetings that she didn't need psychoanalytic training to understand that people compart-mentalize self-knowledge until they see or hear something in the outside world that brings their attention to the material they have repressed. Jay had this experience, and it sounded to Carmen that Jay felt overwhelmed. I likened it to the opening of Pandora's fabled box. Once Jay's knowledge about his lived experience was released and revealed to himself, there was no stuffing it back down, and no way to reseal the box.

After the session ended, Carmen took some time to reflect. She was aware that she felt apprehensive. This student did feel different to her. She had attended continuing education workshops on the needs of transgender students. She learned that they are more prone to suicidality, and that they benefit from being gendered properly, or seen and referred to as the gender they experience. Correct language was important to these students. Carmen felt a certain amount of pressure to make no mistakes, as if one false move would ruin any alliance she could establish with Jay. Could he be that fragile? She did not want to make any mistakes, yet, she was aware that the desire to not make mistakes could be conflated with a feeling of pressure from school administrators, who were perhaps overly concerned with liability issues. From her stance as a clinician, she wanted to address concerns about risk, but not at the expense of reinforcing a student's strengths. This was Carmen's dilemma as well as her thesis. She believed each student must be assessed on his own strengths and challenges. Being a member of a group considered being at more risk of suicide, while certainly a concern, should not result in making it an issue if the student does not present as such, or if he is resilient.

The LGBT Student: At Risk or Resilient?

As Carmen knew, the question of whether, and to what degree, LGBT youth are more at risk is relevant to social workers in school settings. In extension of the debate about formal equality and anti-subordination, questions about LGBT youth's resilience are critical because social workers who would advocate for formal equality in educational settings would argue that segregating LGBT youth does not help them become resilient. After all, society is still homophobic. Learning how to cope with homophobia would be an important skill for LGBT youth to acquire. Conversely, the anti-subordination approach states that some LGBT youth require the protection that segregation offers.

Carmen was taught that clients would be very forgiving if the basics were met: listen closely, be empathic, and be genuine. Did Jay somehow fall outside those guidelines? Were transgender students different, more mercurial? Carmen felt pressure to make sure her interventions were flawless, despite her lack of mileage working with transgender students. As a member of a cultural minority herself, she could appreciate how frustrating it must be for a minority client who becomes a social worker's learning curve client, no matter what. Carmen considered cultural and diversity competence an imperative. To serve this student effectively, Carmen knew that she would have to consult with a specialist and perhaps do research beyond reading her notes from previous continuing education seminars.

Carmen was already aware that LGBT students are now able to present themselves in many public school settings and that they expect to be at least accepted, or perhaps even affirmed and supported. Social workers in many school settings have more resources and knowledge than ever before to assist such students. The internet is one such resource that offers social workers much information about the lives of LGBT students. And for the students themselves, the internet can be a place to socialize and tap into a vast system of resources and information.

Carmen knew that it wasn't always this way. She knew that the LGBT movement was the product of recent history. There were a number of critical and historic events in the latter half of the twentieth century that could be considered as the moment when the movement for acceptance and visibility of LGBT persons began. For social workers, the time to affirm sexual minority identities began in 1973, when homosexuality was declassified as a mental illness. That would make the movement, at least in the realms of mental health and social work, merely forty-three years old.

In less than half a century, unprecedented progress has been made in the area of LGBT rights. Young LGBT students who came of age during this period in history have benefited from such important social progress. Many lesbian or gay high school students that Carmen encountered in her work as a school social worker had told her that to them, being "L," "G," or "B," and in some cases, "T," is unremarkable. The labels and stigma that previous generations had to struggle against do not appear to burden them as much. Many of the non-LGBT students she knows are casually accepting of their LGBT peers. Some may have a gay uncle or lesbian aunt, or have benefited from the instruction of an openly gay teacher. Some know a transgender adult through their parents. Mostly, they take their cues from popular culture. Increasingly, depictions of gay, lesbian, bisexual, or transgender experience are realistic, positive, and non-sensational.

Carmen had been expecting to work with a transgender student at any time in the near future, so Jay's appearance on her caseload was not a surprise. Transgender students had been emerging in the school systems where many of her colleagues worked. Openly gay students were becoming part of everyday life in high schools in the region of the country where she worked. This was likely due to the work of activists in the last twenty years. That transgender students would emerge was a natural next step in the social evolution of the high school environment.

If social work began affirming sexual minorities in 1973, when homosexuality was removed from the *Diagnostic and Statistical Manual of Mental Disorders* (DSM) (American Psychiatric Association, 2013), then transgender persons are still stigmatized by virtue of being classified as having pathology. In order to be recognized as transgender, one must first receive a diagnosis of gender dysphoria. Therefore, social workers in school settings will need to approach transgender youth from a different perspective than they approach gay or lesbian students. Most school social workers Carmen knows report that the appearance of transgender youth in non-urban school systems has been relatively sudden, especially in suburban school districts. The rise in awareness of the needs of gay students was slow when compared to the more rapid appearance of transgender students.

Our First Consultation

Carmen reviewed Jay's file with me. His grades were slightly above average; Carmen suspected that he could do better academically. There were never any problems with discipline, and he had never asked to see a counselor or social worker before. She sensed that he had an agenda beyond just talking but could not imagine what it could be. Jay, in fact, looked like a boy, rather, a boy who wore oversized clothes and hoodies. He kept his hair short, wore a backwards baseball cap when allowed, slumped like a boy, and had facial expressions that Carmen labeled as male. Jay also *moved* like a boy, she told me.

Carmen was a natural school social worker. She could connect with just about any student, regardless of his peer group associations. Jay, though, was harder for her to understand. For example, the notion that Jay could know his gender without relying on his anatomy was initially difficult for her to grasp. I explained to her that gender is a part of self-knowledge, similar to sexual orientation. As such, it resides in our minds. The disconnection between what Jay knew about himself and what he saw reflected in the mirror is part of what creates gender dysphoria.

Carmen told me that Jay had an older brother in the same high school, but the two siblings did not affiliate with the same groups of students. She described Jay's brother as popular and outgoing while Jay was somewhat a loner. When he did join in with other students, they were usually in a more artistic, but somewhat depressive crowd. These were students who played a lot of video games and seemed to be more internet-oriented than the average student. On balance, they seemed like bright underachievers who were too distracted by life's difficulties. I explained that anecdotally, the transgender youth that I see in my practice often isolate and retreat into a world of videogames and internet blogs. When I heard that Jay did this, too, I was not surprised or alarmed. Many transgender youth have full social lives online. The relative anonymity of the internet allows them to present themselves however they want. Jay had an online male avatar and gaming friends that knew him as, well, Jay.

She had seen one of the students with whom Jay affiliates in her work. That student identified as gay and had a history of making suicidal gestures. Carmen recalled from my seminar that there are suicide risk assessment issues particular to the LGBT student. In general, a family history of suicidality is a risk factor when assessing a student who engages in self-harming behavior. For LGBT students, the peer group can substitute for the weight of family history in terms of assessing risk. If one youth in an LGBT student's circle of friends has a history of suicidality, then that youth's risk level may increase (Russell and Joyner, 2001). Most importantly, I explained to Carmen that there are known protective factors for LGB and T youth. Transgender youths whose families are supportive are at a reduced risk for suicide (Ryan et al., 2010).

I thought that it would be useful for Carmen to see what the most recent studies have to say regarding LGBT youth and risks in general, not just suicide. So Carmen and I together reviewed the CDC's recently released report, "Sexual Identity, Sex of Sexual Contacts, and Health-Related Behaviors among Students in Grades 9–12—United States and Selected Sites, 2015" (Kann et al., 2016). The CDC releases this data every two years and this report contained data gathered from the reporting period of September 2014 through December 2015.

The first thing Carmen and I noticed was that the CDC report did not address gender identity. The method was to survey students who identified as lesbian, gay, bisexual, or not sure. For those students who reported being sexually active, the CDC used the "sex" of the partner as a way to operationalize sexual minority status. As stated in the introduction to the report, "sexual identity and sex of sexual contacts can both be used to identify sexual minority youth" (Kann et al., 2016, pp. 2–3). Carmen had two questions. First, shouldn't the term "sex of partner" be replaced by "gender of the partner"? The language was confusing, with "sex" being both a verb and a noun. Second, she was puzzled that transgender-identified youth weren't identified in the report. If she wanted to understand transgender-specific risks, would she have to generalize from the data whether or not a student like Jay was represented? Carmen was a critical thinker. She did not want to jump to conclusions. Yet she always assumed that the acronym LGBT meant that transgender persons and gay persons were somehow part of the same cohort.

What Carmen and I did learn was both useful and unsettling. According to the report,

> during the 12 months before the survey, 29.9% of all students; 26.4% of heterosexual students; 60.4% of gay, lesbian, and bisexual students; and 46.5% of not sure students nationwide had felt so sad or helpless almost every day for 2 or more weeks in a row that they stopped doing some usual activities.
>
> *Kann et al., 2016, p. 18*

Sadness and/or hopelessness were what she felt from Jay and his peer group. Whenever she saw students like them, she told me that it felt like she was sitting with tremendously, and unjustly, burdened young people.

Carmen and I were aware that hopelessness and suicidality are correlated. Was that what Jay felt? She continued to review the data, which told that "nationwide, 17.7% of all students; 14.8% of heterosexual students; 42.8% of gay, lesbian, or bisexual students; and 31.9% of not sure students had seriously considered attempting suicide during the 12 months before the survey" (Kann et al., 2016, p. 19). Clearly, sexual minority students could be seen as being more at risk for suicide. Seeing such data saddened Carmen. She knew that working with adolescents would expose her to the possibility of suicide in general. Carmen felt she needed to know more, and asked me about how I assess and think about suicide.

I explained that contemplating suicide was not the same as attempting suicide. Did sexual minority students attempt suicide more? According to the CDC report, yes: "nationwide, 8.6% of all students; 6.4% of heterosexual students; 29.4% of gay, lesbian, and bisexual students; and 13.7% of not sure students had attempted suicide one or more times during the 12 months before the survey" (Kann et al., 2016, p. 20). Again, the rates were higher for sexual minority youth than for heterosexual youth. Next, Carmen wondered, beyond self-report, how could attempts be measured? The CDC looked at whether a physician or a nurse had treated a youth for a suicide attempt during the period the survey was taken. The CDC found that, "nationwide, 2.8% of all students; 2.0% of heterosexual students; 9.4% of gay, lesbian, and bisexual students; and 4.7% of not sure students nationwide had made a suicide attempt during the 12 months before the survey that resulted in an injury, poisoning, or overdose that had to be treated by a doctor or nurse" (2016, p. 21). At a rate of 9.4%, it seemed apparent to Carmen that her sexual minority students would be at higher risk for suicide and possibly self-harm. The CDC defined a suicide attempt as an event that produced physical injury, a drug overdose, or some kind of poisoning (2016, p. 20). I explained to Carmen that this kind of attempt goes far beyond mere parasuicidal gesture, the function of which is to get help or bring people close. The gesture is typically not lethal and usually does not produce injury. An attempt that does produce injury implies serious intent. I explained to Carmen that suicide is about ending pain, not ending life. There must be a lot of distress by the time a person has crossed that cognitive threshold where suicide becomes a possibility. Sexual minority youth who attempt suicide must be in a great deal of pain to use such aggressive means.

Carmen asked if there are any protective factors that would prevent LGBT students from self-harm if they were feeling sad or hopeless. I explained that studies consistently suggest that family support is the key protective factor for LGBT youth, and parental support is crucial for transgender youth in particular (Ryan et al., 2010). Resiliency interested her as well. Carmen wanted to know if schools could play a role in supporting and reinforcing resilience in LGBT youth. I suggested that we look at a recent School Climate Survey produced by GLSEN. According to GLSEN's 2013 School Climate Survey, LGB and T students are considered to be at higher risk for suicide and other forms of self-harm (Kosciw et al., 2014). GLSEN concerns itself with what schools, and GSAs in particular, can do to mitigate the risks associated with being an LGBT student through having a safer, more inclusive social climate in schools. The survey found that 64.5% of LGBT students heard homophobic remarks (2014, p. 16), and that 30% of LGBT students surveyed missed at least one day of school in the past month before completing GLSEN's questionnaire because they felt unsafe or uncomfortable (p. 49). Almost three-quarters of the students reported that they experienced verbal harassment during the past year prior to the administration of the survey (p. 22). Furthermore, almost 40% stated that they had experienced physical harassment because of their sexual orientation (p. 23) and 23% of transgender students described being physically harassed due to their gender presentation. Physical assaults were perpetrated against 16.5% of sexual minority students, and 11.4% of gender minority students were assaulted (p. 23).

In a section titled "Availability of school based resource and supports," GLSEN looked at staff support and its impact on LGBT students. Respondents reported that they were less likely to feel unsafe in schools where there were at least eleven supportive staff members. The GPAs of those LGBT students were higher, also: 3.3 vs. 2.8 for the students who identified less supportive staff members.

Unfortunately, only 39% of the students surveyed reported that they could identify at least eleven supportive staff members in their schools (Kosciw et al., 2014, pp. 56–64).

There was one finding that I thought was particularly salient for Jay. One of the first things Carmen told me about him was that she sensed he had an agenda that he hadn't brought up yet. Understandably, she and her administration had concerns about suicide, but I thought that Jay had other concerns more specific to his day-to-day life as a transgender student. For example, transgender youth do well when they are referred to by their chosen name. The GLSEN survey found that many transgender students were prevented from using their preferred name and that almost one-third were not allowed to wear clothes that did not conform to their assigned gender (Kosciw et al., 2014, pp. 39–40). I suspect that Jay's dysphoria would be much more intense if he could not dress as he did and was not called "Jay" by his peers and school staff.

Other research perspectives exist. Psychologist Ritch C. Savin-Williams has been exploring the resilience question since the notion about LGBT youth and suicide surfaced. Savin-Williams thinks that today's LGBT youth live in a post-gay society. He refers to these youth as the "new" gay teenagers. His concern is that activists, society, and gay affirming mental health professionals, promulgate a "suffering, suicidal script" of LGBT youth (2006, p. 50). Carmen did not want to participate in that. As a Latina, she knew that minorities have strengths that even the most well-meaning members of the cultural majority do not see. Carmen believed that labeling a student as being at risk because of their minority status was a form of stigmatization, and as such, could function to discount the unique nature of an individual minority student's coping strategy. However, Carmen's dilemma persisted. Jay was her first transgender student. She did not yet have the confidence that comes from experience, the kind of confidence that allows a clinician to place judgment ahead of data.

Ultimately, Carmen and I agreed that social workers do not need research to tell us that some youth are more resilient than others, and it would follow that some LGBT youth are more immune to suicide and self-harm than others. While Carmen and I found the survey data useful, we knew from experience that case studies and student narratives could yield valuable information as well. Jay was an N of one. By understanding Jay as an individual case, we could generate as much knowledge about the lived experience of transgender youths as we might from looking at aggregate data. I wanted Carmen to get to know Jay better as a person now that survey research had been reviewed.

Jay and Carmen, Session Three

Jay seemed distracted and remote during his third visit with Carmen. This was out of character for Jay; he had been far more open and verbal during the first two visits. Carmen made a conscious choice to resist the urge to attribute meaning to Jay's mood. Having recently reviewed the data on sexual minority youth, she knew that it would be easy to make up a story about what Jay's affect might mean. But, that didn't mean that she had to be non-directive, either.

"Jay, I can't help but notice that you seem different today—like only half of you is here. How is your day going?" He shrugged, but at least he made eye contact. "I'm just tired, I guess," he replied non-committedly. "So, this is you when you are tired?" Jay smiled slightly, rubbed his eyes, and sat up in the chair. "Better?" he asked with an exaggerated grin. Carmen was about to offer the typical reply she was taught to give in these kinds of clinical interactions: "well, we aren't here for me—we're here for you, so if it's better for you, that's great." Instead, she followed a gut instinct and said, "Jay, what's up with you today? I know you have stuff to tell me about. Let's just talk like we did the first two times. I really am curious to get to know you better, and I think you want me to get to know you. Would it help if I asked you some questions?" She understood the wisdom of letting the student guide the direction of the session, but in some cases Carmen found that asking direct questions was a better use of the time. She also found that sometimes she had to teach the student how to be curious about his feelings, and how to think psychologically.

"What do you want to know," Jay asked. "Everything!" Carmen said with warm enthusiasm, leaning forward slightly. "Let's start with what it's like to be you *today*, right now. I don't think you are tired, I think you have something going on inside that maybe you can't express easily. Take a few seconds to ask yourself if that's true. If my hunch is correct, don't worry about picking the right words— just try to say what you have to say without any screens. You've told me enough already, I won't judge you or change my opinion about you."

"What is your opinion?" Carmen was prepared for this, and she gave him a direct response. "I think you are complicated. I think there are many parts to you. Sometimes, those parts work together, and sometimes they get in each other's way. Today I am guessing that your parts are crowding each other out, so that it's hard to find a voice to speak from." *Smart*, I thought, as Carmen was telling me about her visit with Jay. Talking about Jay's parts was a clever way of addressing things like ego-states or defense mechanisms. He wanted to jump right to his real concern, but decided to ask about something else first. He was afraid to ask about what he wanted because he assumed the answer would be "no." He wanted to be able to hope for "yes."

"You're right about my parts. Mostly, it's my outside parts that bother me. Do I look like a boy or a lesbian to you?" Carmen was surprised at Jay's sudden directness. He was watching her closely. She sat still for a few seconds, reflecting on his question. What does a teenage lesbian look like? More importantly, what does it mean to look like a boy? Then, it occurred to Carmen that what Jay really wanted to know was whether Carmen believed that he was male, not just that she believed that he believed it. In order for her to believe it she had to feel like she was, in fact, sitting with a boy, not a girl who believes she is a boy. She knew that the correct response would be to affirm that he looked like a boy, but that wouldn't be keeping things real, as some of her students would say. She searched her feelings, looked closely at Jay, and knew what was so.

"You know that boy in your English class, Cooper? He looks very much like a boy. And you know that boy Noah, in your math class? Some would say that he looks feminine. But, I know he's a teenage boy. You aren't asking me if I think you look like a boy or even pass as a boy. You want to know if I experience you as a boy when I see you in the hall or in the waiting room or in my office. I do. I'm sorry I didn't make that clear before." Jay's eyes got moist. The social worker was right. That was what he was asking.

Jay believed that his social worker saw him as a boy. He felt immediate relief. Jay had always been caught up in his experience of living in his body, and how he feels when he catches a glimpse of himself in the mirror. Sometimes, he will study his facial features to see what looks male and what doesn't. In fact, he could scrutinize his face until he didn't recognize that it was his face anymore. The same could be said for his entire body, but much of that was in his mind. Paradoxically, Jay could not tolerate seeing glimpses of his body in a mirror, even though he could study his facial reflection. He could not tolerate any visual reminder of his anatomy, especially now that his body was going through changes. He thought he knew what that meant. In some of the transgender forums he followed, like reddit's *ask transgender*, posters would write about gender dysphoria instead of gender identity. The New Oxford American Dictionary defines dysphoria as the antonym to euphoria. The origin of the word is from the Greek word *dusphoros*, which means "hard to bear." Jay knew that living in a body that didn't feel like it should be his was hard to bear. At times, it felt impossible. The opposite of euphoria, a feeling he rarely felt since adolescence began, was an accurate way of describing his lived experience.

There was another reason why Jay asked Carmen if she thought he looked like a boy. He began wearing a chest binder last year. His mother didn't know, since Jay only wore it to school. He wasn't ready to talk with his mother about his dysphoria. The memory of her telling him not go shirtless, despite the fact that it was years ago that she admonished him, was still fresh in his mind. He had a friend order it for him from Amazon. It arrived in an Amazon box, so there would be no way for anyone to know what was inside. Jay was curious to know if Carmen could tell he was binding. As I suspected, and unbeknown to Carmen at this point, Jay had an agenda. He knew that a cycle of gym class would begin next marking period, and he really did not want any students to see the binder. He wanted out of gym class, badly.

"Can I ask you another question?" asked Jay. "I mean you are right that it's important to me that you think I'm a boy instead of only believing that I believe it. If you said that, I would feel like you were labeling me as crazy. But there is another thing I want feedback about." Jay paused, testing the feeling between them. Carmen simply listened; Jay had found his groove in the session, and she knew he would continue talking. "It's about my chest," Jay said. "Can you see it or is it flat?"

Carmen was a little surprised. Jay wore oversize, baggy clothes. It would be hard to notice breast development. "I'm asking because I wear a binder while I am in school. I don't want anyone to see it or my chest. Is that OK? Can that be between us?" Carmen assured Jay that she would not tell anyone. She asked Jay to tell her more about the binder he wore. She recalled that young trans-gender men would wear chest binders, and that they provide some relief but eventually become uncomfortable. Carmen was relieved that his binder was transgender-specific and not something thrown together, like Ace bandages. That approach could be physically harmful. It occurred to Carmen that Jay was thoughtful. Being thoughtful would prove to be an important internal resource for Jay over the long term.

The session ended on an upbeat note. Jay seemed a little lighter, and more present. Carmen made a few notes for herself. First, she thought maybe she would refer Jay to the GSA, but she wanted to look into it more. Second, she found herself wondering if Jay had any sense of his sexuality. Other students his age had discussed sex with her. These days, adolescents are more sexually self-aware. Carmen thought that this is likely due to the internet and how easy it is to access all sorts of information.

Another Consultation with Carmen

Carmen was disappointed. She had referred Jay to the GSA for support, and the session, the fourth visit, went poorly. Suffice it to say the intervention did not work. She didn't understand why. To Carmen, it seemed like the perfect resource. She liked the faculty advisor. The alliance had a nice mix of gay and non-gay students, and the advisor thought that there might be two transgender students who attended regular meetings. Like Jay, they weren't out as transgender, but that wasn't an issue with the other students. I asked Carmen to tell me how Jay responded to her suggestion.

> His face dropped, like I had given him bad news. He just sat there, I couldn't tell if he was sad, angry, or both. I let him have a few minutes, and then I asked him what was bothering him. At first, he said he was fine—just tired—but he knew I didn't buy that. He said that I didn't understand him and that if I did I would never have suggested anything that lame.

Lame? I asked. Carmen went on to say that Jay thought the GSA had nothing to do with him. He had gay friends, and they would not go, either. The way Carmen told it, Jay and his friends saw the GSA as akin to the yearbook committee. I laughed: we certainly do live in a post-gay era. I asked Carmen if she had explored with him what made the GSA lame.

Too many cisgirls and too many popular kids. That's hard to imagine, because the GSA attracts kids just like Jay and his friends. I pressed him for some details. He said that he didn't care about politics—world events—as he called it. He didn't think he'd like sitting around, talking about oppression or making an LGBT history project for the front hall case. He also said that he knew there were no students like him in the GSA, and if there were a trans-cis alliance group he wouldn't go to that, either. Then he just folded his hands and looked away. I've never seen him so annoyed, like I had made a huge mistake or something.

I chuckled, and pointed out that Jay might be what young people refer to as "high maintenance." After only four visits Jay was already devaluing what Carmen was trying to offer.

I explained to Carmen that the disappointment she felt was the same disappointment Jay felt. His devaluing of the GSA and her suggestion was his way of telling her that she had failed, empathically. This could be new and useful information for Carmen. All she needed to do was take a step back, detach, but be curious. I validated that Jay's reaction was out of proportion to the suggestion she made to him. I had two speculations. One, that Jay, like many of the transgender youth I've known, simply don't like support groups because, when in the groups, they become preoccupied with their dysphoria. Many of them will start to compare their body's shape and facial features to those of the other youth in the group. Of course, they never find reassurance through such comparisons. In a way, it is similar to the body dysmorphia that teenagers with eating disorders experience. The difference for transgender adolescents is that their bodies are wrong because their lived experience of their embodiment does not match what they know about who they are. It is like a living paradox, twenty-four hours a day, every day.

My second speculation was that Jay had an agenda that he was not revealing to Carmen. He had been telling her that he just wanted someone to talk to, but his affect was somewhat volatile for someone looking for support and ventilation. In my experience, adolescents that are easily distressed are not telling the social worker everything they should if they want help. It is a form of what was often referred to as resistance. It seemed, to me, that Jay wanted Carmen to read his mind, and then he would punish her with moodiness if she failed. So, if he were resisting, what was Jay enacting and what was he afraid to reveal? Carmen was direct, so she could not be faulted for avoiding addressing things with her students. She was not afraid of conflict or anger. After all, she chose to work with teenagers! I imagined that I would be frustrated, too. Working with adolescents like Jay could feel like trying to nail Jell-O to a wall.

We strategized for the next visit, and I reassured her that Jay would give her opportunities to correct her understanding of him. Carmen agreed that Jay seemed to want something, but wasn't asking. I suspected it had to do with transitioning. Perhaps Jay wanted to begin HRT. Neither Carmen nor I could imagine if there were any issues in school. Jay had been told that he could use the boy's bathroom, but he chose to use the school nurse's bathroom instead. His teachers, at Carmen's suggestion, recently began calling him Jay instead of his birth name, Jacqueline. We brainstormed some more, and agreed that Carmen should simply say to Jay that she thought that there was something he wasn't telling her. I didn't think she should go so far as to apologize for anything from the last session. A simple acknowledgment that there was something she didn't yet grasp would be enough. Jay's job would be to help Carmen help him.

Of course, Jay missed the next session. To her credit, Carmen took it in her stride. She scheduled another visit, but this time she had the teacher send Jay to her office.

Carmen Plays Her Hand

I suggested that Carmen read a chapter in a book by Thomas Szasz that described clinical work in terms of game theory (Szasz, 1988). Older concepts can be very useful in therapeutic relationships that do not lend themselves to manualized approaches. Essentially, game theory conjectures that people follow rules, and assume roles, in all of their pursuits. As applied to clinical work, game theory emphasizes what roles people play, such as social worker and client, and how they are played, over what diagnosis is attached to the person in the role of client. Her relationship with Jay, which had started out so nicely, had quickly devolved into what felt like a game of strategy. I told Carmen that often, the initial phase of a therapeutic alliance might feel like a courtship. Therapeutic relationships are based on hope: in the beginning the connection can feel optimistic. Inevitably, the optimism becomes precarious. Clients may appear to be pulling away after a period in which things feel secure. The goal is to "play your hand" skillfully during this phase, so that a secure alliance will form. By having Jay's teacher send him to his appointment with her, Carmen was making a move in the game. Taking the missed appointment in stride was a style of play.

CARMEN: Jay, what happened on Monday? You knew we had an appointment. After the last visit I would have thought you'd want to give me another chance to understand what I had missed.

JAY: It just slipped my mind. I would have preferred to see you than have to sit through that boring movie in history class. The last session was fine. What do you mean, give you another chance for what?

CARMEN: Jay. Please don't expect me to believe that you weren't irritated in the last visit. I was there, too—haha—I saw it.

JAY: Didn't we talk about it? I thought we did. I'm not mad.

CARMEN: I'm not saying you are mad now. I'm asking about Monday's missed session. I think it means something.

JAY: Like what? I'm a teenager. I forget things.

CARMEN: And you minimize things, too, Jay. [Paused for effect. Jay averted his glance.] I see a pattern here, Jay. We started off really well—I thought we had a good connection. You told me a lot of important things, and then, all of a sudden our relationship became like a game of chess. That's become the pattern. We met six weeks ago. This marking period is almost over, and then there will be a break for a week. Do you think we can get past this before the break? [Paused. Smiling.] And don't say get past what.

Jay had to laugh. He also felt a little hopeful. She knew that the marking period was ending soon. Maybe he would have a chance to ask her about getting out of gym class. His problem, though, was that he didn't know what would be worse, taking gym or hearing the answer he did not want to hear. If she said no, then he would lose the idea and the hope of ever getting out of gym. Jay believed that he had little to hope for anyway. His sense of the future and of the possibilities it offered was limited.

CARMEN: You just laughed, Jay. I take that to mean that I'm on to something, right?

She remembered my advice: detach with curiosity. She waited for Jay to reply.

JAY: You're very smart, Ms. Hernandez. That's why I keep coming back, except for last Monday. I was afraid to come back because there is something important I have to ask you. I'm afraid you'll say no. You've done a lot for me already, like arranging for me to use the nurse's bathroom and now my teachers call me Jay. I know they mean J instead of Jacqueline, but it helps anyway. I'm not ready for too many people to know about me. I'm not sure I'm ready for me to know about me. That's what I meant last month when I said that nobody knows what it's like to be *me*. I don't even know, and not just because I'm a teenager. Being a trans kid is different. That's why I was mad at you for suggesting the GSA. That's not where I want to be. I am like Pinocchio. I want to be a real, normal boy. But I guess my nose grows because you can sense when I'm holding back. I mean if I went to the GSA I would want to go as a cisgender boy who wants to be an ally. I don't even know if I like girls or boys. I pretend to be a lesbian with some kids because it's easier. I don't like it when the bi or gay girls hit on me, though. I might like straight girls if I ever become a guy, but that's like forever away.

CARMEN: I really appreciate you telling me that. You've answered some questions I have. It sounds like you have a question for me, but you are afraid to ask it.

You can ask me anything, Jay, and if it's in my power to say yes I will help in any way. I understand your dilemma, no one wants to hear no for an answer. So here's my deal. If I can say yes, I will let you know right away. I won't say no, but I will look into whether or not I can say yes. At least today you won't have to hear no for an answer.

Jay felt relief. His social worker was smarter than he thought. She understood why he waited so long to ask her about gym class. He asked her his question, explaining that it was not just the locker room he wanted to avoid. He didn't want to wear the girls' gym uniform. He didn't want to have to remove his binder. He didn't want to play girls' sports, even if gym class was co-ed. He didn't want to play gym as a girl. He didn't want to be told he could suit up like a boy, either, because then everyone would know about him. He had been enduring these feelings, and these fears, for at least two years. He explained to Carmen that he just didn't think he could tolerate them anymore.

Jay's Outcome

Carmen told me that she had no idea that Jay was worried about gym class. I wasn't surprised, but I didn't see it coming either. Many of the transgender youth I see avoid gym class and have a range of concerns regarding bathroom use. Some are happy to use the bathroom in the nurse's office or faculty lounge, while others insist on using the bathroom of their experienced gender. Jay wanted to go "stealth," meaning he wanted to pass as androgynous and avoid situations where questions about his gender would emerge.

The gym issue was easy to resolve. The school's administration simply wanted a note from a licensed health care professional. I evaluated Jay for gender dysphoria and wrote a note that excused him from gym class. Carmen continued to see Jay, and I continued to consult with Carmen. I thought that Jay's next task should be to reveal his gender identity to his mother and his brother. Jay was somewhat reluctant, but with Carmen's firm but gentle persuasion he was able to write his mother a letter in which he told her about his gender dysphoria. She was very accepting, and his brother became a source of support at school. At the end of the school year, Jay was in good spirits.

Jay's case is illustrative of what transgender-affirmative case management can look like when it works well. Jay was lucky. Carmen was skilled and open-minded, and the school's administration was progressive. Not all LGBT students experience an outcome such as Jay's. In my clinical experience, Jay is an example of the kind of transgender youth that prefers to "go stealth." Some gay students are like this as well. In Jay's case, he wanted to pass as androgynous and keep to himself until graduation. Jay knew how to keep a low profile. It fit with his overall nature and style.

Carmen was a praiseworthy clinical school social worker. She was open to learning and thinking outside the box. Whether she knew it or not, Carmen was working in accordance with the formal equality theory of educational law mentioned earlier. She helped Jay to work within the environment of the school. She did not stigmatize him by labeling him or referring him to special services. Carmen's work allowed Jay to speak up for himself, and make choices regarding how he wanted to cope. That is social work at its best.

CLOSE READING QUESTIONS

1. In your own words, explain the equality theory of educational law that Healy discusses. Incorporate your understanding of "anti-subordination" in the creation of specialized high schools for LGBT youth. How do these notions work in connection with the inclusion model that Fabbo describes in "Educating Marta"?
2. Read Cuseglio's case study on "Mindfulness Group Work in the School Setting." How does Cuseglio's general assessment of the adolescent experience relate to Jay's adolescent experience? Which of Cuseglio's tactics for working with adolescents might be beneficial to Carmen in the case of Jay? What specific tactics does Healy suggest to Carmen that are specific to working with transgender students?
3. Healy says that "contemplating suicide is not the same as attempting it." Explain how this is true and why this idea is central to the case of Jay.

Prompts for Writing

1. Healy suggests that, according to GLSEN, "LGBT students are more likely to attend school and to feel safer at school if their school has a GSA." Yet Jay did not feel that the GSA at his school was a place where he fit in. Further research GSAs and write about how you would improve the existing model. To start, you could think about how systems theory might help you to involve and educate more students and staff.
2. One reason that Healy was brought in to Jay's school as a consultant is that statistics find transgender youth more prone to suicide than their typical peers. But both Healy and Carmen want to guard against creating a "suffering, suicidal script" for Jay. How can a school social worker take the risk of suicide seriously without prognosticating the worst case scenario?
3. Research gender dysphoria, hormone replacement therapy, and processes for a youth's transition. How does the Social Work Code of Ethics inform your professional relationship to the pathologizing of gender identity? What are your personal feelings about working with transgender students?

References

American Psychiatric Association (2013). *Diagnostic and statistical manual of mental disorders* (5th edn). Arlington, VA: American Psychiatric Publishing.

Brittenham, K. (2004). Equal protection theory and the Harvey Milk High School: Why anti-subordination alone is not enough. *BCL Rev.*, *45*, 869. Accessed online September 18, 2016 at http://lawdigitalcommons.bc.edu/bclr/vol45/iss4/3.

Colapinto, J. (2005). The Harvey Milk School has no right to exist. Discuss. *New York Magazine*, 1–6. Accessed online September 18, 2016 at http://nymag.com/nymetro/news/features/10970/.

Ehrensaft, D. (2016). *The gender creative child.* New York: The Experiment.

Ford, R. T. (2004). Brown's ghost. *Harvard Law Review, 117*(5), 1305–1333.

Gibson, P. (1989). Gay male and lesbian youth suicide. In M. R. Feinleib (Ed.), *Report on the secretary's task force on youth suicide* (vol. 3, pp. 110–142). Washington, DC: US Department of Health and Human Services Public Health Service Alcohol, Drug Abuse, and Mental Health Administration.

GLSEN (2007). Gay-Straight Alliances: Creating safer schools for LGBT students and their allies. Research Brief. New York: Gay, Lesbian, and Straight Education Network. Accessed online September 18, 2016 at www.glsen.org/sites/default/files/Gay-Straight%20Alliances.pdf.

Grossman, A. H., and D'Augelli, A. R. (2007). Transgender youth and life-threatening behaviors. *Suicide and Life-Threatening Behavior, 37*(5), 527–537.

Hetrick, E. S., and Martin, A. D. (1987). Developmental issues and their resolution for gay and lesbian adolescents. *Journal of Homosexuality, 14*(1–2), 25–43.

Kann, L., Olsen, E. O., McManus, T., et al. (2016). Sexual identity, sex of sexual contacts, and health-related behaviors among students in grades 9–12—United States and selected sites, 2015. *Morbidity and Mortality Weekly Reports Surveillance Summary*, 65(No. SS-9), 1–202. Accessed online September 18, 2016 at http://dx.doi.org/10.15585/mmwr.ss6509a1.

Kosciw, J. G., Greytak, E. A., Bartkiewicz, M. J., Boesen, M. J., and Palmer, N. A. (2014). The 2013 national school climate survey: the experiences of lesbian, gay, bisexual and transgender youth in our nation's schools. New York: Gay, Lesbian, and Straight Education Network. Accessed online September 18, 2016 at www.glsen.org.

Martin, A. D., and Hetrick, E. S. (1988). The stigmatization of the gay and lesbian adolescent. *Journal of Homosexuality, 15*(1–2), 163–183.

Remafedi, G., Farrow, J. A., and Deisher, R. W. (1991). Risk factors for attempted suicide in gay and bisexual youth. *Pediatrics, 87*(6), 869–875.

Russell, S. T. (2003). Sexual minority youth and suicide risk. *American Behavioral Scientist, 46*(9), 1241–1257. DOI: 10.1177/0002764202250667.

Russell, S. T., and Joyner, K. (2001). Adolescent sexual orientation and suicide risk: Evidence from a national study. *American Journal of Public Health*, 91, 1276–1281. DOI: 10.2105/AJPH.91.8.1276.

Ryan, C., Russell, S. T., Huebner, D., Diaz, R., and Sanchez, J. (2010). Family acceptance in adolescence and the health of LGBT young adults. *Journal of Child and Adolescent Psychiatric Nursing, 23*(4), 205–213. DOI: 10.1111/j.1744-6171.2010.00246.x.

Savin-Williams, R. C. (2006). *The new gay teenager.* Cambridge, MA: Harvard University Press.

Szasz, T. (1988). *The ethics of psychoanalysis.* Syracuse, NY: Syracuse University Press.

8

RETHINKING DISCIPLINARY STRATEGIES

Reflections on White Privilege in School Social Work

Alexis Kaliades

Pre-Reading Questions

1. How would you define "privilege"? What privileges might you benefit from based on your race, class, gender, or sexual orientation, especially in the context of education?
2. There are many reasons why a student might accuse a school social worker of misunderstanding. How would you respond if a student felt unable to enter into an alliance with you as a clinician because of racial differences?
3. How do you imagine the school social worker's place in systems of discipline? What core social work values might affect the way a school social worker would approach discipline?
4. What are some ways that a school social worker might educate her colleagues on issues of race and class? How could social work values related to race and class influence the culture of a school?
5. What do you know about the term "intersectionality"? Have you ever imagined a school as a context for systematic oppression?

Introduction

Tara sat trembling in my office, on the cusp of erupting, her hands curled into tight fists in her lap. Between sobs, she described the events that had her plucked from English class, earning her a visit to my office and a two-day suspension. My response, deemed inept by her standards, only served to add to her rage and despair. "You just don't get it," she spat. "You're not from here, and you do not know what it is to be black! You don't know what it's like to live in projects. Try and be in here when you're coming from out there." With this claim, Tara had identified the motivation behind years of resistance and academic break-downs, and the reason that I, a social worker with white privilege, had never fully understood her well enough to help. Thus, I began to explore the disconnect between the school staff who were in charge of discipline and the students receiving punishments. As a Caucasian social worker in an urban high school with high proportions of low-income and minority students, I often field questions about my personal history and journey. While these questions may not be as direct as was Tara's declaration, the origin is the same: you are different from me, and it matters.

My experience with Tara was not entirely unique: urban students of color often describe feeling misunderstood and disengaged by white school staff where I work. The experience of feeling this way during interaction with school staff manifests through complex refusal and resistance processes known as disaffection. The processes of disaffection include a variety of behaviors that students exhibit, such as procrastination, distractibility, giving up, frustration, boredom, and anger (Skinner et al., 2009). When feeling misread or judged by white staff, Tara found it impossible to verbalize her unrest with words. As a result, she communicated her feelings through resistance. Tara's disaffection manifested in non-violent ways, yet the school response to her behavior was habitually disciplinary despite the fact that negative interventions do little to curb behaviors but rather further marginalize already marginalized students. Morris (2005) describes zero-tolerance disciplinary methods: "Although many school officials viewed this discipline as a way of teaching valuable social skills, it appeared to instead reinforce race, class, and gender stereotypes and had the potential to alienate many students from schooling" (p. 25). Rather than exercising patience and tending to the emotional needs of students, teachers operating within this disciplinary model respond deliberately to maintain control of the classroom and condemn what they deem inappropriate behavior. School becomes a hostile environment where it is unsafe to challenge one's surroundings and where any misstep is punishable. For an urban student of color, receiving these disciplinary reactions from a white staff member may reinforce the impact of other personal experiences of discrimination and further damage student attachment to school.

These school policies have rendered the classroom, which once served as a safe haven for external difficulties, a space dominated by adverse emotion and marred by privilege. In an effort to preserve peace and productiveness, discipline practices following the zero-tolerance model automatically and increasingly pull children out of the classroom and into a school social worker's office for a variety of infractions. However, the regular practice of removing disruptive students from school in an effort to create safer environments has not been substantiated to be effective (Skiba, 2008; Skiba and Peterson, 2000). Rather, these methods generate anger and rage within the students, their families, and the very teachers and staff imposing them. The result is a breeding ground for misinterpretation of behavior for both students and staff. While there is potential for this void to exist within any relationship, it is drastically damaging when it occurs for African-American students at the hands of a white staff member in a supposedly protective environment.

Of further significance is the well-documented research that illustrates the overrepresentation of minority and low socioeconomic students receiving disciplinary punishments. Skiba et al. (2002) note, "The current results are highly consistent with a large body of previous literature in finding that schools and school districts that rely on school exclusion as a disciplinary tool run a substantial risk of minority disproportionality in the application of those punishments" (p. 338). This disproportionality of exclusionary and punitive school practices perpetrates a history of abandonment, segregation, and discrimination for African-American students. The exposure to these disciplinary practices increases the likelihood of minority students engaging in criminal behavior and processing through the justice system. This trend, known as the school-to-prison pipeline, denotes how discipline techniques (e.g. detention, out of school, suspension, disciplinary alternative education placements) experienced by African-American males alienate them from the learning process by steering them from the classroom and academic attainment and toward the criminal justice system (Darensbourg et al., 2010). Though it is preferential to have students remain in class to avoid missing content, these modern discipline practices following the zero-tolerance model redefine students as pariahs. Negative interventions do little to curb behaviors and further marginalize students by providing a "bad" label, setting the stage for future defiance or impulsiveness. These discriminatory systems establish barriers for students of color that are in addition to the daily challenges for the average adolescent student. Considering the existence of these inequities, it is abhorrent that exclusionary tactics not only remain a one-size-fits-all solution to perceived school infractions, but that more school staff have not stood up to speak against these practices.

However, speaking up for change is a tall order. Change would require the uncomfortable acknowledgment of discriminatory systems functioning not only within the school system but also within the school staff themselves. For many white school staff, the memory of being a high school student is drastically different than the daily reality of our minority students within an urban community. Unlike students of color, white students are not forced to examine race and the implications associated with being white. McIntosh (2010) defines this white privilege as "an invisible package of unearned assets which I can count on cashing in each day, but about which I was 'meant' to remain oblivious" (p. 121). White people are awarded an unspoken freedom and ease with which to go through life. As a result, this privilege may translate into white staff incorrectly understanding the experience of a minority student. Moreover, because culture defines which situations are considered dangerous, what separates positive behavior from deviance, how information is received, and how prevention measures are conducted, differences in race may result in disputes within the classroom. Bergeron (2008) describes this as a sense of "cultural disequilibrium" (p. 5), which results when the experiences of teachers are incongruent with those of their students. This has implicit implications for interaction within the classroom, as methods that may have been motivating within a white middle-class community are not effective within a minority or low socioeconomic school community. As a white social worker in a high school with minority populations, I can attest that such practices have potentially devastating repercussions for students who are receiving an education outside the white middle-class paradigm.

Moreover, my relationship with Tara compelled me to consider my presence as a white social worker in a minority school and how the overarching impression of white privilege has created systems that do not resonate at high schools with minority populations. Of specific interest is the idea that white privilege functions negatively by generating white fragility, "a state in which even a minimum amount of racial stress becomes intolerable, triggering a range of defensive moves" (DiAngelo, 2011, p. 57). In other words, white people are not used to dealing with racial stress, and their efforts to protect against it are like self-imposed limitations on understanding the actual challenges and realities that students of color face. Because the cultural environment defines how students interpret and respond to surroundings, any response to student behavior which lacks tolerance and self-awareness cannot be successful. In this phenomenological case study, I examine how the intersecting subjectivity of a white social worker and an African-American student reveals the inefficacy of modern discipline models. However, it is not enough to simply concede that these inequalities exist. Despite the discomfort it may induce, it is imperative for white school staff to contemplate how their whiteness manifests consciously and unconsciously within student interactions.

Disturbances in Development

By the time Tara arrived as a freshman, she had a significant history of run-ins with previous teachers and administrators. Tara's dense file went as far back as kindergarten, where she was described as an oppositional child with difficulty managing affect. Yet an evaluation from kindergarten revealed that Tara did not start out as an unhappy child. Her behavior became unpredictable only after the separation of her mother and father around age three.[1] As one of five children to a single mother in a family of low socioeconomic status, Tara often expressed feelings of loneliness. Trauma struck again when her father passed away suddenly at age seven.[2] Without the ability to put her despair into words, Tara would erupt in fits of rage toward her classmates and teachers when she was challenged. Further compounding this despair was a soon-to-follow classification from the Child Study Team, extracting Tara from the classroom where she had spent most of her year. Isolated and labeled, Tara became indignant.[3] The disrespect of being called "retarded" by her classmates was too much to bear; her aggressive tendencies increased, and she began to settle into her identity as a recidivist. Her response to these injuries became vindictive: she exploded at students when they teased her and tormented teachers when they challenged her. Tara was an exquisite example of how a traumatic home environment, systems that classify black students more often than white students, and racial health disparities can affect a student's propensity to endure difficult feelings. With little support for processing this series of disappointments and losses, Tara's despondent life at home translated into a chaotic life at school. Disappointingly, Tara's outbursts were met with impatience and corrective actions instead of understanding and empathy. The school response further frustrated and enraged Tara, thus contributing to the likelihood of future transgressions.

As a result, Tara's inability to manage frustration within stressful school situations was solidified by the time she entered high school. I have found that most students are quite capable of finding something to lament about, whether a heavy workload or stringent school rules; even the most devoted and dedicated students occasionally express some form of displeasure or discontent. While some students take a moment to acknowledge this displeasure or aggravation and carry on, others are incapable of tolerating the frustration and remaining productive. One such student was Tara, whose infectious laugh, contagious smile, and captivating charisma overflowed on her best days. On her worst, her rage could create a palpable sense of unease or distress for anyone in the room. Tara's fiery temper and razor sharp tongue lanced anyone she deemed worthy of her wrath. Tara's tenure as a high school student read like a rap sheet, but the motivation behind her behavior continuously stumped administrators and frustrated her teachers. In spite of the detentions, suspensions, and behavior modification plans, Tara inevitably ended up sitting in front of our principal or in my office. When it came time to examine what was responsible for perpetrating her behavior rather than correcting it, the blame always came back to Tara. Described by her teachers as an "unreachable, stubborn, and irrational kid," I wondered how the school escaped culpability for these repeated episodes. Without the open acknowledgment of racial privilege, the school staff did not have to confront their own roles in upholding a system that perpetuated Tara's behavior and the stressors that led to it.

Powerless to Feelings

The distress that Tara endured in her personal history made her easily susceptible to stress and disapproval in all aspects of her life. Perhaps one of Tara's most intense struggles was managing her reactions when she was overwhelmed or overstimulated. It was well known that when Tara had a feeling, she would act on it. If she felt that a teacher or classmate were wronging her in any way,

Tara would pounce, regardless of the consequences. Jensen (2009) explains these reactions: "Impulsivity is a common disruptive classroom behavior among low-SES students. But it's actually an exaggerated response to stress that serves as a survival mechanism: in conditions of poverty, those most likely to survive are those who have an exaggerated stress response" (p. 26). Tara's exaggerated and rowdy responses to these stressful situations were indeed a survival tactic. In actuality, these behaviors indicate the residual effect of the traumatic past experienced by African-Americans. Leary and Robinson (2005) explain: "as a continuing legacy of slavery, African Americans today have recognized that the society around them does not always respect them and have developed a hypersensitivity to, and anger about being disrespected" (p. 694). Tara almost exclusively responded to perceived disrespect and feelings of shame with intense and explosive anger, emanating a visceral need to thwart those who frustrated her. Unable to endure such unpleasant emotions, she would discharge her aggravation by trying to induce retributive embarrassment. Successful in that retribution or not, she would indubitably suffer the consequences of punitive discipline.

On the wide spectrum of emotions that Tara experienced, feelings of shame created the most conflict. Just past the halfway mark of her junior year, Tara was required to speak in front of the class as part of a group presentation. During the group preparation for the presentation, Tara became apprehensive and omitted some speaking points while reading her part. The teacher, a white man, chastised Tara for unpreparedness and promptly requested the group move on to the next segment of the project. Enraged by this dismissal, Tara ferociously erupted, hurling profanity at her teacher and destroying a poster for the project as she stormed out of the room. Tara was quickly apprehended, issued a suspension, and placed with me while we waited for her mother to pick her up. Upon my exploration, I learned that Tara felt deeply disrespected and rejected in front of her classmates. While the teacher's intention had been to move onto a more productive way to spend the practice time, Tara viewed this exchange as a slight by an uppity white person. This expression not only revealed Tara's insecurity and feelings of judgment by a rigid authority figure, but also her susceptibility to feelings of being discarded. According to Dupper et al. (2009), "The strong correlation between race, income level, and school exclusion suggests that schools must do a better job of addressing potential cultural conflicts and misunderstandings between teachers and students of color" (p. 8). These misunderstandings are common within the school setting and must be alleviated by considering how staff expressions are interpreted by students. It must be argued that the outcome of this exchange would have been different had her teacher responded to her nervousness with empathy and understanding rather than frustration.

Throughout Tara's four years, I received countless visits from frustrated and concerned teachers seeking advice. "Sometimes she is just so disruptive, and she refuses to do her work. Why can't she learn how to act?" her white math teacher lamented one day. The concept of "acting right" was always a point of contention for Tara and many of her teachers. If Tara was feeling resistant to participating in class any particular day, she would refuse to do her work by sitting dormant in her seat or placing her head on her desk. On these instances where her resistance was not disruptive but passive, she would still endure a punitive consequence for disobedience. It was apparent that this white teacher could not tolerate a challenge from Tara in any form, so the response was a vindictive punishment to an "insubordinate" student. Tara was generally outspoken about behaviors she identified as being representative of her race. If this white teacher felt victimized by Tara, then was sending her out of the classroom a way to avoid a racially charged incident? When tensions arise within classroom exchanges, this may expose the inner-workings of white fragility. While exclusionary discipline tactics are intended to keep the classroom safe, it seemed that Tara's teacher was not in fact unsafe, but rather uncomfortable. White people often confuse comfort with safety and state that we don't feel safe when what we really mean is that we don't feel comfortable (DiAngelo, 2011). In the context of a classroom, power imbalance exists where the teacher is omnipotent, and the student is expected to follow the rules as determined by the teacher. When this power is tested and further complicated by underlying racial inequality, the result is a disruption in white privilege and then a reflexive response to restore the power differential.

Tara often attempted to challenge authority by inducing frustration in her teachers when she herself experienced those feelings. Once, after becoming frustrated by an assignment, Tara began to engage loudly with her classmates, refusing to complete the in-class assignment. Afterwards, when I asked what had happened, she reflected, "Nothing happened. It's because I'm black." With these words, Tara was expressing how she had internalized a self image of being "bad" as a result of her race. Ogbu (2004) explains this through the "acting White" theory, which describes how historical racial oppression creates oppositional collective identities against white mainstream prerogatives in African-American youth. At some point in her earlier education, Tara had learned what was perceived as appropriate behavior in the classroom. When she acted opposite of the expected behavior, she identified the reason as a cultural motivation beyond her control. The implication is that the current discipline model is a manifestation of the history of oppression and injustice suffered by African-Americans and may result in specific behavioral responses. As such, punitive disciplinary actions are a symbolic repetition and must be omitted from the response to student behaviors, for at the root of Tara's individual and unique needs are intense social and emotional challenges that are felt widespread by students and their families in at-risk communities. Better understanding of these social and emotional challenges is a requisite component of social justice, for which all schools should strive.

The negative effects of Tara's history of exclusion spread like shockwaves throughout her life and the people connected to her. Gibson and Haight (2013) state, "Suspensions were described by many as morally problematic, that is, unjust, harmful to children, negligent in helping children with underlying problems such as bullying, undermining caregivers' racial socialization, racially suspect, and emotionally difficult for caregivers" (p. 266). The strain that suspension placed on Tara and her mother was significant because it perpetrated a consistently recusant message. A particularly volatile meeting between Tara, her mother, the principal, and me occurred at the beginning of Tara's sophomore year. Accompanying Tara back to school after a four-day suspension, Tara's mother immediately became defensive to the principal's criticism. There was plenty of conversation in that meeting, but all that was left on the table were feelings of disrespect and resentment. Again, I was left wondering about the efficacy and cultural competence of an educational system that invokes such ferocious rage within a mother and daughter. I invited Tara and her mother up to my office to decompress and to end the meeting on a more positive note. I closed my door and turned to see tears streaming down the cheeks of both Tara and her mother. I saw a mother grieving for her daughter and a teenager imprisoned by her own feelings. I remember feeling wordless at that moment, paralyzed by their sadness. In the confines of my small office, I was suffocating with uncertainty. What could I say that would offer any comfort? The desperation to protect my own fragility and fill the gap between us had prevented me from realizing that perhaps nothing fruitful could be said at that moment. Still, rather than speaking, I sat with them and waited, and they cried in silence.

When Tara became uncontrollably enraged, I would often find her isolated from other students, alone with her overwhelming feelings. My approach to Tara in these situations was always docile, careful not to further stimulate or agitate. Shrieking, the story of the incident in question would explode out of her, her deep victimization echoing in the empty office and through the adjacent hallways. Once during an in-class activity, an intense battle had transpired as a result of Tara's wearing a sweater over her school uniform. Shocked, I listened as Tara described the repartee between her and her white Spanish teacher, who refused to start class until Tara was in her complete uniform. As the teacher became more insistent and combative, Tara became embarrassed and combative. The dispute resembled bickering between two teenagers rather than between a teacher and student. While Tara's version omitted the profanity, most notably she fixated on the imbalance of blame. Tara noted, "I'm going to get suspended, but she gets to just come back tomorrow and go back to teaching, no questions asked." In effect, she was correct: the teacher's behavior was not suitable for a teacher/student exchange. Here was a conflict in which both parties were expressing vulnerability: Tara for suffering the embarrassment of being singled out, and the teacher for being undermined by a student. Tara had always been taught to stand up for herself, and felt she needed to defend against the shame. Hughes et al. (2006) call this racial socialization, "the processes through how families of color experience and discuss social inequalities and injustices and how they teach children to manage them" (p. 748). Parents are the first source of information on which experiences are perceived as harmful or dangerous. For a white teacher and an

African-American student, there may be significant gaps in the perception of what constitutes safe behavior. When either the student or teacher feel unsafe, the corresponding behaviors can lead to further negative stimulation by the student or ineffective response to student behavior by the teacher.

Considering the Role of Whiteness

To combat the negativity, I made sure my approach to Tara always communicated how important I considered her well-being. Depending on how her threshold had been tested that day, she could vacillate between demonstrating affection and suspicion. She loved to tease me about my clothing and my hair; I gamely endured her jokes, and we cozily enjoyed the banter. Whether she was currently enraged or fond of me, she was relentless in acknowledging my whiteness, but I often missed that she was trying to communicate with me about racial privilege; Caucasian hair texture and even nose shapes afford power in contexts of white supremacy (Leonardo, 2004).[4] She had an explanation for how every facet of my life was a product of my race. She fantasized that I lived in a large mansion and drove an expensive Mercedes Benz, which was ideal since I was probably commuting from a suburb far away. While her image of me changed from year to year, there was an underlying theme that always remained: she was convinced that because I was white, my life had been and always will be easy. The most poignant acknowledgment of white privilege is that it ceases to exist unless it is deliberately considered. Landsman and Lewis (2010) state, "Privilege resides in the fact that White people can move about, can experience life, can apply to college, for loans, for jobs without being denied entrance or freedom based on their skin color—and never for a moment have to think about it" (p. 15). Tara was confirming interpretation in her assessment; she never attributed my perceived success as a result of my hard work or discipline. She was convinced that I had not experienced struggle and that, as a result, I could not comprehend the struggles she had already endured and would endure in her future.

To a large extent, she was correct. I grew up with all the members of immediate and extended family playing active roles in my everyday life. I had a comfortable home, with plenty of space so that I could find respite from my family when needed. I never felt insecure about my parents' support, and I felt confident about where my life would take me after high school. I did know struggle, but the enormity and immediacy of my struggle was profoundly different from Tara's. In the context of her education, Tara's consistent receipt of punishment generated a sense of distrust toward most figures of authority. Whereas I felt safe to grow and learn within my school, Tara felt perpetually targeted and under surveillance. Unlike Tara, I was comfortably secure as a student, yet I was also acutely unaware that this security was a result of my status as a white person. Gump (2010) posits that "Subjects who occupy the subject position *White*, for example, may be unaware of the entitlement and privilege the position bestows" (p. 46). Like many other white school staff, my personal experience as a white student in a predominantly white school had forced an impression in my mind of how students and teachers interacted with each other. I had failed to contemplate how the societal impressions of being white would function in my work with non-white students.

Such was the basis of Tara's interpretation and the reason she felt that I could never truly be in her corner. It frustrated her that anyone could have it that easy, and with that, a deep seed of guilt was nestled inside me and planted. Toward the end of her senior year, Tara walked out of her creative writing class and into my office as a preventative measure. She wanted to exit before she "blacked out on the teacher." I invited her to stay with me so she could manage her affect in a safe place and discharge the energy she wanted to direct at her teacher. During Tara's decompression, our conversation unfolded as such:

TARA: You won't understand, we're too different. You didn't grow up here, and you don't know how bad it is here.
ME: Just because we look different, doesn't mean I don't understand you or what it's like to be you. Maybe you could explain it to me.

Looking back, my white privilege in the form of color-blindness—the idea that race should take a back seat to one's individuality, thus discounting one's relationship with her environment—was seeping into our exchange (Richeson and Nussbaum, 2003). How could I reduce our differences to our looks or insist that I was capable of fully understanding her experience? On what grounds could I indicate it was Tara's responsibility to correct my ignorance? Even though my goal was to listen and empathize, I was making assumptions. My white fragility was firing away, and I was quickly negating the existence of racial imbalance and selfishly aiming to alleviate the discomfort created by my own unawareness. DiAngelo (2011) describes this void: "Because race is constructed as residing in people of color, whites don't bear the social burden of race" (p. 62). Herein lies the phenomenological examination of what it is to be a minority student in a school with white staff. While I have never been required to really consider my race, Tara was constantly reminded of her own by systems in her everyday life.

The constant reminders of Tara's race did not exclusively manifest in negative systems or in stereotypes. In the spring of her senior year, Tara interviewed for jobs and colleges fairly frequently. Diverse members of the school staff all had tips to benefit our students during these processes. One day while reviewing potential job interview questions, Tara interrupted me mid-suggestion to ask, "Oh, so I should try to sound white?" Again, my white fragility began to percolate at the hard line being drawn in the sand. "Um . . . well, how do you mean?" I responded. Tara picked up the answer sheet and purred gently through all the answers, with a noticeable difference in both her tone and her vernacular.

"It sounds more professional that way," she remarked. Another instance struck a similar chord: I was meeting with Tara and fellow white school staff when another student came in to ask directions to the baseball game Friday night. The other staff member provided the directions, but also offered advice on traveling to a predominantly white suburb for the evening. "Don't go above the speed limit. If you are flagged to pull over, do so immediately. Oh, and wear your school colors so it's clear you're a teenager." While these messages were presented in a protective manner, Tara and her classmate received the message that at baseline, their race put them at a disadvantage. Conversely, white privilege ensured that I was never in the position where I had to correct my behavior to alleviate myself as a target or seem more viable.

Overcompensation by African-American students to avoid victimization reveals situational racism which is difficult for teachers with white privilege to acknowledge. As a white woman I can attest: it is difficult to admit participation in a system that is discriminatory. However, the generalizability of these incidents makes it impossible to deny that this inequity exists. Disparities truly shine when teachers and staff pass judgment on what constitutes a student violation. Simmons-Reed and Cartledge (2014) explain, "African-American students are more likely to be suspended for discretionary offenses (offenses that may or may not require suspension based on safety concerns) than nondiscretionary offenses (carrying a weapon or drugs)" (p. 98). Tara's displeasure with staff was often manifested in such discretionary offenses. Her acts of defiance ranged from subtle to overt; on countless incidences, Tara would avoid class completely or leave the classroom without permission. Any number of factors could affect Tara's willingness to follow school policy, none of which were acknowledged by the staff. Rather than engage and risk exposing themselves, staff response to Tara's defiance became an automatic call to have her removed. Tara always maintained that she was unfairly targeted by her teachers, often for violating the electronics policy. One such incident occurred after Tara, having failed to surrender her phone, exploded into a profanity-filled rant. Both Tara and her teacher were highly agitated after this account. The dual agitation signals a sense of solidarity, as both people at opposite ends of the spectrum expressed negative emotions as a result of an incompetent system. Had the teacher assuaged her concern that she was not the only student being reprimanded, she may not have responded so aggressively. If the initial response to Tara had been more sensitive and exploratory, the subsequent negative emotion and reaction may have been avoided.

Discussion

This school environment continues to remain particularly bleak for minority students from low socioeconomic stratas. According to the United States Census Bureau, in 2015, 30.5% of African-American families with children in the household under the age of eighteen were living below the US poverty threshold.

The theory of intersectionality links these two social characteristics that influence every aspect of a child's life experience. Murphy et al. (2009) say, "Intersectionality posits that an understanding of a person's social location, that is, his or her place in society that is formed by the intersection of social constructions that mark privilege or oppression, is essential to capturing the complexity of that person's experiences" (p. 7). These social constructs have serious implications for how individuals and groups interpret their environment, behave, and adapt to the world. The experience of living in poverty can encumber a student's ability to feel optimistic about life, let alone academic success. Whereas some students can imagine a life post high school, students living in poverty suffer from limited perception and may not be able to picture a fulfilling life. Valois et al. (2002) describe this stagnancy: "Poverty creates frustration and feelings of relative deprivation, injustice, and anger, as well as self-devaluation and hopelessness" (p. 459). When an adolescent experiences these thoughts and is then met by an intolerant school discipline system, these feelings are repeated. Consequently, it is no wonder that minority students, specifically male African-American students, are amongst the most affected by these practices.

As the focus of these discipline practices is to confine and control student conduct, there is little consideration of the diverse personal history which informs student behavior. From birth, there are countless familial, social, and environmental circumstances that influence how a child learns to perceive and respond to the world. For example, children from families with low socioeconomic status are often neglected: not necessarily in basic needs, but in the sense of attention and support. Jensen (2009) states that "Low-income parents are often overwhelmed by diminished self-esteem, depression, and a sense of powerlessness and inability to cope—feelings that may get passed along to their children in the form of insufficient nurturing, negativity, and a general failure to focus on children's needs" (p. 17). Children who are deprived of affectionate attention or subjected to harsh criticism may become legitimately burdened. A severely criticized child made to feel perpetually ashamed may have difficulty tolerating feelings of shame and embarrassment. Because of the retributive quality in classroom management practices, students often experience feelings of shame when corrected by teachers or school staff. The result is further condemning for the student who is incapable of enduring such humiliation, as she will inevitably erupt with anger and fury. Lewis (1971) describes this relationship between shame and rage as the futile attempt by a shamed person to alleviate feelings of powerlessness or exact revenge on the person inflicting the shame. I have witnessed countless students who became overwhelmed by feelings of shame and exploded with profanity-filled rage as a result. While punishment is the inevitable response to such an episode, the perception of the incident by the staff and administration determined the severity of the sentence.

Herein lies the theory-to-practice problem that plagues the current discipline models being employed within the school setting. Administration hears "defiance" and immediately springs to retributive action. While it cannot be denied that student and staff safety is paramount, there are deeper and complex factors that are contributing to the behavior that cannot be cured easily or quickly. Unfortunately, school-based social work practice often relies heavily on services that were requested by administration to increase protective factors and decrease risk factors in reference to youth truancy and school refusal. These results-based services create a severe discrepancy by preventing the most appropriate services from being provided. Interventions that focus on providing adolescents with emotional understanding and support are negated in lieu of punishment and negative discipline. While the goal of these interventions is to discourage the student from exhibiting the same behavior again. If the corrective action is unpleasant enough, it may successfully discourage the student from engaging in similar future behaviors. However, controlling behavior through retaliation is not resolving any internal issues within the student. Discipline may treat behavior, but it certainly does not address the student's mind or motivation.

A perspective that addresses this motivation and encompasses all the inner workings of the mind is person-in-environment. Under person-in-environment, behavior is an interaction with the environment where one influences the other, with no separation. Based on this perspective, the person and the environment are interconnected and constantly interacting. This concept heartily negates the dualistic structure of the existing discipline model which only aims to treat behavior. Accordingly, it is imperative for schools to consider the personal history and culture of students when creating and implementing discipline systems. For while these students may give the impression of delinquency, there are far more deeply rooted and underlying issues that contribute to behaviors and prevent academic success. Within the context of the classroom and without uttering a word, teenagers have the ability to tell their life stories. Whether it be consistent cooperation or acts of defiance and resistance, entire histories can be communicated when we examine the way students interact with the school staff. The way in which a student relates to school staff tells us everything about how the student has related to the important adults in her life up until this point. The characteristics of adolescent behavior and the challenges they face during this phase of development must be considered as they mature and pass through the tumultuous teen years. Adolescents can be impulsive as their ego is still not able to cope with pressures that they experience. At baseline, adolescence is a trying time for even the most well-adjusted youth. Between unpredictable hormones, rising sexual tension, peer pressure, and struggling with self-expression, youth are often overwhelmed and may use poor judgment. When these pre-existing factors are compounded by trauma, oppression, poverty, or neglect, the adolescent's ability to function and cultivate relationships is further hindered.

Given the unique life experiences of each student by the time she reaches high school, it is hard to imagine how a one-size fits-all model would be applicable in responding to all student behavior. The majority of the students have been subjected to many disadvantages throughout their short lives. For such youth that have endured trauma or neglect, the punitive school discipline system may induce difficult feelings associated with their personal histories. "Children raised in poverty rarely choose to behave differently, but they are faced daily with overwhelming challenges that affluent children never have to confront, and their brains have adapted to suboptimal conditions in ways that undermine good school performance" (Jensen, 2009, p. 14). When there is a school system that has a system of order based on rejection and betrayal, these feelings are further perpetrated within a punitive school discipline system. Administratively motivated, generalizable services may be ineffective due to culturally specific presenting issues to the youth population. For the at-risk youth population, there may be serious implications without outlets or support systems. When youth experience overwhelming feelings, they are often helpless in their ability to strike out against those who arouse these emotions. Youth may not be aware that their behavior is potentially harmful, and as a result may be highly vulnerable or resistant to prevention and intervention. As students pass to higher grade levels and graduate, they also face new decisions that come along with this growth and transition. Students benefit from guidance and as they undergo these important transitions and integrate into the community as young adults.

However, the current punitive disciplinary model does not lend itself to protecting student's self esteem and helping them manage difficult feelings. Acts of defiance or resistance were Tara's way of communicating her story or experience; these acts are not always received with compassion. Tara responded to my empathy and attention. What I have noticed is that if students feel that an authority figure is truly engaged in what they are saying, whether it is about home or about their dissatisfaction with school lunch that day, they will realize some comfort in being heard and understood. This concept is elucidated further by Simmons-Reed and Cartledge (2014), "Another speculation, with some empirical support, is that a strong teacher-pupil relationship may play a protective role for African-American children at risk for aggressive behavior . . . Strengthening student-teacher relationships may help teachers better understand students' actions and their perceptions of discrimination and unfairness" (p. 101). While this sentiment is indubitably accurate, it is impossible to foster and cultivate these relationships if there is a system in place which allows for unjustly perceived discipline by school staff. Youth are unconsciously motivated to please the significant adults in their lives. If a child has a history of disappointment or distrust with those significant adults, these feelings will be conveyed to any future adults. When this transfer occurs, it is difficult for youth to form relationships with teachers, resulting in misinterpretation and tension. As a result, it is culturally competent to encourage school staff to create relationships with students as early as possible to reduce risky behaviors and promote positive interactions. The stronger the relationship, the less opportunity for student infraction. This equals less negatively perceived behavior and less negative interventions resulting in suspensions.

Tara's experiences demonstrate that when students are suspended for acting out, we miss the chance to try to understand what their actions are trying to tell us. In Tara's case, by excluding her we were repeating a pattern that was already operating in her life. She admitted to feeling rejected at school and at home and as a result, acted disruptively. Tara internalized the labels and criticisms that were applied to her. Schools must do better in providing outlets for emotions that are difficult to control. We must offer empathy, professional help, and acceptance rather than punishment. It is our responsibility to build self-esteem in our students rather than to engage in interventions that add to feelings of inferiority. Many students are reacting to previous experiences or are trying to forget past trauma, but do not have the capacity to imagine or "fantasize" about their futures. Where non-impulsive people can fantasize or ponder about difficult emotions, at-risk youth such as Tara become overwhelmed and aggressive. Instead of criticizing her response, I help her fantasize about a life past high school. Once this life becomes more familiar, we can discuss behaviors that will help her head toward that life, not away from it. By providing my students with a safe avenue to reflect on their feelings, I can help them begin to heal and become productive.

Conclusion

The school system should avoid the risk of shaming and shunning implicit in modern punitive discipline practices and instead should empower students to gain confidence, express themselves with conviction, and respect the dignity of others. When students are suspended, feelings of past exclusion or neglect are reinforced. Negative interventions such as those grounded in punishment also add to feelings of inferiority and impulsivity. Youth benefit from connections that provide an empowering environment and the opportunity to increase self-esteem. By creating outlets where students can manage difficult emotions, it is possible to build character and resilience. Exploring the complexities interwoven within the fabric of each student offers the opportunity to provide them with services which best fits their unique needs. There is currently a significant incongruity with implementing discipline practices that are also sensitive and engaging to the adolescent mind within the school setting.

Current policies are intended to create safe school environments, and those who break the rules are suspended or expelled. But these policies must be carefully evaluated and changed. In laying down a strict rule, the effect of such a decision must be carefully studied. For students that come from a history of oppression or trauma, these exclusionary practices are not culturally sensitive or effective. A culturally competent approach to interaction with students is a necessity to fostering cooperation, engagement, and trust. When students believe the school understands their journey, they have room to succeed. Negative discipline methods imposing paternalistic and corrective principles rouse resistance and distrust from students. This distrust only further perpetuates the harmful patterns, leaving all members of the school community in its wake. It is well established that children learn from what we do, not from what we say. If we adopt an attitude of control and zero tolerance for adolescents, it does not help them to develop values of tolerance, differences, and diversity. How do they learn to understand and forgive others if we do not give them an experience of consideration for their own mistakes? Given the potentially oppressive personal experiences of minority students, any approaches that deny inclusivity demonstrate a significant lack of cultural consciousness and a hostile school environment.

As such, any barriers to effective student and teacher relationships must be examined. Of significant importance is how race unfolds for white social workers at urban schools with minority populations. Reflections on the context of race and how it may interfere with student relationships may produce discomfort. It is imperative that we, as school social workers, do not run from this discomfort, but wholeheartedly embrace it. It is not enough to simply acknowledge that white privilege and white fragility exist and function within the school setting. The revelation of this privilege is the key to dissolving the obstacles to engagement with minority students. Working with marginalized populations demands an examination of the roles of oppression and power within the community and in the context of individual issues. As white staff, we cannot ignore how our own unique intersectional experiences and histories interact with the experiences of minority students.

CLOSE READING QUESTIONS

1. Look at the footnotes that Kaliades provides that serve to connect Tara's circumstances with the disproportionate health outcomes of African-Americans and over-classification of African-American students. Why does Kaliades includes these footnotes in connection to Tara's case?

2. How does Kaliades account for Tara's impulsivity and low-frustration tolerance, and how are these behaviors connected to racial stressors?

3. Reread Kaliades's definitions of white privilege and white fragility. Which moments in the case study help Kaliades to recognize her own white privilege and white fragility? Bonus: use DiAngelo's article on white fragility as cited in Kaladies's references to further explore the concept and to think about how it has played a role in your life.

Prompts for Writing

1. Think about how the Social Work Code of Ethics relates to Kaliades's position on zero-tolerance discipline policies, her perpetuation of white privilege through "color-blindness," and/or the ways that "white supremacy," as Blay (2011) defines it in note 4 below, has informed social work practice in schools.
2. In this case study, Tara makes the connection that "acting white" is, in a sense, "acting right." In trying to educate a school staff about the complexity of this issue, what would you say? What do you think is the most productive way to address the school staff's frustration over Tara's behavior?
3. Kaliades shows that she tries to respond to Tara with empathy in order to establish an alliance with Tara. How is "empathy" and the therapeutic alliance complicated when the school social worker (and/or staff) and her client do not share the same racial classification?

Notes

1. Single parents are less able to support their children's schooling through supervision and monitoring in reference to both behavior and school work (Zill, 1996), thus sometimes resulting in lower expectations of their children's academic progress and accomplishments (Entwisle et al., 1998).
2. Black people have higher mortality rates and lower life expectancy than other demographic groups. Differences in the burden of cardiovascular diseases, including heart attack, diabetes, and stroke, are among the most important contributors to these differences (Wong et al., 2002).
3. In the context of race, African–American students are overrepresented in special education, particularly in the categories of intellectual disability (ID) and emotional disturbance (ED) (Skiba et al., 2008).
4. Blay (2011) defines "white supremacy" as "an historically based, institutionally perpetuated system of exploitation and oppression of continents, nations, and peoples classified as 'non-White' by continents, nations, and peoples who, by virtue of their (white) skin pigmentation and/or ancestral origin from Europe classify themselves as 'White' . . . this global power system is structured and maintained not for the purpose of legitimizing racial categories as much as it is for the purpose of maintaining and defending a system of wealth, power, and privilege" (p. 6).

References

Bergeron, B. (2008). Enacting a culturally responsive curriculum in a novice teacher's classroom: Encountering disequilibrium. *Urban Education*, 43(1), 4–28. DOI: 10.1177/0042085907309208.

Blay, Y. (2011). Skin bleaching and global white supremacy: By way of introduction. *The Journal of Pan African Studies*, 4(4), 4–46.

Darensbourg, A., Perez, E., and Blake, J. J. (2010). Overrepresentation of African American males in exclusionary discipline: The role of school-based mental health professionals in dismantling the school to prison pipeline. *Journal of African American Males In Education*, *1*(3), 196–211.

DiAngelo, R. (2011). White fragility. *International Journal of Critical Pedagogy*, *3*(3), 54–70.

Dupper, D., Theriot, M., and Craun, S. (2009). Reducing out-of-school suspensions: Practice guidelines for school social workers. *Children & Schools*, *31*(1), 6–14.

Entwisle, D. R., Alexander, K. L., and Olson, L. S. (1998). Family configuration. In D. R. Entwisle, K. L. Alexander, and L. S. Olson (Eds.), *Children, schools & inequality* (pp. 99–120). Boulder, CO: Westview Press.

Gibson, P., and Haight, W. (2013). Caregivers' moral narratives of their African American children's out-of-school suspensions: Implications for effective family-school collaborations. *Social Work*, *58*(3), 263–272. DOI: 10.1093/sw/swt017.

Gump, J. (2010). Reality matters: The shadow of trauma on African American subjectivity. *Psychoanalytic Psychology*, *27*(1), 42–54. DOI: 10.1037/a0018639.

Hughes, D., Rodriguez, J., Smith, E., Johnson, D., Stevenson, H., and Spicer, P. (2006). Parents' ethnic-racial socialization practices: A review of research and directions for future study. *Developmental Psychology*, *42*(5), 747–770.

Jensen, E. (2009). *Teaching with poverty in mind: What being poor does to kids' brains and what schools can do about it*. Alexandria, VA: ASCD.

Landsman, J., and Lewis, C. W. (2010). *White teachers, diverse classrooms: Creating inclusive schools, building on students' diversity, and providing true educational equity*. Sterling, VA: Stylus Pub.

Leary, J. D., and Robinson, R. (2005). *Post traumatic slave syndrome: America's legacy of enduring injury and healing*. Portland, OR: Joy DeGruy Publications.

Leonardo, Z. (2004). The color of supremacy: Beyond the discourse of white privilege. *Educational Philosophy and Theory*, *36*(2), 137–152.

Lewis, H. (1971). Shame and guilt in neurosis. *Psychoanalytic Review*, *58*(3), 419–438.

McIntosh, P. (2010). White privilege and male privilege. In E. F. Provenzo, Jr. (Ed.), *The teacher in American society: A critical anthology* (pp. 121–134). Thousand Oaks, CA: Sage Publications.

Morris, E. W. (2005). "Tuck in that shirt!" Race, class, gender, and discipline in an urban school. *Sociological Perspectives*, 1, 25. DOI: 10.1525/sop.2005.48.1.25.

Murphy, Y., Hunt, V., Zajicek, A. M., Norris, A. N., and Hamilton, L. (2009). *Incorporating intersectionality in social work practice, research, policy, and education*. Washington, DC: National Association of Social Workers.

Ogbu, J. U. (2004). Collective identity and the burden of "acting White" in Black history, community, and education. *Urban Review*, *36*(1), 1–35.

Richeson, J., and Nussbaum, R. (2003). The impact of multiculturalism versus color-blindness on racial bias. *Journal of Experimental and Social Psychology*, 40, 417–423.

Simmons-Reed, E. A., and Cartledge, G. (2014). School discipline disproportionality: Culturally competent interventions for African American males. *Interdisciplinary Journal of Teaching and Learning*, *4*(2), 95–109.

Skiba, R. (2008). Are zero tolerance policies effective in the schools? An evidentiary review and recommendations. *American Psychologist*, *63*(9), 852–862. DOI: 10.1037/0003-066X.63.9.852.

Skiba, R. J., Michael, R. S., Nardo, A. C., and Peterson, R. L. (2002). The color of discipline: Sources of racial and gender disproportionality in school punishment. *Urban Review*, *34*(4), 317–342.

Skiba, R. J., and Peterson, R. L. (2000). School discipline at a crossroads: From zero tolerance to early response. *Exceptional Children*, 66(3), 335–346.

Skiba, R. J., Simmons, A. B., Ritter, S., Gibb, A. C., Rausch, M. K., Cuadrado, J., and Choong-Geun, C. (2008). Achieving equity in special education: History, status, and current challenges. *Exceptional Children*, 74(3), 264–288.

Skinner, E. A., Kindermann, T. A., Connell, J. P., and Wellborn, J. G. (2009). Engagement and disaffection as organizational constructs in the dynamics of motivational development. In K. R. Wentzel and A. Wigfield (Eds.), *Handbook of motivation at school* (pp. 223–246). New York: Routledge.

Valois, R., MacDonald, J., Bretous, L., Fischer, M., and Drane, J. (2002). Risk factors and behaviors associated with adolescent violence and aggression. Proceedings of the 2nd Scientific Meeting of the American Academy of Health Behavior, March 24–27, Napa Valley, CA. *American Journal of Health Behavior*, 26(6), 454–464.

Wong, M., Shapiro, M., Boscardin, W., and Ettner, S. (2002). Contribution of major diseases to disparities in mortality. *New England Journal of Medicine*, 347(20), 1585–1592.

Zill, N. (1996). Parental schooling & children's health. *Public Health Reports* (1974), (1), 34.

9

MINDFULNESS GROUP WORK IN THE SCHOOL SETTING

Ralph Cuseglio

Pre-Reading Questions

1. What do you know about mindfulness? How do you imagine that mindfulness practice would be useful, specifically to adolescents in this era?
2. How might group work offer school social workers insight into a student's lived experience in ways that individual casework cannot?
3. What particular stressors exist for school social workers? What options for self-care might be most useful for both school social workers and their students?

I was the only social worker for a school population of 1,800 students in an urban community that sorely lacked social and mental health services. Students' presenting problems ran the gamut from basic needs deficits (lack of food, shelter, and medical care) to child abuse and neglect to mental health issues. With each passing year, my caseload for individual therapeutic counseling continued to grow, becoming more than I could manage alone. There were simply not enough hours in the school day to meet with each individual student in need of support. I was feeling burnt out; inevitably, exhaustion and compassion fatigue developed, and on occasion, their effects negatively impacted my work.

After several years—yes, *years*—of advocating for more support, the school district hired an additional social worker and approved my request to supervise Master's-level interns to better meet the students' socio-emotional needs. As for my part, I found ways to meet the high demand for services by capping the limit of student sessions based on severity of the presenting problem, history of mental health issues, and social support affiliation (i.e. participation in the school's peer program and/or gay/straight alliance). I also guided students toward membership in community programs and church groups. Yet, in spite of my efforts, the high and varied demands of the student population continued to feel overwhelming. I told myself that I could not continue to count the days until the next school break any longer. I needed a more immediate solution to help the students—and myself.

First and foremost, I knew self-care was in order. In contemplating various self-care options, I ultimately made a decision to pursue mindfulness meditation with results that seemed too good to be true. Over the course of several months, my stress level, mood, and relationship to myself and others improved in ways that seamlessly carried over into my professional life and work with students. Like any good social work researcher, I was initially skeptical of my subjective observations. "Placebo effect?" I wondered, until I recalled the notion that a social worker's subjective experience is a valuable therapeutic tool. Emotionally intelligent social workers pay great attention to their own feelings as well as those of their clients (Howe, 2008). My clinical training emphasized this, too: a social worker's attention to his own feelings serves as the barometer for what is relationally occurring in therapeutic treatment.

My understanding of mindfulness-based theory and its practice seemed to endorse a similar yet more global philosophy of presence and attunement to the experiences of self, others, and one's surroundings. With this in mind, I began to ponder how mindfulness-based practices could be beneficial to the adolescents whom I treat. I decided that by creating a mindfulness group in the school, I could not only provide an effective treatment option, but I could also meet with more than one student at a time, thus cutting down my individual caseload. In years past, I had conducted several groups based on data trends. I designed groups to address the following need trends: anger management, social skills, self-esteem issues, social anxiety, anxiety support, immigration and acculturation, and stress management. However, I often found that there was not enough time in the school year to address the wide variety of presenting problems that students demonstrated.

I believe that a group designed to educate students about mindfulness-based practices could have the greatest overall benefit because the challenges of adolescent development, compounded by the digital age, present a need for applicable means of emotion management and tools to help navigate the daily experiences of life with compassion. Research demonstrates that mindfulness practices have significant benefits to youths' self-regulation capacity, emotional and behavioral reactivity, and levels of psychological stress and anxiety (Bögels et al., 2008; Flook et al., 2010; Greenberg and Harris, 2011; Schonert-Reichl and Lawlor, 2010; Semple et al., 2005, 2010). This chapter is a case study of my first mindfulness group in a school setting, a measure that efficiently offered students valuable skills in a social context.

What Is Mindfulness?

Both "mindful" and "mindfulness" are terms that have become quite popular in recent years; however, their use often reveals a diluted misappropriation of these terms. Mindfulness is not about achieving an enlightened, euphoric state. Mindfulness is concerned with "paying attention in a particular way: on purpose, in the present moment, and nonjudgmentally" (Kabat-Zinn, 1994, p. 4). Mindfulness is "bringing one's complete attention to the present experience on a moment-to-moment basis" (Marlatt and Kristeller, 1999, p. 68). Based upon this seemingly basic notion, a mindful individual attempts to fully engage with his lived experience. Mindfulness is not gender specific, nor is it socially based; it crosses all socioeconomic and cultural barriers—important considerations in any diverse group environment (Tadlock-Marlo, 2011). Breathing exercises and techniques promoting awareness are compatible with a multiplicity of cultural traditions (Canda and Furman, 1999). When practiced correctly, these techniques, which originate in Buddhist spiritual efforts to mitigate suffering, can lead to long-lasting positive effects for the individual (Hanh, 1976). A core tenet of the practice is observation of all stimuli, without emotional attachment: a non-judgmental acceptance of internal experiences (i.e. thoughts, feelings, and perceptions) and external experiences (i.e. sights, sounds, smells, body sensations, and tastes). These internal and external experiences are not analyzed nor deemed right or wrong, normal or abnormal, true or false, good or bad, important or insignificant (Marlatt and Kristeller, 1999). They are merely to be observed.

In the West, mindfulness is a relatively new concept, one steadily growing since the 1990s, largely popularized by Jon Kabat-Zinn. Kabat-Zinn, a molecular biologist by trade and Zen practitioner, writes that he wanted to unite "dharma practice together with [his] work life into one unified whole, as an expression of right livelihood and in the service of something useful that felt very much needed in the world" (Kabat-Zinn, 2011, p. 286). As a result, he founded the Stress Reduction Clinic in 1979, while at the University of Massachusetts Medical School. Kabat-Zinn writes about the Mindfulness-Based Stress Reduction (MBSR) program practiced at the UMass Stress Reduction Clinic in the book *Full Catastrophe Living: Using the Wisdom of Your Body and Mind to Face Stress, Pain, and Illness* (1990) and how it is used to counteract stress, balance the body and mind, and facilitate well-being and healing. Kabat-Zinn, like many mindfulness teachers, promotes a secular version of mindfulness practice. Secular mindfulness practice is also an essential treatment component of several psychotherapeutic modalities. Marsha Linehan (1993), founder of Dialectical Behavior Therapy (DBT), writes that "The DBT tenets of observing, mindfulness, and avoidance of judgment are all derived from the study and practice of Zen meditations" (pp. 21–22). Mindfulness-Based Cognitive Therapy (MBCT) most often used in the treatment of depression and anxiety disorders uses traditional Cognitive Behavioral Therapy (CBT) strategies combined with mindfulness-based practices, while Acceptance and Commitment

Therapy (ACT) uses acceptance and mindfulness strategies in conjunction with commitment and value-based based interventions.

Mindfulness and Modern Adolescent Development

By its very nature, mindfulness offers a conscious and proactive response to distress and can enhance emotional regulation capacities. Exposure to mindfulness during adolescence is well-timed; Piaget defines adolescence as the Formal Operational Stage of Cognitive Development, which includes the capacity to think in abstract terms, as well as an enhanced capacity for self-knowledge, self-correction, and self-reflection (Inhelder and Piaget, 1958; Piaget, 1972). Mindfulness practices can help adolescents to feel empowered by recognizing, via experiential learning, that they possess the internal capacities for self-control and well-being. This recognition begins with an understanding that the self is separate from one's thinking, feeling states, and physical reactions. Through this realization, adolescents can be empowered to stop negative thought processes through the use of mindful breathing techniques, a pause whereby adolescents can first center their attention on the breath. The result is a distancing from distressing thoughts or emotions, which in turn can minimize maladaptive behavioral reactions and additional suffering to self and others. In short, adolescents learn that they possess the internal capacity for self-control over thoughts and feelings, rather than vice versa (Kostanski and Hassed, 2008). Mindfulness practices can help adolescents to recognize that external situations are often out of their control and that their energy is better spent accepting or "being with" circumstances rather than trying to change, solve, or avoid them.

Adolescence is a significant developmental period in the human lifespan, a period of rapid change physically, sexually, cognitively, psychologically, and socially. It is a "greenhouse" for the cultivation of identity, purpose, and the understanding of self and others (Roeser and Pinela, 2014). Key tasks in adolescent development include separation/individuation, which refers to a final separation from parents and the integration of a separate identity, the consolidation of a gender identity, and the adoption of a peer group that reflects one's own values and purposes. Adolescents straddle an imaginary line that separates childhood and adulthood, often with one foot firmly planted in the former and the other cautiously tapping, or in some cases, stomping on the latter. They are continuously seeking to understand who they are and their place in the world, and in doing so, they test boundaries and limits as they attempt to separate from their parents.

Adolescents can be highly self-conscious yet seemingly over-confident at the same time, a paradox that is only reinforced by the norms and pressures of modern society. At no time in history have adolescents faced the number of challenges that are posed in modern day. The digital age has changed the way they communicate, obtain information, and see themselves. They want to be at the center of it all, and often will talk of Fear of Missing Out (FOMO). Their lives are forever documented on social media, and self-esteem is measured in likes, followers, and virtual friends; at a time when experimentation is a normative right of passage, a catalogue of missteps and mistakes widely available in perpetuity for all to see. This heightens the potential for unmanageable anxiety and therefore their need for tools to manage such anxiety.

In this environment where the illusion of constant connection and gratification are the norm, many adolescents struggle with downtime, silence, or being un-occupied for even short periods of time. They are often over-stimulated by being constantly bombarded with information. As a result, adolescents may come to expect continuous stimulation by sources external to them. Most often, their phones serve this purpose. When feeling lonely, bored, and seeking distraction, adolescents will immediately turn to their phones, reinforcing a reliance on them and on being connected, especially during moments when the adolescent is seeking to avoid or cope with difficult emotions. As a result, they are not challenged to develop inner resources to deal with uncomfortable feelings of loneliness or to derive the benefits of solitude. Moreover, connectivity via the smartphone can also be a trigger for negative emotions. It is easier now than ever to feel bullied and ostracized by peers on social media. While once adolescents could have a respite from the judgmental eyes of peers, now they are in constant contact with the sometimes cruel words of peers. Their phones are with them twenty-four hours a day. Stretching far beyond the confines of school building walls, harassment can now take place anonymously on a grand scale through a medium that inhibits observation of the sensory cues that allow for victim empathy. The same omni-present technology that promotes connectivity and relationships has the potential to create deeply painful feelings that can be overwhelming to the developing adolescent.

Given the specific risk factors and age-related experiences in this stage of development, adolescents are prone to feelings of distress. The demands of managing school, peer pressure, sexual activity, romantic relationships, parental conflict, and individuation, all during the digital age can culminate to threaten adolescent well-being. Romeo (2010) posits that the intersection of stress and the developing adolescent brain can create a climate of dysfunctional emotional development. Thus, in order to meet the demands of this developmental stage, adolescents must have a high level of socio-emotional competence (Broderick and Jennings, 2012). Emotional regulation, the ability to positively manage one's emotions during stressful situations, is increasingly understood as the key to well-being and positive adjustment throughout the lifespan (Eisenberg et al., 2010). As MacPherson et al. (2010) point out, adolescents that struggle to manage difficult emotions are more prone to engage in harmful risk-taking behavior than those with greater capacity for distress tolerance. Further, difficulties in emotional regulation capacities are a feature of many adolescent mental health problems, including depression, anxiety, conduct problems, deliberate self-injury, and substance abuse (Campos et al., 2004). Offering adolescents an antidote to stress is crucial, and doing so in a school environment is altogether possible.

Group Work

School social workers are charged with addressing the developmental and socio-emotional needs of students as well as helping foster students' academic success (Johnson and Johnson, 2005; Littrell and Peterson, 2001; Steen and Kaffenberger, 2006; Webb et al., 2005). Demands placed on social workers include: individual and supportive counseling, crisis management, classroom meetings and guidance, parent, teacher, and administrative consultations, student observation and assessment, case management, an abundance of required paperwork and documentation, and partnering with and referring to outside supportive services (Bemak et al., 2005). This combined with high student to social worker ratios can make it exceedingly difficult to meet the expectations placed upon them. Thus, individually meeting with students may not be the most effective or economical use of time and resources (Akos et al., 2007; Sayder, 2008). Research has demonstrated that group work is an effective intervention in schools (Akos et al., 2004; Johnson and Johnson, 2005; Shechtman, 2002) and serves as a way to better meet the often varied needs of students. Group work, therefore, must be a vital part of any school social worker's repertoire, especially when working in a high school.

Shechtman et al. (1997) posit that there are several advantages to group work with adolescents that include: a shared space in which to relate to one another, an emphasis on generalizing behaviors practiced in the group to real-life situations, the provision of multiple perspectives and feedback that serves to increase members' self-esteem, and the positive self-regard that occurs in response to helping peers. Group work offers specific insight, absent within the context of individual treatment, that can only emerge from peer-based social interaction (Bemak et al., 2005). It also provides for the experience of universality: that students share circumstances and challenges in common with peers (Fleming, 1999; Steen et al., 2007). School group work also offers students the opportunity to shift and shape their perspectives through peer interaction, discussion, and negotiation (Akos et al., 2007; Van Velsor, 2004). Kulic et al. (2004) contend that "The group format is a logical choice . . . given the amount of time children and adolescents spend in groups with their peers, both in and out of the classroom," and it "provides the context within which children and adolescents will receive preventative interventions and will practice and utilize them in their 'real lives'" (p. 139).

In the development of any group, it is important to first assess the normative and specific needs of the population being served. Normative needs are universal to the population and include the developmental tasks of the group members, where specific needs reflect problems particular to individuals (e.g. anger management, grief, substance abuse, child abuse, illness, etc.) (Malekoff, 2004).

I chose to form a psychoeducational/skills group, which promotes coping strategies, problem-solving, and healthy decision-making in an effort to prevent problems (Gerrity and DeLucia-Waack, 2007). The group objective was to enhance members' intrapersonal and interpersonal strengths through mindfulness, instead of targeting student deficits or problems.

As I established my group, school faculty and staff were contacted via e-mail and asked to recommend students whom they believed could benefit from or might be interested in a mindfulness group. The e-mail included a general description of mindfulness to educate them, which they were encouraged to share with students, as well as information regarding where they could access additional information on mindfulness. In the days leading up to a general information meeting about the group, I spread the word through daily morning announcements, fliers that were hung around the school, and promotional advertisements featured on hallway video screens. Only ten students attended the general information meeting, where I gave a fifteen-minute presentation that provided information about the frequency, duration, and location of the group, and also some background on mindfulness and its benefits. When informally polled, two students were recommended by teachers, four attended in response to the morning announcements, one saw a hallway flier, one came to support a friend, and two students attended because I had personally pitched the group during their individual counseling sessions. Six students, 14–19 in age and split evenly by gender, would come to attend the group's first official meeting and would remain for its entirety.

The group was conducted for a total of eight weeks, with one-hour weekly meetings. Meetings followed the same format, beginning with a sitting meditation, followed by group discussion of the previous week's exercises. A new mindfulness skill was then introduced and practiced, followed by a brief discussion to clarify skill application and to answer practice-related questions. Finally, I explained practice assignments. Each session closed with a five-minute sitting meditation. The mindfulness skills taught are listed and described in Table 9.1.

Malekoff (2004) writes that a formal curriculum should not be so rigidly followed that opportunities for interaction and spontaneity are missed. Flexibility is key when facilitating group work with adolescents. Providing members with opportunities for interaction can facilitate group cohesion. All group members must be involved in discussion and activities in order for members to feel accepted, open, and honest in the group setting. The social worker is responsible for making this happen. Facilitating adolescent groups offers a unique challenge because the social worker must simultaneously balance the role of knowledgeable leader and group member. Thus, social workers must assume a position of uncertainty and fluidity, with attention to moments when it would be more useful to turn control over to group members rather than to demonstrate authority (Malekoff, 2004). This intuition about when to back off conveys respect for members' strengths and their ability to make valuable contributions to the group.

TABLE 9.1 Mindfulness Skills

Skill	Description	Skill Introduction
Sitting Meditation	A guided practice of mindful awareness for 5–20-minute intervals aimed at calming both the body and mind through use of the following: sensations of breathing, relaxation of body parts, acceptance of unpleasant feelings, attention to sounds in the environment.	Week 1, Ongoing
Deep Listening	Members are taught, then invited to fully listen to what is being expressed by others without distraction, judgment, or the need to offer advice and comment.	Week 3
Mindful Moments	Teaches members to pause and fully focus on their experience in the present moment. During each group session, the social worker invited members to pause intermittently at the sound of a bell. The ringing of the school bell was also identified as an opportunity to pause all activity and take a mindful breath.	Week 2
Group Discussion	Discussions allow members to ask questions about the application of mindfulness practices and to share their experiences utilizing mindfulness-based strategies in daily life. This is also a time to receive support and encouragement from the social worker and other members of the group.	Ongoing
Mindful Eating	A guided practice aimed at being attentive to the sensory perceptions and feelings involved in eating.	Week 5
Walking Meditation	A guided practice that teaches members how to focus their attention on the movement and sensations of their bodies while walking or engaging in physical activity.	Week 6
Loving-Kindness and Compassion Meditation(s)	A guided practice that focuses on feelings of positivity (i.e. care, concern, and love) for oneself and others. Attention is given to opening the heart and mind to allow for deeper feelings of kindness to emerge and while working to gradually let go of feelings of negativity, regret, and resentment.	Week 4
Practice Assignments	At the conclusion of each session, members were asked to practice the mindfulness skill(s) learned during that session in their daily lives. Their practice experiences were reviewed during the following week's Group Discussion.	Ongoing

The Group in Session

The group concludes a ten-minute breathing meditation at the start of the meeting, and I ask about positive or negative experiences over the past week to check in.

LUCY: Something that happened this week at home . . . and I used my breath and it worked!

I am curious about what Lucy is going to say. I take a deep breath. The group members begin to direct their attention toward Lucy.

LYNETTE: This is our chance to use deep listening skills. [She laughs.]

I am happy that Lynette made this joke. It lightens the mood. Moreover, it's clear that she understands the concept of deep listening and when to utilize it. But it also gives me an opportunity to compliment Lynette and briefly reinforce the skill.

ME: You're absolutely right, Lynette! Well done. This is a great opportunity to practice. What can we remember about deep listening?
DEV: It's about listening with your heart. You know . . . to try and understand the other person without judging them, being completely about 'em. [A long pause.] And not talking or giving advice.
LUCY: Well, I was at home. It was like the middle of the day on Sunday, and I wanted to go hangout with my friends in the park, and my mom is like, "Did you do your chores?" I was like, "Yeah. Can I go?" She goes, "You have school tomorrow," which makes no sense because it is in the middle of the day. I did my homework. Then she starts yelling at me, "No. Because then I have to let your brother out, too. I don't want him on the streets." I wanted to be like, "Fuck you, bitch! That's not my problem," and just walk out. I was so mad. Yo, I've done that so many times when she acts like that.

[The school bell rings. The group goes quiet. I notice a few students have closed their eyes. I take a deep breath.]

Mindfulness teaches that practice can be done at longer intervals while sitting or lying down, but can also be done at different times throughout the day as a way to take a momentary pause, suspend thinking, check in with our bodies, and remind ourselves that we are alive. The sound of a bell is often employed as a reminder to practitioners to do this. This skill termed "Mindful Moments" was taught to members during Week 2.

Dev breaks the silence.

DEV: So what'd you do?
LUCY: I did that [referring to the mindful break at the sound of the school bell]. I remembered what you said [looking at me]. When you're too angry walk away and breathe deep. I took a really deep breath and didn't say anything.

Then, I left the kitchen and went to my room. But yo, I was still sooo mad! I was like walking back and forth in my room. I kept picturing my mom's face yelling at me. Then, I sat on my bed for like 5 minutes with my eyes closed and just kept paying attention to my breathing. I kept having thoughts about it, but I just kept trying to pay attention to my stomach moving. I felt better after a while.

ME: That sounds really frustrating. You did an amazing job of calming yourself down though. You were able to "just be" with this unpleasant feeling.

LUCY: Yeah. I still think my mom was being dumb. But, walking out or cursing at her never makes me feel better. I always feel guilty or wind up crying about it.

JORGE: Aw, hell! I hate when my moms does that shit.

ME: You can relate, Jorge, huh? [Jorge slouches in his chair, spreading his legs wide.] Parents can cause us to feel frustrated sometimes. Mine do, too. What about the rest of the group? [I scan the circle and see some heads nodding.] Anything else about the experience you want to share, Lucy?

LUCY: [Pauses.] I feel like it worked. I mean paying attention to my breathing helped. That's the first time I really did that.

DEV: Can't believe you didn't put your moms on blast, yo! [Sighs.]

LUCY: I do all the time. I started to think about it though. She's stressed, worried about my brother. She's raising us alone. I just know it's gotta be hard on her.

I reflect on whether Lucy realizes in that she responded compassionately to both her herself and mother in the moment. I decide to explore this further for Lucy and the overall benefit of the group.

ME: Can I ask you a question Lucy? You seem to be talking about having understanding for your mom. Like you are trying to understand that she's struggling in her own way. Putting yourself in her shoes. I'm wondering where that came from?

LUCY: I have no idea. [Long pause.] I think just not going back at her so quick. If I just blacked out on her it would have just made it worse. Taking a breath and meditating just gave me time to chill. I guess I thought about the situation and my mom later. I wasn't as mad. Besides, I talked to my friend the next day . . . I didn't miss anything.

ME: [I smile.] It sounds to me like you helped yourself and your mom suffer a little less. You spared each other more anger and sadness. I'm glad you brought that in. Thanks for sharing that with the group, Lucy.

Our minds spend much of the time generating thoughts about past and future events, in spite of the fact that the past has already occurred and the future has yet to begin. In Lucy's case, we read that her thoughts continue to return to the conflict with her mother. Adversely perceived events can trigger a cascade of negative thoughts as well as rumination, a continuous recalling of a stressful event with co-occurring feelings of negativity that exacerbate negative mood states (Farb et al., 2012). In situations like these, the mindfulness practice of observing the breath can be particularly helpful. Focus on the breath helps to quiet negative thoughts, regulate painful emotions, and activate the parasympathetic nervous system, which relaxes the body. We can see how this transpires in Lucy's situation and how she utilizes her breath to self soothe. She turns her attention to the breath as a way to bring her cognition to her body in the present moment. Although Lucy's attention repeatedly drifts off the breath, she continues to return her attention to it. Mindfulness practice emphasizes taking notice of when this occurs and teaches the meditator to gently and non-judgmentally return the focus to the breath. Much like exercising the body, attention to the breath becomes strengthened with regular practice. It is worth noting that Lucy's experience of mindful breathing comes during the fourth session. This was approximately one month since the group's first meeting, when mindful breathing was introduced, and students were asked to practice mindful breathing meditation for a minimum of five minutes daily.

In family settings, mindfulness is often used to help members build understanding and appreciation for others, develop a sense of calmness before reacting to events, and to enhance personal self-awareness (Christensen et al., 2004; Gehart and Pare, 2008). The fact that Lucy shares her experience demonstrates an integration of mindful breathing outside a meditative exercise during an interpersonal family conflict in which she became angry. Considering the disclosure of similar experiences prior to this one, I imagine that had she not used this skill, it is likely the outcome would have been significantly different. By focusing on her breath, Lucy is able to have a different experience during and immediately following a conflict with her mother. Attention to breath initially allowed Lucy to pause and refrain from an impulsive acting out of her anger. According to Broderick and Jennings (2012), mindfulness-based skills are particularly suited to address the tendency to respond in automatic, unconscious ways to activating stimuli. The practice of mindful breathing can support a non-reactive stance toward one's impulses. In Lucy's case, the application of a mindful break was able to "increase the gap between impulse and action" (Boyce, 2005, p. 40), and it allowed for "problem solving and behavior under more conscious and reflective regulation" (Broderick and Jennings, 2012, p. 116), which was demonstrated by Lucy's ability to exit a potentially aggressive confrontation with her mother. Moreover, through the regular practice of sitting meditation over a four-week span, Lucy was able to employ this skill, *in vivo*, immediately following the conflict with her mother. This helped her to emotionally regulate, assume a more accepting stance of her situation, and later reflect empathically on her mother's experience.

Another example: the following dialogue took place during the discussion portion of the group's sixth meeting. A 16-year-old male named Jorge shared his experience of utilizing mindful breathing following an argument with his girlfriend.

JORGE: Yo, Doctor C. I think I want to say something.

ME: What's on your mind, man?

There is a long pause as I look at Jorge. His head turns up to the left, toward the ceiling. But there is a vulnerability in his face that I have not seen before. I am really curious to hear what he has to say.

JORGE: Nah, nah . . . forget it.

LYNETTE: [Frustrated.] You always do that, bro.

ME: That's ok, Jorge. I think the group would like to hear what's on your mind. But, we can come back to you if you change your mind. Anyone else like to share an experience they had this week that relates to mindfulness or our group?

JORGE: Aight! [A pause.] So, I wanted to smoke [marijuana] this weekend, but didn't.

Jorge had previously revealed to the group that marijuana was a coping strategy he used to manage difficult emotions.

ME: Why did you want to smoke?

JORGE: I was *mad* sad on Sunday. Me and my girl got into a huge fight. I said some dumb shit about her old boyfriend, and she stopped texting me.

LUCY: Yo, you broke up?

JORGE: Nah! We chill now. But, I just got real sad. I started to think about what I said. Thinking like, I'm really messed up for saying that shit. Then, I got like all dark and shit. I started thinkin' 'bout my pops. Shit he's going through. I just couldn't stop thinking.

I am surprised by Jorge's vulnerability. I frown and look directly at Jorge, who puts his elbows on the desk, cupping his head in his hands.

JORGE: I was about to hit up my cuz. See if he'd hook me up. Yo, I tried, too, but he never hit me back. So, I was like, "What I'm gonna do?" I texted my boy. He was like, "Yo, what's good? I'm at work." I just didn't respond. I decided just to sleep.

Silence for a few seconds.

DEV: I do that shit sometimes, too.

ME: Sounds like you were really hurting, Jorge.

JORGE: Yeah. But this helped.

I was surprised by his response. I hadn't heard Jorge say anything that pertained specifically to mindfulness. It seemed to me that his intention was to be heard and supported in a space that felt safe.

ME: What do you mean? How so?

JORGE: When I laid down, I started to pay attention to my breath. You know . . . my stomach goin' up and down. It was hard at first. Just kept thinking about shit. But, I just kept doing it [observing his breath]. I didn't even close my eyes. I kept staring down at it. Not even sure how long it was. I was way more chill by the time my cuz hit me back. But, I didn't even want to smoke anymore. I was like, "Yo, I'm good."

ME: It sounds like whatever you were feeling eventually calmed down. Like it wasn't as intense . . . the feelings weren't as strong?

JORGE: Nothing changed though. Just the way I felt. That's the weird shit! It was like I didn't care. But, my girl was still throwin' shade, my pops was still sick, and I'm failing Mr. Rufti's class. But I was like there is nothing I can do about that right now.

ME: Jorge, I think you did care. I can see that you care now, too. It sounds to me like you by using your breath, your thoughts and feelings began to feel less out of your control.

CINDY: [Giggling.] You were in the present moment.

ME: Cindy's right. Your frame of mind changed, Jorge. The way you felt did too. That changed. It doesn't mean that you don't care, but your breath helped you control your emotions. It put you in back charge.

LUCY: It's like what you said, Doctor C. Thoughts are like clouds. They move. Everything is always changing.

ME: Exactly. Everything we feel and think is impermanent. Maybe that's why you didn't feel like you needed to smoke anymore. Your breath anchored you through an emotional storm.

DEV: Yo, that's deep.

ME: [I laugh.] It is. But I didn't make all this stuff up. I am passing on to you what I've learned and what's been helpful to me.

I look at Jorge for a few seconds.

JORGE: What, Doctor C? Why you keep lookin' at me? [Grinning.]

ME: I just want to thank you for talking about your experience. I know it is not easy sometimes . . . not just for you, but everybody. It takes a lot of courage. But, I think the group benefited from what you shared.

DEV: Yo, Gee! [referring to Jorge] I'm be trying that shit next time I want to puff.

ME: [I smile.] I would love that, Dev. But, see that Jorge? You already got Dev thinking about breathing instead of smoking weed.

In reflecting upon Jorge's experience, there are several points worth mentioning, beginning with Jorge's cognition to employ mindful breathing during a stressful life event. Jorge's mind was able to generate mindful breathing as a possible coping option in response to a life stressor. By observing his breath Jorge repeatedly brought himself back in touch with the present moment. Like all of us, Jorge's mind wandered, got lost in thought, and ultimately took his attention away from the here and now. His breath, however, served as an "anchor" or focal point during a distressing emotional experience. In this case, Jorge watched his abdomen rise and fall with each inhalation and exhalation. This is easier said than done, as the meditator's thoughts will drift off the breath. Jorge states, "It was hard at first. Just kept thinking about shit. But, I just kept doing it [observing his breath]." Mindfulness practice emphasizes taking notice when the attention moves off the breath and then to gently and non-judgmentally return one's focus to it. Much like exercising the body, attention to the breath becomes strengthened with regular practice. Jorge's ability to do this demonstrated that he had acquired the knowledge vis-à-vis his engagement in the group and was able to retrieve said knowledge when necessary. Mindful breathing may not have been Jorge's first coping option, but the fact that it was a viable option at all suggested that his membership in the group was having *in vivo* positive consequences. This alone was an indicator of the group's success. Not only did Jorge have the thought that mindful breathing is an option available to him, he chose to utilize the technique, thus indicating that Jorge believed or at least considered mindful breathing to be a potentially effective strategy in the management of his anxiety.

Despite being in an early stage of mindfulness-based practice, Jorge experienced a positive outcome through his use of mindful breathing. In his words, "I was way more chill by the time my cuz hit me back. But, I didn't even want to smoke anymore." I would surmise, based on Jorge's experience, that he would be likely to use mindful breathing in future situations of distress based upon the positive outcome in this particular situation. This, however, would be contingent upon his continued mindful breathing practice during periods of emotional stability when not under duress.

Mindfulness-based strategies, such as those I taught during the group, have the potential to help members to cope with daily stressors in a manner that decreases emotional reactivity and promotes overall well-being. Once an individual is exposed to mindfulness and has begun to integrate the knowledge and skills he acquired, mindfulness-based skills then become a potential coping strategy for future situations of stress. The likelihood of employing a strategy is, in part, contingent upon its efficacy for producing a desired outcome in the past. Coping strategies can take many forms and can be healthy or maladaptive (i.e. they serve to maintain a problematic response. That is, they ultimately interfere with the person's ability to address the problem and may in some cases exacerbate it). For Jorge, marijuana was a maladaptive coping strategy that when previously used, produced a desired effect (i.e. decreased emotional reactivity to a stressor in the past). Jorge had learned and erroneously believed that marijuana was an effective way to cope with stressful events. Without the availability of marijuana, Jorge opted for a mindfulness skill that he had learned during group. By utilizing mindful breathing, he experienced a beneficial outcome, becoming less emotionally reactive to the conflict he experienced with his girlfriend. Mindful breathing thus offered an alternative to getting high and thereby increased his repertoire of healthier options for dealing with stress. Ideally, mindfulness-based strategies become a "go to" coping mechanism that adolescents can utilize to manage difficult, stressful events.

Discussing Compassion in Group

Self-compassion is a proactive, mindfulness-based coping strategy, where action is specifically taken in moments of suffering and where the intention is to self soothe and provide relief. According to Tadlock-Marlo (2011), "Having self-compassion and self-acceptance during the unfolding awareness of reactions is a critical element in mindfulness practice that promotes safety in discovering and understanding self" (p. 223). In a meta-analysis of fourteen self-compassion studies, MacBeth and Gumley (2012) find a negative association between psychopathology (i.e. anxiety, depression, and stress) and self-compassion in healthy adults. Bluth and Blanton (2014) posit, "Mindfulness and self-compassion may function as mediators with emotional well-being" (p. 1307) and engage in a process that can culminate in increased emotional stability in adolescents. Long term, this positively impacts self-perception, efficacy, and promotes increased satisfaction with life.

Mindfulness practice encourages the expansion of compassion beyond the self. Often referred to as "loving kindness," thoughts of warmth, empathy, and understanding are reflected on and wished for others during meditative practice. Roeser and Pinela (2014) describe loving kindness as "characterized by visualization (of self and others) and then the cultivation and extension of feelings of love, kindness, and forgiveness—first toward oneself, and then progressively 'outward' toward a good friend, a neutral person, a difficult person, all four equally, and eventually everyone everywhere" (p. 16). Continued loving kindness practice has been associated with greater emotional awareness, emotion regulation, empathy, and feelings of self-kindness and social-connectedness (Hutcherson et al., 2008).

Following a ten-minute breathing meditation during the group's fourth meeting, I introduce the skill of Loving-Kindness and Compassion Meditation(s).

ME: Today, I want to spend a little bit of time talking about compassion. It closely relates to what we've been talking about here. So, let's . . .
WILLIAM: [Interrupting.] You mean like taking care of people?
LYNETTE: [Sigh.] Yo, just let him finish, bro!
ME: It's ok, Lynette. I was hoping to hear the group's thoughts on what you think it means to be compassionate anyway.

My eyes scan the circle for a response.

DEV: It's like being nice to people.
LUCY: [Uncertain.] Um, treating people the way you want to be treated?
ME: Great! What about you, Jorge? Any ideas?

JORGE: I thought it was like the way you act when your wit' your girl. Yo, like the way boyfriends and girlfriends be actin' when they all close and extra nice.

LYNETTE: [Laughing.] That's passion.

The other members of the group start to laugh as Jorge raises his hands up off the armrests of his chair.

JORGE: [Indignantly.] Damn! I don't even know why I say shit.

ME: [Firmly. Voice slightly raised.] Hold up! Hold up! Let's stop for a moment.

The group begins to quiet down.

ME: Let's take a pause to reset. Let's take a few deep, belly breaths to bring us back to the present moment.

The group members begin to adjust themselves into an upright position in their seats as they look around at one another. Slowly group members are beginning to close their eyes. I guide them through their breathing—in, out, in, out—and bring them back together.

ME: We were discussing compassion. I think what Jorge was saying makes a lot sense. It sounds to me like he is talking about love and kindness. That's the right idea. Treating people with love and kindness.

JORGE: [Righteously.] See, told you!

ME: You did, Jorge. There is even a word for it called meta. It actually means loving-kindness. There is even a meta-meditation. But let me ask, do you think it's possible to practice loving-kindness with other people?

LUCY: Don't we do that all the time?

WILLIAM: Yeah, what's the big deal? I don't get it.

ME: Well, Lucy, to answer your question. Yes and no. It may feel easy to practice loving-kindness toward our family and friends sometimes, and our pets . . . like your dog or cat. Pets are especially easy because they usually love us no matter what. Even when they misbehave it's not really on purpose. They're animals. But when it comes to people, it can be a lot more complicated. Does this make sense?

WILLIAM: Yo, Dr. C. Are you saying like love your enemy?

At this point, I considered the value of interjecting my own personal experience. I thought that it might serve as a useful example, that I could serve as an object with which group members could identify as they attempted to integrate the idea of loving-kindness, and that my disclosure could strengthen members' trust in me and encourage deeper self-disclosure on their part. At the same time, I was aware that I was not an equal member of the group and did not want to risk blurring the boundaries or confusing students. Moreover, I did not wish to take over the discussion but rather to encourage communication among group members. In this instance, I believed that sharing a story had the potential not only to educate but to strengthen group cohesion.

ME: That's interesting, William. I never thought about it quite like that, but I guess I am. Ok, I'm going to give you a real example from my life. There is a person who I see from time to time, a friend of a friend, that whenever I'm around them they're usually pretty rude to everybody. I'm not exactly sure why. So, I really don't like being around them much. But, when I am around them I *try* to show them loving-kindness.

LYNETTE: What do you do?

DEV: Why do you even care? Fuuu. [Stops himself. Pauses.] F' him.

I look at Dev and take a deep breath while making a half smile.

ME: A few of reasons. Being rude back isn't going to make me feel good. Second, that person is suffering in some way. When people are hurtful to others, they're suffering. Something causes them to act that way. They don't feel good about themselves in that moment or maybe even in their lives.

LUCY: But then how do you stop them from hurting you?

ME: Good question . . . [Pause.] Part of it starts with recognizing it's not personal. If you can remember to do that, it helps. It's not an easy thing to remember to do all the time though. By doing this though, it helps you not to react quickly to them. That'll only add to your own stress and anger. So, you're making a choice that's actually better for you. [Pause.] So, it's keeping in mind that the person is in pain and in need of help. It's exactly why they need our compassion.

WILLIAM: That makes mad sense, but I feel like people never do that.

LYNETTE: I always feel like crap after I get into a fight. How I acted, what I say.

JORGE: I think my dad does that shit too, yo. He be coming home from work all pissed off and tired and shit. He be yellin' about dumb stuff. But, he ain't got it easy. He had a tough life.

ME: I hear you, William. It's not easy to do. First, it takes understanding of what we're talking about. Well, actually first it takes being exposed to the information. Then, remembering to practice. Compassion takes practice. Being mindful of doing it, especially when it's hard. And you won't be good at it all the time, because we're human.

DEV: [In a deep voice.] Dee Cee, Geettin' Deeeep!

LUCY: So, wait. If we're all angry or sad and we're tryin' not to take it out on other people, do we just stay shut?

ME: I think that's a great question. What does everyone think?

LYNETTE: Hell no! I can't just stay shut. I have to do something instead of being all grumpy.

ME: There are lots of things you can do. Some healthy, some not so much. But one thing that can help is not fighting the bad feeling.

WILLIAM: Let me guess, we should breathe with it.

ME: Ding! Ding! Ding! That's right. But there's another part. Showing yourself some compassion. Showing yourself some love. We humans are pretty good at beating ourselves up. Generally not so great at being compassionate with ourselves.

DEV: Aight. But, when you love yourself isn't that being conceited?

ME: Love of self can be a good thing too, sometimes. Especially when we are suffering.

WILLIAM: Maybe tell them it's not their fault or it won't feel that way forever.

JORGE: I be like, breathe, Gee!

Laughs from the group.

ME: Nice, Jorge! [I giggle.] But, all good answers. Now ask yourself, "Why wouldn't you do the same for yourself?"

The group members inquisitively look at each other and me.

LUCY: I've never thought that before.

JORGE: Aight. So, I'm failing Mr. Rufti's class. I should just be cool wit' it? Yo, be like, just chill? Cause then, how am I gonna do better?

ME: Um, I'm not sure I'm understanding.

JORGE: Aight, so my mom's be like. "You ain't gonna get nowhere. How you gonna get into college? You ain't trying." All this shit. But, I be saying the same shit sometimes.

ME: Gotcha!

LYNETTE: When I be messin' up, I be doin' the same thing.

DEV: Yuuuppp!

ME: So we're feelin' this as a group. None of us are alone in this.

LYNETTE: I be thinking some mean stuff sometimes.

ME: Can you share any of it?

LYNETTE: [Scrunching her face up and shaking her head.]

ME: That's ok. Maybe I can just give an example. Let's assume you fail a test or you forget to wish your mom a happy birthday. First things I thought of. Anyways, you could have thoughts like, "I'm stupid," "I'm never gonna pass this class" or "I'm a horrible son or daughter" or "She'll never forgive me." But, this only makes things worse. We already feel pain and then our mind takes over with thoughts that can make us feel even worse. [I glance at the clock.] We still have some time. You want to try a loving-kindness meditation?

The discussion that took place during this meeting was one of the most personally gratifying experiences of the entire group. In terms of group dynamics, the group felt cohesive and bonded to one another. Group members were helping to maintain equilibrium by setting boundaries for one another, but also by validating and joining in each other's experiences. This took pressure off me, as group facilitator, to maintain order. Instead, I was able to focus my attention on educating its members, understanding their integration of information, clarifying concepts, and processing their personal experiences.

Tadlock-Marlo (2011) suggests that students can use mindfulness-based techniques to build self-acceptance and an understanding of others' situations. Although, I believe the intimacy of a small group and processing of content for which this allowed was pivotal in its interconnection, the practice of mindfulness-based techniques cannot be underestimated. By engaging in mindfulness, members are learning to be present with their full range of feelings. By experiencing thoughts, feelings, physiological responses, and recognizing characterological aspects of the self in a non-attached and non-judgmental manner, adolescents can become more accepting of themselves and are less prone to self-imposed suffering. The idea is that they can begin to see themselves as more integrated and varied in aspects of self and behavior, capable of change, and not merely the totality of their experiences. Starting with the self, a position of nonattachment and understanding can be gradually transmuted to empathize with another person or accept unfavorable circumstances. As with other mindfulness-based strategies, however, in order to utilize these practices *in vivo*, repeated formal meditation is necessary. Roeser and Pinela (2014) write of loving-kindness meditation that it can "cultivate or augment a number of skills and dispositions including . . . other-oriented dispositions—kindness, empathy, compassion, altruism, forgiveness, generosity," inclusivity, and social-cognitive skills, like perspective-taking (p. 17). Although members of the group had yet to engage in the practice of loving-kindness meditation, they were able to relate their own experiences and that of those close to them to the concept of compassion. These are concepts and skills related to the developmental tasks in the area of adolescent socio-emotional identity, and they can further support prosocial behavior later in adulthood.

As school populations continue to diversify, the understanding of one's self and others, and the shared experience of humanity, in both emotion and behavior are essential to inclusivity and harmony within schools. Adolescents who are more self-aware, have increased emotional regulation capacities, and are capable of perspective-taking are in a unique position to affect change within their school climate. By engaging in mindfulness-based practices in their daily life, adolescents can share mindfully informed perspectives and model compassionate behavior in the classroom and during peer interaction. By engaging in mindfully informed behaviors, adolescents can help to mediate conflict, and safeguard themselves and others from harassment, bullying, and intimidation. Ultimately, this can have far-reaching positive consequences within high schools, with the promise of encouraging peaceful resolution to conflict, thereby decreasing the potential for aggression and school violence.

Closing Thoughts

This group was not created with the intention of producing data that measures outcomes, and there was not a formal measurement tool that assessed whether the group was successful in meeting its objectives to educate students on the concept of mindfulness and its practices, and to have members apply what they learned in their daily lives. Various members did, however, provide positive feedback throughout the duration of the group that points to its benefit and overall effectiveness. I routinely offered opportunities for verbal feedback by asking members about their experiences in group and its content because ongoing assessment is important. The school setting permits opportunities during the occasional cafeteria or hallway run-in, a school event, and an impromptu office drop-in, but the most formal attempt to elicit feedback was during a member's exit interview. Overall, feedback was positive with regard to the group process and having been exposed to mindfulness and its various practices, but members openly shared challenges with daily application of mindfulness techniques, preference for some over others, and the struggle to practice mindfulness on a regular basis. These challenges were not a surprise to me. I have heard similar experiences from longtime mindfulness practitioners and teachers of mindfulness practice, and can relate to these experiences myself.

A social work researcher might argue that because there was not a measurement tool used to assess outcomes and objectives, it is not possible to prove group benefit or effectiveness for its members—which may be true. However, I counter that an individual's phenomenological experience and human connection does not easily lend to quantification via measurement tools and statistical analysis. Throughout the group process, there was an abundance of observational data and feedback from members that pointed to the group being beneficial to its members. To further my point, take a moment to reflect on the following question: how is treatment effectiveness most often measured in clinical social work treatment? In each session and over the course of treatment, it is measured by either the client's or social worker's subjective experience of the treatment and each other. Treatment benefit is purely based on individual perception. I would pose that this is the norm in psychotherapeutic treatment and even further, the gold standard in assessing effectiveness in clinical social work treatment. The effectiveness and benefit are defined by perceptual experience, cognitions, and emotions in relation to an object (i.e. the treatment, the social worker) and the self. In spite of a growing pressure to quantify treatment outcomes in social work, an individual's description of their experience and the social worker's presence and attunement to such is the best tool available to us to gauge outcomes in work with clients.

I recognize, however, that conducting an evaluation for mindfulness group work in high school can yield valuable information. This can be done in a multitude of ways, and a measurement tool to collect data can be specifically designed to measure the specific function of a group. In running a similar group in the future, I would likely collect pre-group and post-group data regarding members' presenting problems and their understanding of mindfulness concepts and practice. I would also consider gathering data through members' self report on adherence to daily mindfulness practice. Lastly, I would plan for follow-up data collection at three months, six months, and one full year following the conclusion of the group to assess for lasting benefits and changes as a result of continued mindfulness practice or lack thereof, as I hypothesize that group members who did not regularly engage in mindfulness-based practices experienced less socio-emotional benefit over time.

Based upon the abundance of scientific research that supports the benefits of mindfulness for adults, my personal experience with mindfulness practices, and my knowledge working with teens in a high school setting, I hypothesized that mindfulness-based practices could be used to address the developmental and socio-emotional needs of adolescents. I believe my experiences of conducting such a group demonstrates the potential benefit and impact of a mindfulness-based practice group in other high school settings and as an effective treatment intervention for school social workers. As my research demonstrates, students evidenced an ability to apply mindfulness-based practices in their daily lives in the face of difficult situations and as a result make healthier and more compassionate choices for themselves and those around them. However, continued research measuring the effectiveness of mindfulness-based practice groups in high schools is necessary to further support my assertion and to explore the various other ways that mindfulness-based practices can be of benefit to adolescents.

CLOSE READING QUESTIONS

1. What are some of the benefits that members in Cuseglio's group experience as a result of being in a group? What significant aspects of group dynamics can you identify in the group process? Quote snippets of dialogue in your answer.

2. Cuseglio states, "A social work researcher might argue that because there was not a measurement tool used to assess outcomes and objectives, that it is not possible to prove group benefit or effectiveness for its members." The case studies in this volume offer a phenomenological account of school social work, one that focuses on the lived experience of school social workers and the students they serve. What have you learned about mindfulness training of adolescents, group work with adolescence, and the challenges of a large caseload for school social workers from this phenomenological perspective? What questions might you still have for a researcher?

Prompts for Writing

1. Design a school-based group based on a problem you have observed. Research group theory for social work practice and describe the process you would use to choose appropriate members for the group, whether the group would be open or closed, and whether it would be ongoing or time-limited. Discuss some of the challenges you would face in implementing such a group and how you would overcome such challenges.

2. Recreate the dialogue from a group you have been a part of or have run. Then reflect upon the group dynamics.

3. Cuseglio engages in the practice of self-disclosure during his group work. Do some research on the role of self-disclosure in group therapy. Write about the risks and benefits of personal disclosure as well as disclosure of thoughts about the group process using the process from this case. How do you feel about disclosing aspects of your personal experience? What would you consider when making a decision about whether or not to disclose?

References

Akos, P., Goodnough, G. E., and Milson, A. S. (2004). Preparing school counselors for group work. *The Journal for Specialists in Group Work, 29*(1), 127–136.

Akos, P., Hamm, J. V., Mack, S. G., and Dunaway, M. (2007). Utilizing the developmental influence of peers in middle school groups. *The Journal for Specialists in Group Work, 32* (1), 51–60.

Bemak, F., Chung, R. C., and Siroskey-Sabdo, L. A. (2005). Empowerment groups for academic success: An innovative approach to prevent high school failure for at-risk, urban African. *Professional School Counseling, 8*(5), 377–389.

Bluth, K., and Blanton, P. (2014). Mindfulness and self-compassion: Exploring pathways to adolescent emotional well-being. *Journal of Child & Family Studies, 23*(7), 1298–1309.

Bögels, S., Hoogstad, B., van Dun, L., de Schutter, S., and Restifo, K. (2008). Mindfulness training for adolescents with externalizing disorders and their parents. *Behavioural and Cognitive Psychotherapy, 36*(2), 193–209.

Boyce, B. (2005). Two sciences of the mind. *Shambhala Sun, 13,* 34–43, 93–96.

Broderick, P. C., and Jennings, P. A. (2012). Mindfulness for adolescents: A promising approach to supporting emotion regulation and preventing risky behavior. *New Directions for Youth Development, 136,* 111–126. DOI: 10.1002/yd.2004.

Campos, J. J., Frankel, C. B., and Camras, L. (2004). On the nature of emotion regulation. *Child Development, 75,* 377–394.

Canda, E. R., and Furman, L. D. (1999). *Spiritual diversity in social work practice: The heart of helping.* New York: Free Press.

Christensen, A., Sevier, M., and Simpson, L. (2004). Acceptance, mindfulness, and change in couple therapy. In S. Hays, V. Follette, and M. Linehan (Eds.), *Mindfulness and acceptance: Expanding the cognitive-behavioral tradition* (pp. 288–310). New York: Guilford Press.

Eisenberg, N., Spinrad, T. L., and Eggum, N. D. (2010). Emotion-related self-regulation and its relationship to children's maladjustment. *Annual Review of Clinical Psychology*, 6, 495–525. DOI: 10.1146/annurev.clinpsy.121208.131208.

Farb, N., Anderson, A. K., and Segal, Z. V. (2012). The mindful brain and emotion regulation in mood disorders. *Canadian Journal of Psychiatry*, 57(2), 70–77.

Fleming, V. M. (1999). Group counseling in the schools: A case for basic training. *Professional School Counseling*, 2, 409–416.

Flook, L., Smalley, S. L., Kitil, M. J., Galla, B. M., Kaiser-Greenland, S., Locke, J., Ishijima, E., and Kasari, C. (2010). Effects of mindful awareness practices on executive functions in elementary school children. *Journal of Applied School Psychology*, 26(1), 70–95.

Gehart, D., and Pare, D. (2008). Suffering and the relationship with the problem in postmodern therapies: A Buddhist revisioning. *Journal of Family Psychotherapy*, 19, 229–319. DOI: 10.1080/08975350802475049.

Gerrity, D. A., and DeLucia-Waack, J. L. (2007). Effectiveness of groups in the schools. *The Journal for Specialists in Group Work*, 32(1), 97–106. DOI: 10.1080/01933920600978604.

Greenberg, M. T., and Harris, A. R. (2011). Nurturing mindfulness in children and youth: Current state of the research. *Child Development Perspectives*, 6(2), 161–166.

Hanh, T. N. (1976). *The miracle of mindfulness: A manual for meditation*. Boston: Beacon Press.

Howe, D. (2008). *The emotionally intelligent social worker*. New York: Palgrave Macmillan.

Hutcherson, C. A., Seppala, E. M., and Gross, J. J. (2008). Loving-kindness meditation increases social connectedness. *Emotion*, 8, 720–724.

Johnson, S. K., and Johnson, C. D. (2005). Group counseling: Beyond the traditional. *Professional School Counseling*, 8, 399–400.

Inhelder, B. and Piaget, J. (1958). *The growth of logical thinking from childhood to adolescence: An essay on the construction of formal operations structures*. New York: Basic Books.

Kabat-Zinn, J. (1990). *Full catastrophe living: Using the wisdom of your body and mind to face stress, pain, and illness*. New York: Dell Publishing.

Kabat-Zinn, J. (2011). Some reflections on the origins of MBSR, skillful means, and the trouble with maps. *Contemporary Buddhism*, 12, 1. DOI: 10.1080/14639947.2011.564844.

Kostanski, M., and Hassed, C. (2008). Mindfulness as a concept and a process. *Australian Psychologist*, 43, 15–21.

Kulic, K. R., Horne, A. M., and Dagley, J. C. (2004). A comprehensive review of prevention groups for children and adolescents. *Group Dynamics: Theory, Research, and Practice*, 8, 139–151.

Linehan, M. (1993). *Cognitive-behavioral treatment of borderline personality disorder*. New York: Guilford Press.

Littrell, J. M., and Peterson, J. S. (2001). Transforming the school culture: A model based on an exemplary counselor. *Professional School Counseling*, 4, 310–319.

MacBeth, A., and Gumley, A. (2012). Exploring compassion: A meta-analysis of the association between self-compassion and psychopathology. *Clinical Psychology Review*, 32(6), 545–552. DOI: 10.1016/j.cpr.2012.06.003.

MacPherson, L., Reynolds, E. K., Daughters, S. B., Wang, F., Cassidy, J., Mayes, L. C., and Lejuez, C. W. (2010). Positive and negative reinforcement underlying risk behavior in early adolescents. *Prevention Science*, 11, 331–342.

Malekoff, A. (2004). *Group work with adolescents: Principles and practice* (2nd edn). New York: Guilford Press.

Marlatt, G. A., and Kristeller, J. L. (1999). Mindfulness and meditation. In W. R. Miller (Ed.), *Integrating spirituality into treatment* (pp. 67–84). Washington, DC: American Psychological Association.

Piaget, J. (1972). *The psychology of intelligence*. Totowa, NJ: Littlefield.

Roeser, R. W., and Pinela, C. (2014). Mindfulness and compassion training in adolescence: A developmental contemplative science perspective. *New Directions for Youth Development*, 142, 9–30. DOI: 10.1002/yd.20094.

Romeo, R. D. (2010). Adolescence: A central event in shaping stress reactivity. *Developmental Psychobiology*, 52, 244–253.

Sayder, S. (2008). Joining up with "not us" staff to run adolescent groups in schools. *Journal of Child Psychotherapy*, *34*(1), 111–126.

Schonert-Reichl, K. A., and Lawlor, M. S. (2010). The effects of a mindfulness-based education program on pre- and early adolescents' well-being and social and emotional competence. *Mindfulness*, *1*(3), 137–151.

Semple, R. J., Lee, J., Rosa, D., and Miller, L. F. (2010). A randomized trial of mindfulness-based cognitive therapy for children: Promoting mindful attention to enhance social-emotional resiliency in children. *Journal of Child and Family Studies*, *19*(2), 218–229.

Semple, R. J., Reid, E. F. G., and Miller, L. (2005). Treating anxiety with mindfulness: An open trial of mindfulness training for anxious children. *Journal of Cognitive Psychotherapy: An International Quarterly*, 19, 379–392.

Shechtman, Z. (2002). Child group psychotherapy in the school at the threshold of a new millennium. *Journal of Counseling and Development*, 80, 293–299.

Shechtman, Z., Bar-El, O., and Hadar, E. (1997). Therapeutic factors and psychoeducational groups for adolescents: A comparison. *The Journal for Specialists in Group Work*, *22*(3), 203–213.

Steen, S., Bauman, S., and Smith, J. (2007). Professional school counselors and the practice of group work. *Professional School Counseling*, 11, 72–80.

Steen, S., and Kaffenberger, C. J. (2006). Integrating academic interventions into small group counseling in elementary school. *Professional School Counseling*, *10*(5), 516–519.

Tadlock-Marlo, R. L. (2011). Making minds matter: Infusing mindfulness into school counseling. *Journal of Creativity in Mental Health*, *6*(3), 220–233. DOI: 10.1080/15401383.2011.605079.

Van Velsor, P. V. (2004). Training for successful group work with children: What and how to teach. *The Journal for Specialists in Group Work*, *29*(1), 137–146.

Webb, L. D., Brigman, G. A., and Campbell, C. (2005). Linking school counselors and student success: A replication of the student success skills approach targeting the academic and social competence of students. *Professional School Counseling*, 8, 407–413.

10

SCHOOL SOCIAL WORK WITH PARENTS

Developmental Guidance Groups in a Preschool Setting

Karen E. Baker

Pre-Reading Questions

1. What do you know about attachment theory? How is it related to the concept of separation?
2. Why is it important for a school social worker to be an available resource for students' parents?
3. What do you know about psychoanalytic theories of development?
4. How do you think becoming a parent changes someone?

It was the fourth week of school when Fisher's mom approached me after drop off requesting to speak with me. Fisher was three at the time and was having his first preschool experience. Prior to beginning school, he had been home with his mom. With misty eyes, Mrs. J. told me that she thought Fisher was doing pretty well with separation and the transition to school. I agreed with her and wondered what was causing her sad feelings. "He seems to be managing this better than me. His teachers told me that he's happy at school. He especially loves the singing. This is exactly what my husband and I want." I spoke with her for about twenty minutes and after listening to her feelings about her son starting to grow up and to separate from her, I pointed out to her the strength it takes to acknowledge and hold her feelings of missing Fisher while he was at school. This was a big change for both of them. Attempting to join with Mrs. J.'s desire to be a good mother, I stressed the fact that Fisher was successful because of his secure attachment to her and his father, something they instilled in him. In addition to my awareness of Fisher's secure attachment, I was also aware that Mrs. J. was experiencing a complex feeling state that included her admiration of her son's achievement, as well as the loss that accompanies the painful job of being a mother. Erna Furman (1982) refers to this pain as "being there to be left," a state that all mothers feel as their children master a developmental step that ushers in the acknowledgment of not being needed as they once were in the earlier stage of development. She notes that when working with mothers, "we hear of their pangs of loneliness and the hurt of their not being needed" (p. 16). She goes on to say that mothers are "always available so as not to be needed, always there to be left, always bearing the pain and anger at being inevitably rejected, and at times, feeling the joy at the children's growing independence and love of life turn bittersweet" (p. 16). When mothers are unable to bear this pain, their children are at risk of feeling as if they have to protect their mothers from such feelings and therefore cannot allow themselves to grow up or they have to separate and grow up in an angry hurtful way.

Upon first glance, this brief emotional dialogue may appear simple, but in fact it is replete with nuance and complexity. It required me to listen carefully and then to bring these deeper matters to light. In doing so, I normalized Mrs. J.'s experience and highlighted the developmental tasks that she and her son were experiencing. These themes of separation and "being there to be left" were addressed with Mrs. J. individually and later in a parent group. This interaction captures a type of conversation that I often have at a preschool where I serve as a clinical social worker-family consultant. The depth of our exchange was significant because in addition to normalizing what Mrs. J. was experiencing, it had the impact of preventing a possible defensive reaction to cling to her son as a means of avoiding her feelings of loss. In turn, this defensive position could interfere with Fisher's developmental task of mastering separation. Partnering with Mrs. J. supported a successful separation process. Ultimately, it facilitated Mrs. J.'s achievement of separateness while staying emotionally connected to her son.

In general, school social work is widely known as an important clinical service delivered in educational settings. Thinking of the school social worker, most imagine providing services to students in elementary, middle, and high school. The focus of clinical work in these settings is to help students navigate their way through conflicts, developmental disturbances, crises, and other mental health issues that are interfering in their social and emotional well-being and academic performance.

It is my impression that people rarely consider clinical social work in preschool settings that are not therapeutic preschools. But imagine being around young children with all their natural curiosity, energy, and sense of wonder as they learn and discover things about themselves and the world. Imagine being able to work with teachers to collaborate in helping children become self-controlled, empathic, kind, resilient, and creative individuals. Imagine the opportunity to work with parents as they strive toward mindful and intentional parenting. And imagine learning about child development and the process of parenthood from this intimate vantage point. This is the work that I have the privilege of doing as a clinical social worker in a small Midwest preschool. I will describe the school, some components of its curriculum, and the psychoanalytic theories that inform my work with parents.

A Psychoanalytically Informed Preschool

The preschool, founded twenty years ago by local psychoanalysts, is a mastery-based preschool that applies psychoanalytic ideas in its curriculum and philosophy of early childhood education. All preschools put into practice their educational philosophy, but as a mastery-based preschool focusing on the needs of the whole child, we are particularly interested in attending to the process of sepa-ration that children and parents experience, strengthening the parent-child relationship, understanding the intra-psychic meaning of behavior, facilitating the achievement of mastery related to internal and external conflicts that pertain to children's relationships, and managing transitions. Moreover, we focus on the development of the child's capacity for self-care, for social development, for conscience development, and for the development of the capacity for concern, pride, empathy, kindness, and respect for others. Mastering these developmental tasks puts children on a forward path to developing strength of character or "emotional muscle."[1]

The school is a private preschool and many parents are drawn to the school because of its philosophy and the family consultant program. It is not a therapeutic preschool in the sense that the children attending the school are not high-risk children with severe emotional and behavioral problems. However, once enrolled and as the school year progresses, it may become evident that some children are struggling with difficulties related to aggression, attachment, or developmental disorders.

I have found in my clinical experience in private practice and in many educational settings that working with children is most effective when parents are included in the process. Parents are the most influential figures in a child's life, yet teachers, administrators, and even some social workers, prefer to limit or marginalize parental involvement and blame parents for the child's problems. Our premise at the preschool is that children and families will be more successful if parents are an integral part of their child's school experience. We underscore the fact that parents are a child's primary attachment and resource; therefore, an important aspect of our work at the school is to support and reinforce the loving bond within the parent-child relationship. Not only do we keep a finger on the pulse of each child's development, but we are also attending to the development of parents. The primary avenue for gaining this support is through the relationship that parents develop with the teachers and their family consultant.

The Family Consultant

Because the school is not a therapeutic preschool, the family consultant program is truly a unique aspect of the school curriculum and sets us apart from other preschools in the area. A social worker-family consultant is assigned to a particular classroom: transitional toddler, junior preschool, or one of the two senior preschool classrooms. Once assigned to a classroom, the family consultants observe weekly in the classrooms for twenty to thirty minutes in an effort to come to know children individually as well as in the context of their school group. In addition, family consultants meet weekly with their teaching team to gain further understanding about each child's experiences. Ideally, the family consultant will follow the group progressively year by year until the children graduate from senior preschool and transition to kindergarten. This provides continuity for the children and their parents and provides the opportunity for family consultants to become well acquainted with the families.

The parents, teachers, and family consultants work together to understand the internal world of the child, child development, as well as the tasks of parenthood. These joint efforts are at the heart of the school's success in working with children and their families.

As members of the school community, parents attend bi-monthly psycho-educational parent guidance meetings. The purpose of the parent meetings is to discuss child development and other parenting matters. The topics at the meetings are most often generated by what is on parents' minds; they are far reaching from toilet mastery, to how to talk with children about adult issues such as school shootings, to how to know when a child is ready for kindergarten. First and foremost in my mind is to invite parents to think about their philosophy of child rearing and to have a clear sense of the values they want to instill in their children. This is something that is woven into every meeting whether implicitly or explicitly.

On occasion, for a variety of reasons, families may request additional, individual meetings with their family consultants. For example, teachers may note that a child has significant impairment in fine motor skills or a speech and language delay requiring intervention. Parents will use the family consultant to discuss their concerns and obtain referrals to occupational therapists or speech and language specialists. But what primarily compels parents to seek additional guidance is problematic behavior that is of concern to the teacher and to them. Most often, this involves a child who is dysregulated in some fashion and is not able to control her aggression or who shows signs of deep withdrawal that impact her ability to connect with her peers or teachers. When there is a child exhibiting such behaviors in the classroom, teachers seek help from the family consultant in an attempt to understand what is giving rise to such behavior—to understand its meaning—and to inform their classroom interventions. If it is determined that the teacher and parent interventions have little impact on the child's behavior, I refer the family to an outside mental health professional. One such child was Alice. She was four years old when her parents enrolled her in the preschool. Prior to this preschool experience, she had been in three daycare settings. Her process of separation was a bumpy road, but with support from the teachers and me, Alice made the transition into the classroom. As the days and weeks progressed, however, it became clear to all of us that Alice was struggling mightily with her impulse control and aggression. Initially, she would grab a toy from another child and run with it, or she would push and hit a child for an assortment of reasons. While it is not uncommon for preschoolers to express themselves physically as they are moving toward mastering their impulses and taming their aggression by learning to assert themselves through verbalization, Alice's behavior continued to escalate, and the teacher's attempts to help her label her feelings, by setting firm limits and expectations and supporting her in conflict resolution, were not having a significant impact on the transformation of her aggression. It was also true that Alice could be kind, and enjoy school, and take advantage of much of what her classroom offered. I was curious about her emotional unevenness and escalating aggression, as were her teachers. I invited the parents in to share with them my concerns and to hear from them about their thoughts and worries regarding Alice's current struggles. Upon their arrival for our meeting, I noticed that I was feeling anxious.

Conversations like the one we were soon to embark upon are difficult, and I was not sure how Alice's parents would respond to my curiosity and recommendations. I was aware that Alice's parents probably knew that I was not a parent myself. I wondered if they, like some parents I had met before, would assume that I could therefore not understand their predicament. Experience had taught me that remaining empathically attuned and near to another's experience does not require sharing it but rather deeply listening with the intent of entering into their point of view. While anticipating their anxiety that I may not be equipped to help them gave me pause, I also knew that my very awareness of the possibility of their doubt would help me to manage my own feelings about what would transpire next. I also knew that some parents would feel judged and that feeling might lead to their resistance to hear me out or worse to anger.

I breathed a sigh of relief as they expressed their own worries about their daughter's aggressive behavior. They informed me that she was exhibiting these behaviors at home as well; she would vacillate between angry outbursts and detached withdrawal. With despair, they reported to me that she would hit and kick them and at times would break her toys. It quickly became apparent that Alice's family was under a great deal of stress. Both parents were intermittently struggling with depression, Alice's father was just laid off from work so financial pressures were mounting, Alice's grandmother had passed away six months earlier, and both complained of feeling overwhelmed and helpless. They were experiencing a great deal of loss and uncertainty. I noticed a tension building in me, and as I listened to them, I simultaneously reflected on the tension I was feeling. In partnering with them on behalf of their daughter, I intended to support them and empathize with their current status as well as offer them techniques to use at home. But I also know that I had to deliver the message that their family was needing more than what the school setting could provide. I spoke frankly with them about these limitations and made a recommendation for referral to a clinical social worker in the community. They readily accepted this recommendation.

One of the joys of working as a family consultant is the opportunity to partner with the teachers as we endeavor to achieve our collective goals of promoting forward development in both the children and their parents. Most Fridays throughout the school year, family consultants meet for an hour with the classroom teachers to discuss individual children, and to share observations, concerns, pleasures, and strategies to use in the classroom and with families. Following that meeting there is a staff meeting that includes all the teachers, the family consultants, and the administrative team of the school. The purpose of these meetings is to discuss pertinent issues in the classroom such as attachment and separation in the first several weeks of school, developmental progression in big block play, the developmental function of superhero play, assessing a child's need for an outside mental health referral, classroom interventions to facilitate a child's social emotional development, to name a few. Each classroom rotates presenting at the meetings. Family consultants also attend two parent-teacher conferences per year.

Parenthood

Parenting is a significant role in an adult's life, replete with complexity and nuance. The transition into parenthood is a normative developmental task within the life span. While normative, this transition is a multifaceted process that brings forward new responsibilities and challenges to one's self, as well as to others. Engaging in the enterprise of parenthood brings joy, satisfaction, concerns, fears, and the need for support and at times guidance.

In addition, it is a time in life that brings with it much hope and possibility for change. Selma Fraiberg (1980) notes that "the baby can be a catalyst. He provides a powerful motive for positive changes in the parents. He represents their hopes and deepest longings; he stands for renewal of the self; his birth can be experienced as a psychological rebirth for his parents" (pp. 53–54). In tandem with this possibility for hope and change is the fact that parenting is hard work that places external and internal demands on the parent as well as the child. It requires parents to be attentive and responsive to the child's needs. The early stages of parenthood are labor intensive as parents figure out their infant's feeding schedule, sleeping pattern, and assess what causes the baby's discomfort. It is common for parents to experience sleep deprivation which adds to the adjustment to parenthood and the challenges in parenting.

It is also true that parenting revives one's own childhood experiences of being parented. It pulls on both mothers and fathers to live up to their ego ideal[2] of being and becoming good mothers and good fathers. I believe that the seeking of this parental ego ideal facilitates the desire to provide a "good enough" environment (Winnicott, 1965) for the baby. It is through this "good enough" environment that consistent emotional involvement, secure attachment and the establishment of a loving connection between the child and the caregiver will facilitate the internalization of positive object relations and an integrated sense of self (Bowlby, 1969).

Verbalization, Mentalization, and Emotional Muscle

In recent years the theory of mentalization and the concept of reflective functioning has garnered much attention in the psychoanalytic world. Borrowing these terms from developmental psychology, Fonagy et al. (2002) put forth their theory of the development of a self, thereby expanding our understanding of the theory of mind. According to Fonagy et al., mentalization is a process by which we realize that having a mind mediates our experience of the world. It is intrinsically linked to the development of the self, to its gradually elaborated inner organization, and to its participation in human society, a network of human relationships with other beings who share this unique capacity. Reflective functioning is the processing mechanism in the mind that allows for mentalization to develop. As Fonagy et al. describe it, reflective function is the developmental acquisition that permits children to respond not only to another person's behavior but to the children's conception of other's beliefs, feelings, attitudes, desires, hopes, knowledge, imagination, pretense, deceit, intentions, and plans. In other words, reflective functioning enables children to "read" other people's minds. It is through this process of coming to know the other and one's self that meaning and a sense of predictability are established. It is the development of the capacity to imagine and understand one's mental state as well as the mental state of another. Their theory builds connections between psychoanalytic thinking and attachment theory. Rather than looking at the form of attachment patterns as templates for future relationships, they have deepened our knowledge by noting that early attachment relationships provide a dynamic system in which mentalization skills and capacities can emerge. They posit that impoverishment within this inter-subjective field of attachment will lead to limitations and interferences in a person's capacity to mentalize. As a clinical social worker who values psychoanalytic thought, I recognize the significance of the role of verbalization and mental representation in the capacity for self-regulation.

The development of language is important as words have the function of creating meaning. Babbling is recognized as a precursor to language acquisition. We've all experienced the pleasure of these early utterances, which begin sometime after birth: the cooing that compels us into these initial exciting engagements with a baby. As the caregiver mirrors and interprets the cooing, the crying, the looking, and so forth, she is facilitating the growth of the capacity to mentalize.

It isn't until about twelve months of age that the words of infants begin to be recognizable. This forward movement in language development facilitates thinking, reflection, organization, and the emergence of an internal symbolic world. Assigning words to emotions, behaviors, and experiences expands the child's capacity for self-awareness and introspection (Tyson and Tyson, 1990), allowing the child to communicate more directly her feelings, wishes, ideas, and fantasies. As Katan (1961) noted in her seminal paper on verbalization, a child's capacity to use words to label feelings, assists her in the containment, control, and modulation of affect. She emphasizes that verbalizing feelings increases the "controlling function of the ego over affects and drives" (p. 184). In essence, verbalization is a significant development that aids in the capacity to mentalize.

The ability to reflect on mental states is a vital ego capacity that has its origins in the early relationship between the infant and her caregiver. When the parent-child interactions take place in a "good enough" environment (Winnicott, 1965), the infant becomes known and understood (Fonagy et al., 2002; Slade et al., 2005). Being known and understood in one's own right, one establishes separateness and the development of an authentic self. In my work with parents, I use the theory of mentalization to guide my thinking and interventions. By doing so, I encourage the capacity for self-reflection, observation, and curiosity, all of which foster healthy adaptations in children and parents.

This intersubjective process of recognition is dependent on the parents' capacity to acknowledge, tolerate, contain, and represent the range of thoughts, feelings, desires, and behaviors their child is experiencing and to then respond in words or through play or non-verbal interactions. Not only do the parents need to make sense of their son's or daughter's mental states, but they must also make sense of their own. This process of making sense of one's own mind and the mind of the baby/child plays a critical role in helping children with self-regulation. According to Slade (2006), this exchange assists the baby/child to develop adaptive and flexible ways of regulating herself and assists the baby/child in establishing consistent, predictable relationships. She goes on to state that when a parent tolerates and regulates her own internal affective states, this allows her to tolerate and regulate these experiences in her child, thereby impacting the child's capacity for self-regulation. This psychic involvement and investment in one's baby/child facilitates the internalization of positive object relations and an integrated sense of self (Bowlby, 1969).

An ongoing parental task involves helping children maneuver through a myriad of developmental challenges, eventuating in mastery. Parents are responsible to help their children differentiate self from object representations,[3] regulate drives[4] and related affects, and foster reality testing[5] (Sugarman, 2003). In other words, it is the parents' task to recognize that this little person is developing separateness throughout all stages of development to become an individual in her own right with her own thoughts, feelings, and desires.

Novick and Novick (2002) have contributed to the theory of self-regulation through their work on the development and treatment of sadomasochism.

They posit that there are two kinds of conflict resolution: the open system which is attuned to reality and is distinguished by competency, creativity, and joy, and the closed system which avoids reality and is characterized by sadomasochism, omnipotent beliefs, and stagnation (Novick and Novick, 2002). The concept of "emotional muscle" was born out of this work and their time devoted to parents, children, teachers, and therapists. Similar to the idea that exercising our physical muscles can lead to developing a healthy body, Novick and Novick use the metaphor of emotional muscle to capture the process of developing a healthy internal life. Emotional muscle includes the concepts of ego strength, ego control, self-regulation, resilience, and development (Novick and Novick, 2011).

In their book, *Emotional Muscle: Strong Parents, Strong Children* (2010), Novick and Novick expertly describe the ego strengths and controls that both children and parents need to master as a pathway of development that contributes to open-system functioning. They emphasize that building emotional muscle happens in relation to reality, within the context of respectful and loving bonds between parents and children. They state that individuals functioning within an open system use their real skills and knowledge to their fullest capacity at any age. In contrast, closed-system functioning employs magical thinking, forcing, and power dynamics. In terms of parenting, an authoritarian parenting philosophy is considered to be a closed system of functioning because, in this mode, parents use their superior strength and power arbitrarily to intimidate children into obedience and submission. In keeping with open-system functioning, parents and teachers strive toward helping children develop individual skills, capitalizing on their real capacities and strengthening their various emotional muscles which will foster resiliency and lead to an adaptive and flexible capacity for self-regulation. In the classroom, helping children develop emotional muscle happens on a daily basis, as it is expected at these young ages children will become dysregulated at different points in time. Likewise, the clinical social worker-family consultant strives toward helping parents strengthen their various parenting emotional muscles which will foster their resilience, and an adaptive, flexible approach to parenting.

Junior Preschool Parent Group

The parent group meetings are set at the beginning of the school year. Because parent meetings are not mandatory, mothers and fathers who attend are hoping to expand their knowledge of child development, share their parenting perspectives, and gain support in the enterprise of raising children. Since the groups are organized based on the classroom their child is in, the meetings provide an intimate setting for parents to connect with other parents from the same class as their child. Sometimes both parents will attend the meeting, but, more often it is one parent while the other stays home with their son or daughter. The groups are informal, self-directed, and open-ended.

The junior preschool classroom is made up of 3-year-olds, many of whom are having their first experience in school. As 3-year-olds move out of the stage of toddlerhood, their next developmental undertaking is to master separation, separateness, self-care, and their feelings. Novick and Novick (2011) assert that there are several emotional muscles that parents of 3-year-olds are in the process of developing: integrating love and separateness, respecting children's privacy, self-reflection, and taking pleasure in their children's new capacities. Some of these tasks were evident during this particular parent group in which seven parents were in attendance.

Nancy arrived for the parent meeting looking tired.

> I'm so glad to be here tonight. It was an awful day. Well actually, that's not exactly accurate. Maggie has been out of town helping her mother move her grandmother into assisted living. I've been solo parenting for three days. Thank goodness, she arrived home a few hours ago. How do single moms, or dads for that matter, do it? Anyway, the hard part of the day was lunch time. I was running a bit late and Phillip [Betsy's 11-month-old brother] was crying because he was hungry. Betsy needed to use the toilet. She's been pretty independent about using the potty on her own, but she suddenly proclaimed that she needed my help. I went to help her and she says NO!

As I empathically listened to Nancy describe her experience with her children that afternoon, I was wondering how the other parents would respond to her anxiety and forthrightness.

She continued to speak with openness. "I was starting to feel stressed because Phillip was still crying, and lunch wasn't ready yet." She described how Betsy was vacillating between the position of help me, and no I will do it myself.

> I became so frustrated, and I lost it. But before I lost it, I noticed she was covering her ears and I had some of my wits about me because I remember saying to her that Phillip was crying because he was hungry and that his crying was loud and it seemed like that was making her uncomfortable—or something like that. But then between Phillip's crying, the push-pull, my wanting to get lunch on the table, I just started yelling. I completely lost it.

In general, Nancy is a loving, thoughtful, and reasonable mother. In my private reverie, I found myself wondering: what was it in that moment that caused Nancy to "lose it"? How did she manage her frustration and speak to herself about it later? What did she do afterwards to help Betsy understand what just happened? I was impressed with her capacity and internal strength, that even in the face of her anxiety, frustration, and, in her mind, loss of control, she was still able to "mentalize" and notice her daughter's discomfort and offer her an idea, an explanation about her discomfort. At this point, I elected to hold my reveries to myself allowing for the group process to unfold. I decided to remain quiet taking a position of partnering with the parents. In the initial phases of the parent guidance groups, parents looked to me as the authority in the room. Over time, my goal is to instill in parents a sense of confidence and authority in their parenting. By holding back, I allow parents to put into practice our previous work of making observations about their children, themselves, and their methods of parenting. The group experience facilitates expanding their capacities to reflect on their children's states of mind as well as their own. Through the intersubjective process of identifying with my curiosity, attitudes about behavior as communication, and reflection, they develop a greater sense of being an authority with regard to parenthood and their method of parenting. A significant accomplishment!

Earlier, I referred to Fraiberg's perspective that children are powerful motivations for positive parental change. I believe this motivation manifests itself unconsciously as well as consciously. This motivation enhances parents' strivings to live up to their ego ideal of being good enough mothers and fathers. By staying quiet at certain moments like this one, I am not interfering in their process of reflecting on the difficult or joyful interactions with their children, which furthers their parental development.

The group discussion continued as one of the dads offered his support and resonance with the conflict. "Oh, I think we've all lost it with our kids at times." All the parents chimed in empathically, echoing my own inner experience of feeling empathy for Nancy and her children. "I just felt so guilty, like I was a really terrible mom." Another mom immediately piped up. "You're not a terrible mom—a stressed mom at that time, but not terrible. But I get what you are saying." She then related an experience of her own when she felt she did not live up to her ideal maternal self. This is a common occurrence within a group modality. In this case, when Nancy shared her experience of "losing it" with her children, she opened the space for parents to safely expose themselves as adults who at times become dysregulated. It is validating for parents to know that other parents have similar moments. This phenomenon of "being in the same boat" reduces shame and guilt and normalizes difficult parenting moments.

This meeting occurred about five months into the school year when the group's working alliance was well established. Her connection with the other parents and confidence that they would be non-judgmental allowed Nancy to bravely reveal herself during an intense time with her children. What she experienced and described was not out of the ordinary. These moments occur in the day-to-day experiences in the lives of mothers and fathers raising young children. It is a moment in time when multiple needs and desires are all converging simultaneously. I empathized with her as well as the other parents about how difficult these moments were for them. I also pointed out that Nancy was trying to support her daughter's independence on the one hand but also recognizing her request for mommy help on the other.

Another mom resonated with the "losing it" theme but shifted the conversation to a different, as she put it, push-pull interaction. "I'm always curious about Carlos's day: what did he do today? What did he have for snack? Who did he play with? The majority of the time, he is not interested in answering my questions. He says things like, 'I don't know. I don't remember.'"

Again, parents were nodding in unison, each acknowledging that they were having a similar experience of their children's reluctance to share their day with them. There was a lull in the exchange at which point I said,

> Ah. All of you are experiencing your 3-year-olds beginning recognition that they have a separate mind from yours. They are realizing that you cannot read their minds as the all-knowing, all-powerful parent. They are now in a place in development where they are beginning to choose for themselves what they want to tell you about their day or about their thoughts.

Nancy said, "Sometimes that's really hard, partly because I'm so interested and curious about her day." "And the other part?" I inquired. Nancy said, "I guess it is the part of me that has to come to terms with not knowing everything that she is doing."

What transpired here during this exchange in the group is another theme that emerges for parents of 3-year-olds. It is a transformative time for parents in which they must come to terms with their child's growing separateness and for them moving from knowing, or imagining that they know, everything about their child's experiences, to one of not knowing. The parental task at this point is to acknowledge their child's growing independence and privacy which is a developmental achievement for the child (Novick and Novick, 2010).

Once again, I supported the parents in this challenge they were facing. I said, "You're curious and interested in your children because you love them and you want to stay connected with them. I'm wondering if any of you have ideas about other ways to learn about your kid's day." In using this intervention, I mitigated the notion that I was the only authority in the room. In so doing, I invited parents to reflect on their desire to connect and engage with their children. Brainstorming with one another, and sharing techniques that have worked for them, served to strengthen their relationships with one another and enhance their parental authority.

Peter's dad, a musician, talked about a technique that he has used when he picks his son up. He would greet his son and then chat with him about the weather or some other benign topic. Eventually, he would get around to talking about a song that he has been singing or writing. To his delight, his son would then begin to talk about the songs he and his classmates were singing that day at school. Rather than ask his son a barrage of questions, he figured out how to initiate conversation that left him feeling good and close to his son.

Another parent shared her technique to engage her daughter in conversation about the school day. She made note of something that she noticed at drop-off. She matter-of-factly said to her daughter, "I noticed at drop-off that Cindy and her mom were carrying a big sack. I was wondering what was in that big sack?" With pleasure, she reported the success of this method. In response to her inquiry, her daughter volunteered that Cindy brought in a snack of fruit rollups and crackers. As opposed to meeting her with a string of questions, she met her with curiosity. This opened the door for her daughter to engage in a brief conversation about some aspect of her school day.

Respecting a child's privacy is one of the "emotional muscles" parents are exercising during this 3-year-old phase of development. It requires parents to surrender the illusion that they know everything about their child's feelings and thoughts and come to terms with the fact that their child has private experiences and a separate internal life of her own. This "muscle" on the part of parents will be exercised throughout all stages of development.

Senior Preschool Parent Group

Over the years that I have been a family consultant at the preschool, the concerns about superhero or bad guy play, which is common in 4-year-olds, emerge as a topic of conversation for parents as well as teachers. I've noticed that expressions of concern with this particular form of play seem to increase when violent world events happen and all of us are inundated with news reports. However, regardless of the timing, it is a form of play that worries parents.

Patrick's dad opened the parent discussion by asking the parents present if their kids were pretending to have guns and playing war or were very focused on the idea of bad guys and superheroes. He noted that he and his wife are very uncomfortable with this kind of play. He informed the group that he and his wife told their son not to play like this at home or at school. I wondered to myself why this play might cause so much anxiety for these parents. I also knew that this would be a very difficult request for their son to honor, not only because several children in the classroom were engaged in this play, but also because this play has developmental significance.

Another mom chimed in, her voice animated as she acknowledged that her son was also engaged in this kind of play. "I had this crazy thought about it the other day. I thought, I hope this doesn't mean he is on his way to becoming a serial killer." The group laughed in unison, but beneath the laughter was a palpable feeling of anxiety. She continued. "I also, quite emphatically, told him that this is not a game we play at home and I didn't want him to play it at school either." At this point, I acknowledged that they were experiencing this form of play quite differently from other forms of play they witnessed or participated in with their children. Before addressing the anxiety, I took an educational approach with them about superhero play, explaining that this play is about villains, heroes, and saving the day. Good triumphs over bad! I told them that similar to the idea that behavior is the language of children, fantasy play is the repository for the work of children (Paley, 1988). I explained that this is the space children create to communicate their big feelings, their fears, and their curiosities. The classroom and the home play spaces are the perfect stages for these dramas to unfold.

Hoffman (2004) advocates for guided play, a philosophy that the teachers support. According to Hoffman, using this approach, children learn through the play to use power wisely, differentiate real from pretend violence, internalize controls, achieve a sense of feeling strong and powerful, settle conflicts without harming anyone, and act with compassion when someone needs help. Through the play children are learning how power works in the world and are seeking answers to their questions. By banning the play, parents communicate to their children that this is forbidden because there is something about it that is too dangerous and scary.

A few of the parents mentioned that they were relatively comfortable with the superhero play. One mom said that even if parents tried to ban this play, children would figure out how and when they could play out their good guy and bad guy fantasies. She went on from there and said, "I feel confident that this is a form of play they will move on from." This same mom wondered why these two parents were so concerned about it. This was one of those moments that illustrates the trust and comfort that developed amongst these parents. While this was certainly a curiosity that was on my mind as well, it is not likely that I would have made that inquiry because it seemed to me that I would have been treading toward working therapeutically as opposed to working from a guidance and educational perspective.

There was a brief silence before Patrick's dad courageously revealed that while he hadn't linked this before, he thought it possible that his anxiety had to do with growing up with an alcoholic father who, when intoxicated, would become violent. He worried whether this play was a precursor to his son becoming violent later in life. The mom who emphatically banned this play also confided that the aggression in the play frightened her because of her own history of physical abuse. Feeling safe to disclose one's vulnerabilities occurs in the context of the group because of the members' working alliance and trusting relationships that develop over the course of time.

In using an educational approach to help the parents recognize the function of bad guy and weapon play, from a developmental perspective, these two parents were able to step back from their original perspective and reflect on their anxieties, linking them to their past experiences. They could then differentiate their worries from their child's intent in the play. Through this process of differentiating, they came to realize in a significant way that their child had desires and intentions in the play that were different from their beliefs, imaginings, and attitudes about the meaning of the play.

Upon further contemplation, I was left with the impression that the parents' anxieties were out of synch with the intentions of their sons. Their anxious reaction and defensive position of "laying down the law" of no gun or superhero play confused their children and perhaps caused some conflict of loyalty in their children. After all these 4-year-olds are in the throes of conscience formation, learning right from wrong, and wanting to please their parents, while at the same time wanting to feel a sense of belonging and playing with their classmates. Operating with the best of conscious intent, these parents ran the risk of imposing their fears of aggression and its imagined potential to become out of control and dysregulated onto their young children. Because of their personal histories and lack of awareness of the function of the play, they were not able to recognize the potential for containment and mastery within the play. This educational approach freed the parents up to address the deeper motivation for attempting to shut down the play. While there wasn't a magical shift and immediate acceptance of this form of play, they were more able to actively engage in reflecting on their attitudes and beliefs. This process of reflecting and thinking about how they were feeling about the play assisted them in coming to know their child's developmental need in the play, mitigated their anxiety, and helped to inform their engagement with their children in relation to the play; this lessened the potential for a power struggle with their sons.

Discussion

School social workers are commonplace in elementary, middle, and high school, but rarely seen in non-therapeutic preschools. School social workers provide services to children and adolescents with behavioral problems and mental issues that interfere with their social-emotional well-being and academic performance. While teachers and parents at the preschool consult with me when they are concerned about dysregulated behaviors, for the most part the work conducted with parents, teachers, and children, centers around normative developmental stages and the tasks of parenthood. It seems to me that a significant difference in my role as a social worker in this preschool, as opposed to social workers in other school settings, is that the work I do can be considered proactive and preventative rather than reactive. I am called upon daily to support normative development as opposed to being summoned by teachers and administrators to intervene in a crisis or when the behavior of children is so dysregulated that it becomes disruptive to the classroom environment. The preschool's mastery-based philosophy and curriculum places a strong emphasis on the loving parent–child bond as well as on the importance of other relationships with teachers, family consultants, and friends. Attending to the significance of these early relationships and experiences, as well as the process of separation and separateness, conscience development, and understanding the deeper meaning of behavior, is critical to development as they lay the foundation for internal structure that is so important to character development.

Raising children requires a solid and supportive community with mothers and fathers taking the lead. The parent groups become a part of a family's network of support. The groups empower moms and dads to parent with love and confidence as they are encouraged to question and reflect upon the everyday experiences and interactions with their children and family. Mentalization and the ability to reflect on interactions with one's self and others strengthen their emotional muscle and their ability to listen, and to think more deeply about behavior. As they expand their knowledge about developmental phases and what their children are communicating through their behavior and fantasy play, they begin to feel more competent in their parenting.

Although the groups are not psychotherapy groups, the guidance offered and interventions I put into practice are informed by my psychoanalytic understanding of the phases of parenthood, mentalization, and the development of emotional muscle. Through this work, parents make significant changes and gain important insights into their child rearing practices, their children, and themselves. The vignettes presented demonstrate the remarkable parental capacity to trust and help one another with some of the intimate aspects of their family life as they used the group to share and compare their experiences, their triumphs, and their difficulties with parenting. Frequently, I find myself sitting back, admiring parents as they bravely grapple with questions about separation, reactions to transitions, toilet mastery, aggression, the media, what it is like when in-laws visit, whether to allow their children to play with toy guns and enact superhero scenarios, the topic of death, kindergarten readiness, and so much more that pertains to the ordinary day-to-day aspects of raising young children.

Other themes that emerge in the parent meetings, as noted in the vignette of Fisher, are the feelings of loss that accompany the admiration of children advancing to the next developmental step, regardless of what that next phase may be. It is important to underscore, that as the group process deepens, parents talk more openly about their family histories, the methods they were raised with, and the choices they are making to parent similarly or differently, based on what they are learning by participating in the parent groups.

At times the group dynamics or parental anxieties and concerns are palpable. It is during these times that the parents may actively look toward the clinical social worker as having "the answer" they are seeking. In these moments it becomes important to stand back and reflect on the question and the needs of the parents at that point in time. Parents often rely on the family consultant as the designated child expert or authority in the room. Through our experience and knowledge we have much to offer the parents; however, there are times when we don't have the answers they are hoping we possess. It is during these times that we must confront our own limitations and the reality that there is no all-knowing person in the room. This can echo the pressures parents feel in relation to their children.

These moments can provide an opening for family consultants to assist parents with their own limitations as well as being opportunities to help parents reflect on a range of feeling states such as helplessness, discouragement, or worry. These are opportune moments for the social worker to assist parents in open-system functioning.

Using techniques of listening, being empathically attuned to the parents, putting situations they bring to the group into perspective, using an educational approach about child development and its meaning, encouraging self-reflection and reflecting on their child's experience is helpful and relieving to parents. These interventions promote parents' feeling understood, held, supported, reassured, and encouraged to question and expand their perspectives on parenting. Engaging with parents in this capacity promotes an open system of functioning that is attuned to reality and characterized by competency, creativity, and joy. The group milieu fosters dynamic interactions between the parents and me, and that expands their mentalization skills and self-reflection. Partnering with parents brings pleasure to my work life; in turn, my role as a social worker in the preschool setting helps parents to enjoy their role as parents and impacts family relationships.

Earlier, I referred to the idea that as clinical social workers facilitating parent guidance groups, we are not the only resource in the room. It is gratifying to observe parents exercising an investment in their children as well as in their relationships with the other mothers and fathers in the group, the family consultants, and the teachers. When this occurs, I know that my commitment to partnering with parents has paid off. As a result, the parents become tremendous resources to one another. I have experienced them offering astute and helpful observations, support and advice to one another that parents internalize and use. It is not uncommon to have parents borrow words and ideas not only from me, but from another parent as they integrate a new strategy into their parenting or expand their understanding of a given situation related to their child. This internalization that results from the group dialogue is a powerful process that facilitates mindful parenting and strengthens the loving attachment between the parent and child. Such mindfulness and intentionality in parenting serves as a compass to guide parents' actions and responses to their child, keeping in mind the child's well-being and level of development. I have witnessed parents and children expand their capacity for mentalization as well as strengthen their "emotional muscles" when using this method of parenting. The ways in which parents listen and respond to their children impacts the strength of the bond that will develop between them. This process facilitates emotional sturdiness and helps children develop a sense of their inner world and a capacity for relating.

It is common knowledge that the way parents listen, respond, and communicate with their children has a profound impact on their development. And so it is also true that the way clinical social workers-family consultants and parents listen to one another and respond to one another impacts the development of parenting and fosters a sense of community at the preschool.

CLOSE READING QUESTIONS

1. Describe "emotional muscle" in your own words. How does Baker help parents to develop emotional muscle?
2. What do you learn from Baker's work with the parents of very young children that could be applied to work with parents of adolescents? Is it feasible to apply Baker's thinking on school social work with parents in Sandoval-Arocho's case of Leo, Fabbo's case of Marta, Healy's case of Jay, or Verdicchio's case of Caroline?
3. What does Baker mean when she writes: "an authoritarian parenting philosophy is considered to be a closed system of functioning"? What is fundamentally important about maintaining an open system of functioning? How does Baker guide parents toward an open system of functioning?

Prompts for Writing

1. Much of the foundational work on attachment is focused on the relationship between mothers and their children. Research modern attachment theory to write about how fathers and/or family structures that might be considered non-traditional could be better included in a school social worker's interaction with children's caregivers.
2. Baker writes of her fear that parents will challenge her authority since she does not have her own children. What are your fears in working with parents? How would you manage and address them? What types of countertransference might manifest for you when working in a school setting?
3. School phobia is a problem that social workers often encounter in work with young children. Using Erna Furman's (1982) "Mothers Have to Be There to Be Left," develop a theory about school phobia that includes the mother (and father) and that offers understanding of the significance of separation in early childhood development.

Notes

1. Emotional muscle is a metaphoric concept coined by Novick and Novick (2010) to capture the process of developing a healthy internal life. This concept will be further explicated later in this chapter.
2. The psychoanalytic term ego ideal refers to the conscious and unconscious inner image of one's self as one wants to become.

3. Object representations is a psychoanalytic term taken from the theory of object relations. A representation is a complex cognitive schema containing psychic elements of affect and impulse referred to as the structure of the self or of the object. The object refers to the internal image of the primary caretaker.
4. In psychoanalysis, drives refer to sex and aggression. They are considered instinctual because they are in part biologically driven. As such, they need to be integrated and regulated within the overall organization of one's personality.
5. Reality testing refers to an individual's capacity to distinguish between wishes and/or fears and reality.

References

Bowlby, J. (1969). *Attachment and loss: Volume I, attachment*. New York: Basic Books.

Fonagy, P., Gergely, G., Jurist, E., and Target, M. (2002). *Affect regulation, mentalization, and the development of the self*. New York: Other Press.

Fraiberg, S. (1980). *Clinical studies in infant mental health: The first year of life*. New York: Basic Books.

Furman, E. (1982). Mothers have to be there to be left. *Psychoanalytic Study of the Child*, 37, 15–28.

Hoffman, E. (2004). *Magic capes, amazing powers, transforming superhero play in the classroom*. St. Paul, MN: Redleaf Press.

Katan, A. (1961). Some thoughts about the role of verbalization in early childhood. *Psychoanalytic Study of the Child*, 16, 184–188.

Novick, J., and Novick, K. K. (2002). Two systems of self regulation. In J. R. Brandell (Ed.), *Psychoanalytic approaches to the treatment of children and adolescents: Tradition and transformation* (pp. 95–122). Binghamton, NY: Haworth Press.

Novick, K. K., and Novick, J. (2010). *Emotional muscle: Strong parents, strong children*. New York: Xlibris.

Novick, K. K., and Novick, J. (2011). Building emotional muscle in children and parents. *Psychoanalytic Study of the Child*, 65, 131–151.

Paley, V. (1988). *Bad guys don't have birthdays: Fantasy play at four*. Chicago: University of Chicago Press.

Slade, A. (2006). Reflective parenting programs: Theory and development. *Psychoanalytic Inquiry*, 26, 640–657.

Slade, A., Sadler, L., De Dios-Kenn, C., Webb, D., Currier-Ezepchick, J., and Mayes, L. (2005). Minding the baby: A reflective parenting program. *Psychoanalytic Study of the Child*, 60, 74–100.

Sugarman, A. (2003). Dimensions of the child analyst's role as a developmental object: Affect regulation and limit setting. *Psychoanalytic Study of the Child*, 58, 189–213.

Tyson, P., and Tyson, R. (1990). *Psychoanalytic theories of development: Integration*. New Haven, CT: Yale University Press.

Winnicott, D. W. (1965). *The maturational processes and the facilitating environment: Studies in the theory of emotional development*. Madison, WI: International Universities Press, Inc.

INDEX